Holy
Trinity

Three Hypostases

Jesus

Christ

One Divine

Indivisible

Non-composite

Substance

Son of
God

Son of
Man

Father
Son
Holy Spirit

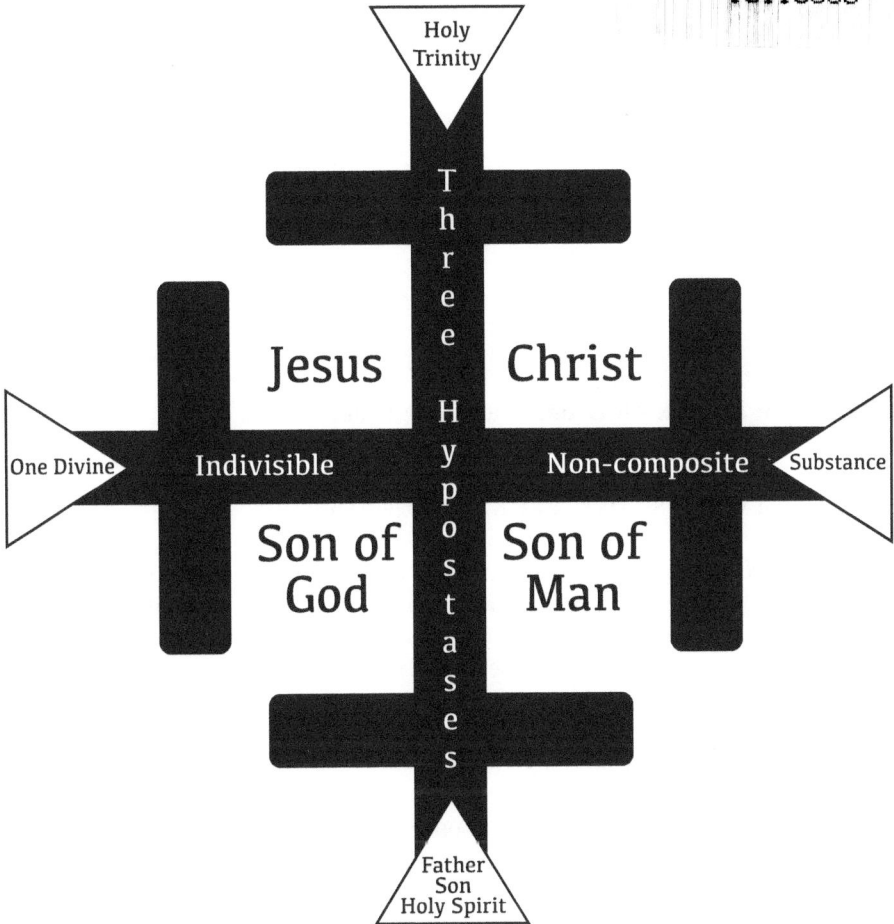

Fundamentals of Christianity — 3rd Edition

Vol. 1—From the Alexandrian Fathers on Trinitarian Theology

By Fr. D. Abba Moses

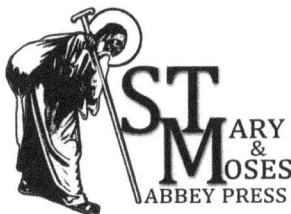

ST MARY
&
MOSES
ABBEY PRESS

Fundamentals of Christianity — 3rd Edition.
Volume 1: From the Alexandrian Fathers on Trinitarian Theology
By Fr. D. Abba Moses

Designed & Published by:
St. Mary & St. Moses Abbey Press
101 S Vista Dr., Sandia, TX 78383
stmabbeypress.com

Library of Congress Control Number: 2020942102

I dedicate this work to You, O Holy, Glorious and Fearsome Trinity. May this work be for the glory of Your Holy Name and may You forgive and absolve Your lazy and disobedient servant.

I also dedicate this work to you, the reader, whoever you may be. I love you very much and pray that this work be an aid in initiating and/or maintaining your own personal relationship with the Glorious and Amazing Holy Trinity. Never give up.

Contents

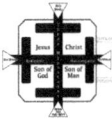

Introduction

"The sound faith which Christ gave us, the apostles preached, and the Fathers, who met at Nicæa from all this world of ours, have handed down";[1] "and yet not even the three hundred laid down nothing new, nor was it in any self-confidence that they became champions of words not in Scripture, but they fell back upon fathers, as did the others, and used their words."[2] And "what our Fathers have delivered, this is truly doctrine; and this is truly the token of doctors, to confess the same thing with each other, and to vary neither from themselves nor from their fathers; whereas they who have not this character are to be called not true doctors but evil."[3] Therefore, "if you wish to be children of the fathers, do not hold the contrary of what they wrote."[4]

"I wrote this... though I am **scarcely** capable of such a thing";[5] consequently, "If it should happen that we fail to explain the more appropriate matters through the weakness of our understanding or the presence of much obscurity, then it befits those who will read it to be forebearing,"[6] because, "the interpretation of the divine mysteries is **extremely** difficult."[7] "I therefore ask . . . those who hear, to take my letter [writing] in good part, and if anything is lacking in it in respect of piety, to set that right, and **inform me**. But if it is written, as from one unpracticed in speech, below the subject and imperfectly, let all allow for my feebleness in speaking."[8]

---

1   Athanasius of Alexandria. (1892). To the Bishops of Africa. In P. Schaff & H. Wace (Eds.), A. T. Robertson (Trans.), *St. Athanasius: Select Works and Letters* (Vol. 4, p. 489). New York: Christian Literature Company.

2   *Ibid.* (Councils of Ariminum and Seleucia, p. 473)

3   *Ibid.* (De Decretis or Defence of the Nicene Definition, p. 153)

4   *Ibid.* (Personal Letters, p. 571)

5   Athanasius and Didymus. (2011). *Works on the Spirit: Athanasius's Letters to Serapion on the Holy Spirit, and, Didymus's on the Holy Spirit.* (J. Behr, Ed., M. DelCogliano, A. Radde-Gallwitz, & L. Ayres, Trans.) (Vol. 43, p. 54). Yonkers, NY: St Vladimir's Seminary Press.

6   Cyril of Alexandria. (2018). *Glaphyra on the Pentateuch, Volume 1 Genesis.* (N. P. Lunn, Trans.) (Vol. 137, p. 52). Washington, DC: The Catholic University of America Press.

7   Cyril of Alexandria. (2013–2015). *Commentary on John.* (J. C. Elowsky, T. C. Oden, & G. L. Bray, Eds., D. R. Maxwell, Trans.) (Vol. 1, p. 3). Downers Grove, IL: IVP Academic: An Imprint of InterVarsity Press.

8   Athanasius of Alexandria. (1892). Personal Letters. In P. Schaff & H. Wace (Eds.), A. T. Robertson

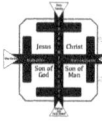

This collection is just a beginning, please add to, correct and improve what needs to be, for the glory of His Name; yet, "I do not think just anyone should attempt this, however, but only those who are enlightened by grace from above,"[9] namely, those who have been shown, "the divine and holy light, that is, to receive knowledge of the holy and consubstantial Trinity,"[10] because, "It is **dangerous** for ordinary people to speak about the essence that transcends all things and about its mysteries, and **doing so risks penalty.**"[11]

"In my love to you and for the sake of your good, I forget my companion, laziness, and imitate your zeal towards good and your untiring labors, and this, above all, through **fear** of God's condemnation, which threatens every man who buries his talent. Moreover, I wished thus to obey the precepts which our fathers and spiritual fathers have given us, enjoining us to transmit, to other God loving men, that which we learned from them. May God, the Father of love, the generous Bestower of all blessings, Who granted speech even to senseless beasts, grant me helpful words and open my slow, dumb lips for those who can hear. May He give you and your companions a wise ear to hear rightly what I have to say, and to live unswervingly in the way which pleases Him. For it is written that without Him we can do nothing good or salutary for the soul (John 15:5), and 'Unless the Lord builds the house, those who have built it have labored in vain.'"[12, 13]

(Trans.), *St. Athanasius: Select Works and Letters* (Vol. 4, p. 574). New York: Christian Literature Company.

9   Cyril of Alexandria. (2013–2015). *Commentary on John*. (J. C. Elowsky, T. C. Oden, & G. L. Bray, Eds., D. R. Maxwell, Trans.) (Vol. 1, p. 1). Downers Grove, IL: IVP Academic: An Imprint of InterVarsity Press.

10   Ibid. (Vol. 2, p. 32).

11   Ibid. (Vol. 1, p. 1).

12   (Ps 126:1 LXX)

13   Patriarch Callistus and Ignatius of Xanthopoulos. (1992). *Writings from the Philokalia on Prayer of the Heart*. (Kadloubovsky E., G.E.H. Palmer, Trans.) (p. 165). New York: Faber and Faber, Inc.

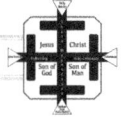

Definition of the word "hypostasis" (ὑπόστασις):

I. Older definition → Substance or Essence[14]

A. "Having accepted then these men's interpretation and defense of their language, we made enquiry of those blamed by them for speaking of One Subsistence,[15] whether they use the expression in the sense of Sabellius, to the negation of the Son and the Holy Spirit, or as though the Son were non-substantial, or the Holy Spirit impersonal.[16] But they in their turn assured us that they neither meant this nor had ever held it, but we use the word Subsistence thinking it the same thing to say Subsistence or Essence"; "But we hold that there is One, because the Son is of the Essence of the Father, and because of the identity of nature. For we believe that there is one Godhead, and that it has one nature, and not that there is one nature of the Father, from which that of the Son and of the Holy Spirit are distinct." "Well, thereupon they who had been blamed for saying there were three Subsistences agreed with the others, while those who had spoken of One Essence, also confessed the doctrine of the former as interpreted by them."[17]

B. "For the Apostle proclaims the Son to be the own Radiance and Expression, not of the Father's will,[18] but of His Essence[19] Itself,

---

14   οὐσία

15   It should be noted that the translator for Saint Athanasius' works, in the NPNF series translated the Greek word 'hypostasis' as subsistence; this is seen by how he translated Hebrews 1:3 in quote 'B.'

16   ἀνουσίου, ἀνυποστάτου, the words are rendered 'unessential' and 'not subsisting' in another connection.

17   Athanasius of Alexandria. (1892). <u>Tome or Synodal Letter to the People of Antioch</u>. In P. Schaff & H. Wace (Eds.), A. T. Robertson (Trans.), *St. Athanasius: Select Works and Letters* (Vol. 4, pp. 484–485). New York: Christian Literature Company.

18   *De Syn.* 53, n. 9.

19   οὐσία and ὑπόστασις are in these passages made synonymous; and so *infr. Orat.* iv. 1, f. And in iv. 33 fin. to the Son is attributed ἡ πατρικὴ ὑπόστασις. Vid. also *ad Afros.* 4. quoted *supr. Exc. A*, pp. 77, *sqq.* Ὑπ. might have been expected too in the discussion in the beginning of *Orat.* iii. did Athan. distinguish between them. It is remarkable how seldom it occurs at all in these Orations, except as contained in Hebrews 1:3. Vid. also p. 70, note 13. Yet the phrase τρεῖς ὑποστάσεις is certainly found in *Illud Omn.* fin. and in *Incarn. c. Arian.* 10. (if genuine) and apparently in *Expos. Fid.* 2. Vid. also *Orat.* iv. 25 init.

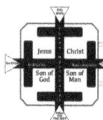

saying, 'Who being the Radiance of His glory and the Expression of His Subsistence.'"[20, 21]

C. "Now subsistence is essence, and means nothing else but very being, which Jeremiah calls existence, in the words, 'and they heard not the voice of existence.'[22] For subsistence, and essence, is existence: for it is, or in other words exists."[23]

D. "But as for those who say 'there was a time when he did not exist' and 'he did not exist before being begotten' and that he was made of nothing, or declare that God's Son comes from a different basis[24] or substance[25]...these the Catholic and Apostolic Church anathematizes. We follow at every point the confession of the holy fathers. . ."[26]

II. Latter definition → Individual Subject

A. "For the Triad, praised, reverenced, and adored, is one and indivisible and without degrees.[27] It is united without confusion, just as the Monad also is distinguished without separation. For the fact of those venerable living creatures [Is 6; Rev 4:8] offering their praises three times, saying 'Holy, Holy, Holy,' proves that the Three Subsistences[28] are perfect, just as in saying 'Lord,' they

---

20   Heb 1:3; the Greek word used in this verse is hypostasis

21   Athanasius of Alexandria. (1892). <u>Four Discourses against the Arians</u>. In P. Schaff & H. Wace (Eds.), J. H. Newman & A. T. Robertson (Trans.), *St. Athanasius: Select Works and Letters* (Vol. 4, pp. 429–430). New York: Christian Literature Company.

22   ὕπαρξις, Jer 9:10, LXX.

23   Athanasius of Alexandria. (1892). <u>To the Bishops of Africa</u>. In P. Schaff & H. Wace (Eds.), A. T. Robertson (Trans.), *St. Athanasius: Select Works and Letters* (Vol. 4, p. 490). New York: Christian Literature Company.

24   ὑποστάσεως

25   Οὐσίας

26   Cyril of Alexandria. (1983). <u>Third Letter to Nestorius</u>. L. Wickham (Trans.), *Cyril of Alexandria: Select letters* (p. 17). Oxford: Oxford University Press.

27   ἀσχηματιστός

28   τρεῖς ὑποστάσεις. This expression is a link between this tract and the *Expositio* (§ 2), and is one of the indications it bears of an early date. At this time we see that Athanasius speaks of Three "Hypostases," but qualifies his language by the caveat (*Expos.* 2) that they are not μεμερισμέναι. In this he follows his Origenist predecessor Dionysius, and the language of the present passage is that of Basil or the Gregories.

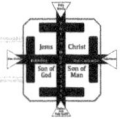

declare the One Essence."[29]

B. "Since there is one essence of the true and natural divinity understood in three hypostases (I mean in the Father and the Son and the Holy Spirit)."[30]

Synonyms for latter definition of the term "hypostasis"

I. Person[31]

A. "Lest he of Samosata should find an excuse to call Him man, as distinct in person from God the Word."[32]

B. "For whole the Holy Trinity opens out, as it were, into three distinct subsistences, or separate Persons, it is as though it contracts into the one nature of Deity."[33]

C. "For while the holy and adored Trinity is of the same substance, one would not for that reason ascribe the Incarnation to whatever Person one chose. For only the Son become man, and not the Father, nor the Holy Spirit."[34]

But it is not the language of Athanasius himself in his later years.

29   Athanasius of Alexandria. (1892). On Luke 10:22 (Mt 11:27). In P. Schaff & H. Wace (Eds.), A. T. Robertson (Trans.), *St. Athanasius: Select Works and Letters* (Vol. 4, p. 90). New York: Christian Literature Company.

30   Cyril of Alexandria. (2013–2015). *Commentary on John*. (J. C. Elowsky, T. C. Oden, & G. L. Bray, Eds., D. R. Maxwell, Trans.) (Vol. 2, p. 212). Downers Grove, IL: IVP Academic: An Imprint of InterVarsity Press.

31   From the Latin *persona*; In the same way that all humans share one essence but all are each unique individual human beings, or persons.

32   Athanasius of Alexandria. (1892). Personal Letters. In P. Schaff & H. Wace (Eds.), A. T. Robertson (Trans.), *St. Athanasius: Select Works and Letters* (Vol. 4, p. 579). New York: Christian Literature Company.

33   Cyril of Alexandria. (2018). *Glaphyra on the Pentateuch, Volume 1 Genesis*. (N. P. Lunn, Trans.) (Vol. 137, p. 94). Washington, DC: The Catholic University of America Press.

34   Ibid. (p. 122)

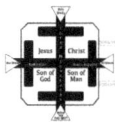

D. "For our part, we say that he [the Son] is distinct not from the essence but from the person of the Father."[35]

E. "The nature of the divinity is, and so is believed to be, one. Even though it is expanded into the Father and the Son and the Holy Spirit, it does not have an absolute and complete gap, I mean between each of the persons indicated... The divine nature is one, in the person and hypostasis of the Father and of the Son and of the Holy Spirit."[36]

II. Subsistence

A. "For whole the Holy Trinity opens out, as it were, into three distinct subsistences, or separate Persons, it is as though it contracts into the one nature of Deity."[37]

B. "When we consider the Father and the Son and the Holy Spirit, though we do truly assign them their own distinct subsistences, it is our habit to adorn them with a unity of nature. It is as though by means of this identity of essence we were raising up together[38] the length, the width, and the height by that one cubit, so completing the ark."[39]

C. "He genuinely depicts in himself the one who begat him, the one from whom he exists. However, he will not for that reason lose his own subsistence, nor will the Father lose his. Neither will their complete likeness cause any confusion of the hypostases so that we understand the Father who begat to be the same in number as the Son who was begotten of him. We will confess the identity of nature for both, but the proper subsistence of each one surely

---

35 Cyril of Alexandria. (2013–2015). *Commentary on John*. (J. C. Elowsky, T. C. Oden, & G. L. Bray, Eds., D. R. Maxwell, Trans.) (Vol. 2, p. 171). Downers Grove, IL: IVP Academic: An Imprint of InterVarsity Press.

36 Ibid. (p. 176).

37 Cyril of Alexandria. (2018). *Glaphyra on the Pentateuch, Volume 1 Genesis*. (N. P. Lunn, Trans.) (Vol. 137, p. 94). Washington, DC: The Catholic University of America Press.

38 Var. "we were closely connecting."

39 Ibid. (p. 95)

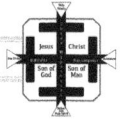

follows so that we should think of the Father as really the Father and the Son as the Son."[40]

D. "He [the Son] is not by nature foreign to the Father, as the enemies of God no doubt think, but he is and is understood to exist in his own person and in his own distinct subsistence. After all, he is the Son, not the Father."[41]

The Divine Hypostases truly <u>individually</u> and <u>simultaneously</u> exist and are not just varying names of <u>one</u> Divine Hypostasis

I. "It is not a Trinity in name alone and in linguistic expression, but in truth and actual existence. For just as the Father is 'He Who Is,' [Ex 3.4] so too is his Word 'He Who Is' and God over all [Rom 9.5]. And the Holy Spirit is not without existence, but exists and subsists truly."[42]

II. "They believed in a Holy Trinity, not a trinity in name only, but existing and subsisting in truth, both a Father truly existing and subsisting, and a Son truly substantial and subsisting, and a Holy Spirit subsisting and really existing do we acknowledge."[43]

III. "Because he was 'with God,' we recognize him as another besides

40   Cyril of Alexandria. (2013–2015). *Commentary on John*. (J. C. Elowsky, T. C. Oden, & G. L. Bray, Eds., D. R. Maxwell, Trans.) (Vol. 1, p. 10). Downers Grove, IL: IVP Academic: An Imprint of InterVarsity Press.

41   Ibid. (Vol. 2, p.171).

42   Athanasius and Didymus. (2011). *Works on the Spirit: Athanasius's Letters to Serapion on the Holy Spirit, and, Didymus's on the Holy Spirit*. (J. Behr, Ed., M. DelCogliano, A. Radde-Gallwitz, & L. Ayres, Trans.) (Vol. 43, p. 97). Yonkers, NY: St Vladimir's Seminary Press.

43   Athanasius of Alexandria. (1892). <u>Tome or Synodal Letter to the People of Antioch</u>. In P. Schaff & H. Wace (Eds.), A. T. Robertson (Trans.), *St. Athanasius: Select Works and Letters* (Vol. 4, p. 484). New York: Christian Literature Company.

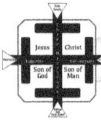

the Father, and we believe that the Son exists on his own."[44]

IV. "The Father is different from the Son by virtue of his own hypostasis. He is not introduced as a Son-Father, like some uneducated heretics think."[45]

The Divine Hypostases:

I.   The Father:

A. Is the only One who will ever have this title

1.   "Hence the one and only Father is the Father of the one and only Son, and only in the case of the divinity have the names 'Father' and 'Son' always been stable and always are."[46]

B. Is first, the Son second and the Holy Spirit third[47] because there is a Divine order, or ranking, observed; yet, **without** causing the Divine Hypostases to no longer be equal to each other in **every** way except Their individual Divine Hypostatic Attributes.

1.   "Seeing that there is such an order and unity in the Holy Trinity, who could separate either the Son from the Father, or the Spirit from the Son or from the Father himself?"[48]

---

44   Cyril of Alexandria. (2013–2015). *Commentary on John*. (J. C. Elowsky, T. C. Oden, & G. L. Bray, Eds., D. R. Maxwell, Trans.) (Vol. 1, p. 13). Downers Grove, IL: IVP Academic: An Imprint of InterVarsity Press.

45   Ibid. (p. 161).

46   Athanasius and Didymus. (2011). *Works on the Spirit: Athanasius's Letters to Serapion on the Holy Spirit, and, Didymus's on the Holy Spirit*. (J. Behr, Ed., M. DelCogliano, A. Radde-Gallwitz, & L. Ayres, Trans.) (Vol. 43, p. 78-79). Yonkers, NY: St Vladimir's Seminary Press.

47   Contemporary worship, viz.: we worship You O Christ with Your good Father and the Holy Spirit, is not contrary to this truth. It is not changing the order within the Trinity; rather, it is showing Who the prayer is directed to

48   Athanasius and Didymus. (2011). *Works on the Spirit: Athanasius's Letters to Serapion on the Holy Spirit, and, Didymus's on the Holy Spirit*. (J. Behr, Ed., M. DelCogliano, A. Radde-Gallwitz, & L. Ayres, Trans.)

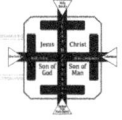

2. "Indeed, when the disciples heard the words: Baptize them in the name of the Father, and of the Son, and of the Holy Spirit [Mt 28.19], they did not futilely investigate why the Son comes second and the Spirit third, or why the whole is a Trinity. . . . For the faith was not to be stated otherwise than as the Savior stated it, the he is the Son and the other is the Spirit, nor was it right to change the manner in which they have been ranked together."[49]

3. "On the other hand, for a different reason it would be wrong also to understand the Father as being between both, since he is the one who is named first in the sequence of the confession of the holy and consubstantial Trinity. We do not in any way claim that by taking precedence to the Son and the Spirit in the listing he is superior to them, which would be an idle and rash statement; rather, our position and belief is that from eternity he has the Son originating from him, and what exists did not have existence without his Spirit; instead, as soon as the Father is understood to be God, immediately the existence of the one whose Father he is came into play, as likewise his divine and holy Spirit. Since, however, he is like a fountainhead of the one begotten by him, he is appropriately named first. I cannot understand how he is *between* Son and Spirit."[50]

4. "For the Triad, praised, reverenced, and adored, is one and indivisible and without degrees."[51, 52]

5. "Where, indeed, can one see inferiority or superiority in the selfsame substance?"[53]

(Vol. 43, p. 84). Yonkers, NY: St Vladimir's Seminary Press.

49   Ibid. (p. 134).

50   Cyril of Alexandria. (2008). *Commentary on the Twelve Prophets*. (T. P. Halton, Ed., R. C. Hill, Trans.) (Vol. 116, p. 368). Washington, DC: The Catholic University of America Press.

51   ἀσχημάτιστός

52   Athanasius of Alexandria. (1892). On Luke 10:22 (Mt 11:27). In P. Schaff & H. Wace (Eds.), A. T. Robertson (Trans.), *St. Athanasius: Select Works and Letters* (Vol. 4, p. 90). New York: Christian Literature Company.

53   Cyril of Alexandria. (1983). On the Creed. L. Wickham (Trans.), *Cyril of Alexandria: Select letters* (p.

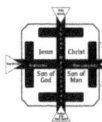

C. Is called:

1. Fountain:

    a. "The Father is called Fountain and Light. . . . The Father is the Fountain."[54]

2. Light:

    a. "The Father is called Fountain and Light . . . Thus the Father is Light and his Radiance is the Son"[55]

3. Mind

    a. "And this one may see from our own experience; for if when a word proceeds from men[56] we infer that the mind is its source, and, by thinking about the word, see with our reason the mind which it reveals, by far greater evidence and incomparably more, seeing the power of the Word, we receive a knowledge also of His good Father."[57]

    b. "[A]. A word is always from the mind and in the mind; and just as surely, the mind is in the word. . . . For the mind is always the root and origin of the word, and furthermore the word is the fruit and offspring of the mind. The mind, however, is never without the word, even if it gives birth to the word; and the word, never without the quality and appearance of the mind begetting it, as if this quality and appearance were its proper nature,—the word, I say, having been chosen, goes forth, damaging in no way the mind that

107). Oxford: Oxford University Press.

54   Athanasius and Didymus. (2011). *Works on the Spirit: Athanasius's Letters to Serapion on the Holy Spirit, and, Didymus's on the Holy Spirit*. (J. Behr, Ed., M. DelCogliano, A. Radde-Gallwitz, & L. Ayres, Trans.) (Vol. 43, p. 82). Yonkers, NY: St Vladimir's Seminary Press.

55   Ibid.

56   Cf. *de Sent. Dionys.* 23.

57   Athanasius of Alexandria. (1892). Against the Heathen. In P. Schaff & H. Wace (Eds.), A. T. Robertson (Trans.), *St. Athanasius: Select Works and Letters* (Vol. 4, p. 28). New York: Christian Literature Company.

has given it birth. . . .

"[B]. But really, how should the force of both of the examples,[58] since they pertain to us, apply in the case of the Father and the Son?

"[A]. Because the conveying of the word is from the mind to the outside, and because its generation is without passion, and certainly because that which was born is not cut off but still remains firmly in the mind that conceives it, and the mind conceiving it has it wholly in itself, ... it is clearly seen that the examples are applicable.[59]

c. "He has been sent, rather, in the same way as a word from the mind, as the sun's rays from the sun itself. For these examples are emergent, so to speak, from the items in which they exist since they seem to come out, but they exist naturally and inseparably in the items from which they come. When a word has come forth from the mind and a ray from the sun, let's say, we should not at all suppose that for this reason what begat them is deserted by what has gone out. Instead, we will see the former existing in the latter and the latter existing in the former. A mind, after all, will never be without words, and a word will never fail to be shaped by the mind in it."[60]

4. Unoriginate, as not Himself coming from a Source:

   a. "The Father has no personal cause."[61]

58 ἀμφοῖν τοῖν παραδειγμάτοιν is a splendid usage of the dual number.

59 Jurgens, W. A. (Trans.). (1970–1979). *The Faith of the Early Fathers* (Vol. 3, p. 214). Collegeville, MN: The Liturgical Press.

60 Cyril of Alexandria. (2013–2015). *Commentary on John*. (J. C. Elowsky, T. C. Oden, & G. L. Bray, Eds., D. R. Maxwell, Trans.) (Vol. 1, p. 271). Downers Grove, IL: IVP Academic: An Imprint of InterVarsity Press.

61 Athanasius of Alexandria. (1892). Councils of Ariminum and Seleucia. In P. Schaff & H. Wace (Eds.), J. H. Newman & A. T. Robertson (Trans.), *St. Athanasius: Select Works and Letters* (Vol. 4, p. 475). New York: Christian Literature Company.

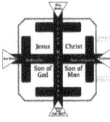

5. An Arche,[62] within the Holy Trinity, in reference to Itself

   a. "Above all as Father, as beginning, as source . . ."[63]

   b. "But if they ask according as Asterius ruled it, as if 'what is not a work but was always' were unoriginate, then they must constantly be told that the Son as well as the Father must in this sense be called unoriginate. For He is neither in the number of things originated, nor a work, but has ever been with the Father, as has already been shewn, in spite of their many variations for the sole sake of speaking against the Lord, 'He is of nothing' and 'He was not before His generation.' When then, after failing at every turn, they betake themselves to the other sense of the question, 'existing but not generated of any nor having a father,' we shall tell them that the unoriginate in this sense is only one, namely the Father."[64]

   c. "The Word has His being, in no other beginning[65] than the Father, whom[66] they allow to be without beginning, so that He too exists without beginning in the Father."[67]

   d. "Gentiles who maintain and think, on account of the Trinity, that we profess many gods.[68] For, as the illustration shews,

---

62   ἀρχέ; a beginning, origin, first cause; Liddell, H. G. (1996). *A lexicon: Abridged from Liddell and Scott's Greek-English lexicon* (p. 121). Oak Harbor, WA: Logos Research Systems, Inc.

63   Athanasius and Didymus. (2011). *Works on the Spirit: Athanasius's Letters to Serapion on the Holy Spirit, and, Didymus's on the Holy Spirit*. (J. Behr, Ed., M. DelCogliano, A. Radde-Gallwitz, & L. Ayres, Trans.) (Vol. 43, p. 97). Yonkers, NY: St Vladimir's Seminary Press.

64   Athanasius of Alexandria. (1892). Four Discourses against the Arians. In P. Schaff & H. Wace (Eds.), J. H. Newman & A. T. Robertson (Trans.), *St. Athanasius: Select Works and Letters* (Vol. 4, pp. 324–325). New York: Christian Literature Company.

65   ἀρχῆ, vid. *Orat.* iv. 1.

66   In this passage 'was from the beginning' is made equivalent with 'was not before generation,' and both are contrasted with 'without beginning' or 'eternal;' vid. the bearing of this on Bishop Bull's explanation of the Nicene Anathema, *supr. Exc. B,* where this passage is quoted.

67   Athanasius of Alexandria. (1892). Four Discourses against the Arians. In P. Schaff & H. Wace (Eds.), J. H. Newman & A. T. Robertson (Trans.), *St. Athanasius: Select Works and Letters* (Vol. 4, p. 379). New York: Christian Literature Company.

68   *Serap.* i. 28 fin. Naz. *Orat.* 23, 8. Basil. *Hom.* 24 init. Nyssen. *Orat. Catech.* 3. P. 481.

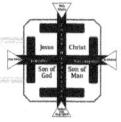

we do not introduce three Origins or three Fathers."[69]

e. "Therefore, since the Son is older than even the ages themselves, he will elude any notion that he came to be in time. Through all time, he 'was' in his Father as in a source according to his own statement, 'I came from the Father and have arrived.' Therefore, since the Father is considered as source, 'the Word was in him' because the Word was his wisdom, power, imprint, radiance and image. . . . It would not be wrong in the least to think that the Son exists in the Father as in a source.[70] For the name 'source' in this case indicates only what something is from."[71]

f. "The Son exists in the Father and from the Father. He did not come into existence from outside of the Father or in time but exists in the substance of the Father. The saints too refer to God the Father as the 'beginning'[72] of the Son only to indicate whom he is 'from'. . . . The Father is the beginningless beginning of the Son's nature, so to speak, but only in the sense of source because the Son's existence is 'from' the Father."[73]

g. "Notice once again the vigilance of the Spirit bearer. He taught above that the Word was in the beginning, that is, in God the Father, as we said."[74]

h. "He [the Father] is the source of the creating Word."[75]

---

69   Athanasius of Alexandria. (1892). <u>Four Discourses against the Arians</u>. In P. Schaff & H. Wace (Eds.), J. H. Newman & A. T. Robertson (Trans.), *St. Athanasius: Select Works and Letters* (Vol. 4, p. 402). New York: Christian Literature Company.

70   The word for "source" (πηγή) denotes a spring of water

71   Cyril of Alexandria. (2013–2015). *Commentary on John*. (J. C. Elowsky, T. C. Oden, & G. L. Bray, Eds., D. R. Maxwell, Trans.) (Vol. 1, p. 7). Downers Grove, IL: IVP Academic: An Imprint of InterVarsity Press.

72   Αρχή.

73   Cyril of Alexandria. (2013–2015). *Commentary on John*. (J. C. Elowsky, T. C. Oden, & G. L. Bray, Eds., D. R. Maxwell, Trans.) (Vol. 1, p. 8). Downers Grove, IL: IVP Academic: An Imprint of InterVarsity Press.

74   Ibid. (p. 10).

75   Cyril of Alexandria. (2013–2015). *Commentary on John*. (J. C. Elowsky, T. C. Oden, & G. L. Bray, Eds., D. R. Maxwell, Trans.) (Vol. 1, p. 31). Downers Grove, IL: IVP Academic: An Imprint of InterVarsity Press.

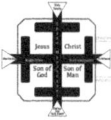

i. The Son and the Holy Spirit have the Father as a mutual Arché; however, the specific relation of Them to the Father, the Arché, is not the same but unique to Each

1) The Son **alone** is eternally **begotten** from the Father

A) "He gave His only begotten Son."[76]

B) "For the Father and the Son were not generated from some pre-existing origin,[77] that we may account Them brothers, but the Father is the Origin of the Son and begat Him; and the Father is Father, and not born the Son of any; and the Son is Son, and not brother."[78]

C) "We declare that the only-begotten Word of God, begotten from the very substance of the Father."[79]

2) The Holy Spirit **alone** eternally proceeds:

A) From the Father

i. "The Spirit, **who proceeds from the Father** (John 15:26) and, being proper to the Son, is given by Him."[80]

ii. "For the Holy Spirit indeed proceeds from God the Father, but belongs also to the Son. It is even often called the Spirit of Christ, though proceeding

---

76 Jn 3:16

77 Vid. *de Syn.* § 51.

78 Athanasius of Alexandria. (1892). Four Discourses against the Arians. In P. Schaff & H. Wace (Eds.), J. H. Newman & A. T. Robertson (Trans.), *St. Athanasius: Select Works and Letters* (Vol. 4, p. 314). New York: Christian Literature Company.

79 Cyril of Alexandria. (1983). Third Letter to Nestorius. L. Wickham (Trans.), *Cyril of Alexandria: Select letters* (p. 17). Oxford: Oxford University Press.

80 Athanasius and Didymus. (2011). *Works on the Spirit: Athanasius's Letters to Serapion on the Holy Spirit, and, Didymus's on the Holy Spirit.* (J. Behr, Ed., M. DelCogliano, A. Radde-Gallwitz, & L. Ayres, Trans.) (Vol. 43, p. 55). Yonkers, NY: St Vladimir's Seminary Press.

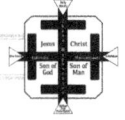

from God the Father."[81]

iii. "The Holy Ghost then proceeds from God the Father as from the fountain; but is not foreign from the Son."[82]

iv. "So also the Holy Ghost, by reason of His being equal in substance, is joined in oneness to the Son, even though He proceed from God the Father."[83]

v. "He says that the Paraclete is 'the Spirit of truth,' and then he declares that he 'proceeds from the Father.'"[84]

vi. "After completing their account of Christ the thrice-blessed fathers call to mind the Holy Ghost, declaring their belief in him just as in the case of the Father and the Son. He is consubstantial with them; he pours out (or proceeds)[85] from, as it were, the fount of God the Father and is bestowed[86] on creation through[87] the Son-he breathed, remember, on the holy apostles saying: 'Receive the Holy Ghost.'"[88]

B) Through the Son

i. "Though the Spirit proceeds from the Father, he

---

81 Cyril of Alexandria. (1859). *A Commentary upon the Gospel according to S. Luke*. (R. P. Smith, Trans.) (p. 45). Oxford: Oxford University Press.

82 Ibid. (p. 296)

83 Ibid. (p. 371)

84 Cyril of Alexandria. (2013–2015). *Commentary on John*. (J. C. Elowsky, T. C. Oden, & G. L. Bray, Eds., D. R. Maxwell, Trans.) (Vol. 2, p. 247). Downers Grove, IL: IVP Academic: An Imprint of InterVarsity Press.

85 ἐκπορεύεται

86 Χορηγεῖται

87 διὰ

88 Cyril of Alexandria. (1983). On the Creed. L. Wickham (Trans.), *Cyril of Alexandria: Select letters* (p. 129). Oxford: Oxford University Press.

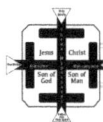

nevertheless comes through the Son and is his own."[89]

ii. "Look—look—he calls the 'Spirit of truth' (that is, of himself) the 'Paraclete,' and he says that he 'proceeds from the Father.' Just as the Spirit belongs to the Son by nature, being in him and proceeding through him, so also the Spirit belongs to the Father. . . . Instead we should believe that he sends the Spirit to sanctify his holy disciples because the Spirit belongs to him, just as the Spirit certainly belongs to God the Father. . . the Son supplies the Spirit from the Father. . . the Spirit who comes from God the Father. . . According to the ignorance of the godless, the Son is declared to be foreign to the essence of the Father, from which the Spirit, who is supplied by him, proceeds."[90]

iii. "We too may firmly believe that the Holy Spirit is not alien to the Son but is of the same substance with him and proceeds through him from the Father."[91]

3) It is wrong to investigate how begetting and procession occur.

A) "Nor again is it right to seek how the word is from God, or how He is God's radiance, or how God begets, and what is the manner of His begetting.[92]

89 Cyril of Alexandria. (2013–2015). *Commentary on John*. (J. C. Elowsky, T. C. Oden, & G. L. Bray, Eds., D. R. Maxwell, Trans.) (Vol. 2, p. 188-189). Downers Grove, IL: IVP Academic: An Imprint of InterVarsity Press.

90 Ibid. (p. 246)

91 Ibid. (p. 367)

92 Eusebius has some forcible remarks on this subject. As, he says, we do not know how God can create out of nothing, so we are utterly ignorant of the Divine Generation. It is written, He who believes, not he who knows, has eternal life. The sun's radiance itself is but an earthly image, and gives us no true idea of

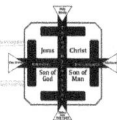

For a man must be beside himself to venture on such points; since a thing ineffable and proper to God's nature, and known to Him alone and to the Son, this he demands to be explained in words."[93]

B) "That he was begotten of God the Father, we know and believe. But how, we say is inaccessible to every mind, and the investigation of it is most dangerous. For we must not investigate things that are too deep or search out things that are too difficult."[94]

4) The Begetting and Procession are indescribable

A) "His ineffable generation from God the Father."[95]

B) "We believe that the first birth of the Word from God is understood to be timeless and beyond thought."[96]

C) "His ineffable birth from God the Father is completely unknown."[97]

5) The begetting of the Son and the Procession of the Holy Spirit are eternal processes, having no beginning nor end.

A) "His [the Word] own everlasting and genuine

that which is above all images. *Eccl. Theol.* i. 12. So has S. Greg. Naz. *Orat.* 29. 8. vid. also Hippol. *in Noet.* 16. Cyril, *Cat.* xi. 11. and 19. and Origen, according to Mosheim, *Ante Const.* p 619. And instances in *Petav. de Trin.* v. 6 § 2. and 3.

93   Athanasius of Alexandria. (1892). Four Discourses against the Arians. In P. Schaff & H. Wace (Eds.), J. H. Newman & A. T. Robertson (Trans.), *St. Athanasius: Select Works and Letters* (Vol. 4, p. 367). New York: Christian Literature Company.

94   Cyril of Alexandria. (2013–2015). *Commentary on John*. (J. C. Elowsky, T. C. Oden, & G. L. Bray, Eds., D. R. Maxwell, Trans.) (Vol. 1, p. 292). Downers Grove, IL: IVP Academic: An Imprint of InterVarsity Press.

95   Cyril of Alexandria. (1859). *A Commentary upon the Gospel according to S. Luke*. (R. P. Smith, Trans.) (p. 474). Oxford: Oxford University Press.

96   Cyril of Alexandria. (2013–2015). *Commentary on John*. (J. C. Elowsky, T. C. Oden, & G. L. Bray, Eds., D. R. Maxwell, Trans.) (Vol. 1, p. 365). Downers Grove, IL: IVP Academic: An Imprint of InterVarsity Press.

97   Ibid. (Vol. 2, p. 47)

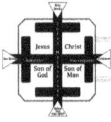

generation from the Father."[98]

B) "The timeless generation by God the Father resulting in the individual existence of the Son."[99]

C) "The ineffable and eternal generation of the Son."[100]

D) "For since the Father is always Father, and does not pass in time from begetting potentially to begetting in actuality, the one through whom he is Father must always exist with him."[101]

E) "His ineffable and timeless birth from the Father."[102]

j. The Son and Holy Spirit are generated from the <u>Essence</u> of the Father

1) "The Father's essence was the origin and root and fountain of the Son."[103]

2) "The Son, begotten from the Father's essence, is coessential with Him."[104]

3) "The Son is of the Father's Essence and coessential with Him."[105]

---

98   Athanasius of Alexandria. (1892). <u>Four Discourses against the Arians</u>. In P. Schaff & H. Wace (Eds.), J. H. Newman & A. T. Robertson (Trans.), *St. Athanasius: Select Works and Letters* (Vol. 4, p. 372). New York: Christian Literature Company.

99   Cyril of Alexandria. (2008). *Commentary on the Twelve Prophets*. (T. P. Halton, Ed., R. C. Hill, Trans.) (Vol. 116, p. 235). Washington, DC: The Catholic University of America Press.

100   Cyril of Alexandria. (2013–2015). *Commentary on John*. (J. C. Elowsky, T. C. Oden, & G. L. Bray, Eds., D. R. Maxwell, Trans.) (Vol. 1, p. 6). Downers Grove, IL: IVP Academic: An Imprint of InterVarsity Press.

101   Cyril of Alexandria. (2013). *Festal Letters, 13–30*. (J. J. O'Keefe & D. G. Hunter, Eds., P. R. Amidon, Trans.) (Vol. 127, p. 35). Washington, DC: The Catholic University of America Press.

102   Cyril of Alexandria. (2013–2015). *Commentary on John*. (J. C. Elowsky, T. C. Oden, & G. L. Bray, Eds., D. R. Maxwell, Trans.) (Vol. 1, p. 365). Downers Grove, IL: IVP Academic: An Imprint of InterVarsity Press.

103   Athanasius of Alexandria. (1892). <u>Councils of Ariminum and Seleucia</u>. In P. Schaff & H. Wace (Eds.), J. H. Newman & A. T. Robertson (Trans.), *St. Athanasius: Select Works and Letters* (Vol. 4, p. 474). New York: Christian Literature Company.

104   Ibid. (p. 479)

105   Ibid. (<u>To the Bishops of Africa</u>, p. 492)

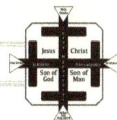

4) "The Word . . . Who shone forth from the substance of God the Father."[106]

5) "The Word being God, and sprung from the very substance of God the Father."[107]

6) "The Son shows that he is from the substance of God the Father when he says at one point, 'I came from the Father and have arrived. I am going to the Father again.' How then will he not differ from him in hypostasis and number since all reason convinces us to think that something that comes from something else is different from that from which it has come?"[108]

7) "The Spirit is of the substance of God the Father... the Spirit is certainly from the substance of God the Father."[109]

8) "[The Holy Spirit] proceeding from the very essence of God the Father."[110]

k. The entire Holy Trinity can be considered an Arché, in reference to all Creation; examples include:

1) Creating

A) "Let Us make man. . . "[111]

B) "The Father creates and renews all things through

---

106   Cyril of Alexandria. (1859). *A Commentary upon the Gospel according to S. Luke*. (R. P. Smith, Trans.) (p. 308). Oxford: Oxford University Press.

107   Ibid. (p. 642)

108   Cyril of Alexandria. (2013–2015). *Commentary on John*. (J. C. Elowsky, T. C. Oden, & G. L. Bray, Eds., D. R. Maxwell, Trans.) (Vol. 1, p. 11). Downers Grove, IL: IVP Academic: An Imprint of InterVarsity Press.

109   Ibid. (p. 97)

110   Ibid. (Vol. 2, p. 296)

111   Gen 1:26 LXX

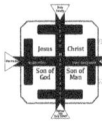

the Word in the Holy Spirit. . . .'[112]

C) "By saying that the world was made through him, he raises our mind to consider the Father, and he introduces the words 'through whom' along with the words 'from whom.' That is because all things are from the Father, through the Son, in the Holy Spirit."[113]

D) "The Father creates through the Son."[114]

E) "Therefore, by saying that it is the work of the one who sent him, he himself is shown to be its fulfiller because all things are from the Father, through the Son and in the Spirit."[115]

2) Authority over all Creation

A) "Now the blessed Evangelist here seems to call the Father the 'beginning,'[116] that is, the authority over all things, so that the divine nature clearly transcends all things. That nature has all originate beings under its feet and is practically borne aloft over those things that are called into being through it. . . . Therefore, since he [the Word] springs from the free Father and is himself free, he will possess with the Father the beginning (or dominion) that transcends all things."[117]

---

112   Athanasius and Didymus. (2011). *Works on the Spirit: Athanasius's Letters to Serapion on the Holy Spirit, and, Didymus's on the Holy Spirit*. (J. Behr, Ed., M. DelCogliano, A. Radde-Gallwitz, & L. Ayres, Trans.) (Vol. 43, p. 91). Yonkers, NY: St Vladimir's Seminary Press.

113   Cyril of Alexandria. (2013–2015). *Commentary on John*. (J. C. Elowsky, T. C. Oden, & G. L. Bray, Eds., D. R. Maxwell, Trans.) (Vol. 1, p. 58). Downers Grove, IL: IVP Academic: An Imprint of InterVarsity Press.

114   Ibid. (p. 12)

115   Ibid. (p. 131)

116   The word for "beginning" in John 1:1 (ἀρχή) also means "dominion."

117   Cyril of Alexandria. (2013–2015). *Commentary on John*. (J. C. Elowsky, T. C. Oden, & G. L. Bray, Eds., D. R. Maxwell, Trans.) (Vol. 1, p. 8). Downers Grove, IL: IVP Academic: An Imprint of InterVarsity Press.

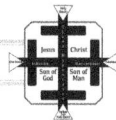

3) Distribution of blessings

    A) "Blessings come to us through the entire holy Trinity, and God the Father is found to be entirely all in all, through the Son in the Spirit."[118]

D. Is never called:

1. Grandfather

    a. "In the Scriptures the Spirit is never called a son, lest he be considered a brother. Nor is he called a son of the Son, lest the Father be thought of as a grandfather."[119]

    b. "It is not otherwise than that the Father is Father and not grandfather, and the Son is the Son of God and not the father of the Spirit, and the Holy Spirit is Holy Spirit and not grandson of the Father nor the brother of the Son."[120]

    c. "Our faith is in the Father and the Son and the Holy Spirit: the Father who cannot be called grandfather, the Son who cannot be called father, and the Holy Spirit who is given no other name than the one he has. It is not permitted to exchange the names of this faith: the Father is always Father, and the Son always Son, and the Holy Spirit is and is said to be always Holy Spirit."[121]

2. Son

    a. "It is impossible to say that the Father has a father."[122]

    b. "In their case the Father's name has always been 'Father'

---

118   Ibid. (p. 223)

119   Athanasius and Didymus. (2011). *Works on the Spirit: Athanasius's Letters to Serapion on the Holy Spirit, and, Didymus's on the Holy Spirit.* (J. Behr, Ed., M. DelCogliano, A. Radde-Gallwitz, & L. Ayres, Trans.) (Vol. 43, p. 78-79). Yonkers, NY: St Vladimir's Seminary Press.

120   Ibid. (p .133)

121   Ibid. (p. 135)

122   Ibid. (p. 77)

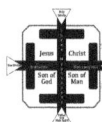

and the Son's name always 'Son.' And just as the Father could never have been a son, so too the Son could never become a father. And just as the Father will never cease to be only a father, so too the Son will never cease to be only a son. . . . "[123]

c. "The Father is a father and not a son."[124]

II. The Son, Who was incarnate for our salvation, and is also called Jesus Christ is:

A. The only Son of the Father, being His Only-Begotten

1. "Hence the one and only Father is the Father of the one and only Son, and only in the case of the divinity have the names 'Father' and 'Son' always been stable and always are. . . "[125]

2. "Indeed, just as the Son is the only-begotten offspring."[126]

B. Called:

1. Angel of the Lord

    a. "The custom with the holy prophets to refer to the Word of God as an angel insofar as he announced to them and made clear the will of the God and Father."[127]

---

123   Ibid. (p. 78-9)

124   Cyril of Alexandria. (2013–2015). *Commentary on John*. (J. C. Elowsky, T. C. Oden, & G. L. Bray, Eds., D. R. Maxwell, Trans.) (Vol. 2, p. 179). Downers Grove, IL: IVP Academic: An Imprint of InterVarsity Press.

125   Athanasius and Didymus. (2011). *Works on the Spirit: Athanasius's Letters to Serapion on the Holy Spirit, and, Didymus's on the Holy Spirit*. (J. Behr, Ed., M. DelCogliano, A. Radde-Gallwitz, & L. Ayres, Trans.) (Vol. 43, p. 78-79). Yonkers, NY: St Vladimir's Seminary Press.

126   Ibid. (p. 85)

127   Cyril of Alexandria. (2007). *Commentary on the Twelve Prophets*. (T. P. Halton, Ed., R. C. Hill, Trans.) (Vol. 115, p. 38). Washington, DC: The Catholic University of America Press.

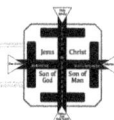

2. Arm of the Father[128]

    a. "They call the Son the right hand and the arm of God the Father."[129]

    b. "Often Holy Scripture calls the Son the **arm** of the Father, for he is God's power."[130]

    c. "The Son is called the hand and arm of God the Father."[131]

    d. "The Son is his power and his arm."[132]

3. Our Bridegroom

    a. "Its heaven-sent Bridegroom—namely, Christ."[133]

    b. "The bridegroom from heaven, that is, Christ."[134]

4. Our Brother

    a. "And in consequence He is called our brother, as having become man."[135]

    b. "When He put on a created nature and became like us in

---

128   This does not mean that He is a portion of the Father

129   Cyril of Alexandria. (2013). *Festal Letters, 13–30*. (J. J. O'Keefe & D. G. Hunter, Eds., P. R. Amidon, Trans.) (Vol. 127, p. 166). Washington, DC: The Catholic University of America Press.

130   Wilken, R. L., Christman, A. R., & Hollerich, M. J. (Eds.). (2007). *Isaiah: Interpreted by Early Christian and Medieval Commentators*. (R. L. Wilken, A. R. Christman, & M. J. Hollerich, Trans.) (p. 394). Grand Rapids, MI; Cambridge, UK: William B. Eerdmans Publishing Company.

131   Cyril of Alexandria. (1859). *A Commentary upon the Gospel according to S. Luke*. (R. P. Smith, Trans.) (p. 370). Oxford: Oxford University Press.

132   Cyril of Alexandria. (2013–2015). *Commentary on John*. (J. C. Elowsky, T. C. Oden, & G. L. Bray, Eds., D. R. Maxwell, Trans.) (Vol. 1, p. 11). Downers Grove, IL: IVP Academic: An Imprint of InterVarsity Press.

133   Cyril of Alexandria. (2007). *Commentary on the Twelve Prophets*. (T. P. Halton, Ed., R. C. Hill, Trans.) (Vol. 115, p. 104). Washington, DC: The Catholic University of America Press.

134   Ibid. (p. 269)

135   Athanasius of Alexandria. (1892). Four Discourses against the Arians. In P. Schaff & H. Wace (Eds.), J. H. Newman & A. T. Robertson (Trans.), *St. Athanasius: Select Works and Letters* (Vol. 4, p. 354). New York: Christian Literature Company.

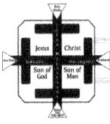

body, reasonably was He therefore called both our Brother and 'First-born.'"[136, 137]

c. "The Word's condescension[138] to the creatures, according to which He has become the 'Brother' of 'many.'"[139]

d. "The Word who for us has become like us,[140] a human being, that is, according to the economy, that we might be above ourselves, and beyond the limits of humanity, being called God's children,[141] and having as our brother him who is above all creation."[142]

e. "Having the Only-Begotten as firstborn and brother in the flesh."[143]

f. "The Word by God the Father, yet humbled Himself unto emptying, even to becoming our brother, by being made like unto us, and similar in all things to the inhabitants of the earth, sin only excepted."[144]

g. "And we are made also sons of God, and win for ourselves brotherhood with Him Who by nature and verily is the

---

136   Rom 8:29. Bishop Bull's hypothesis about the sense of πρωτότοκος τῆς κτίσεως has been comment-ed on *supr.* p. 347. As far as Athan.'s discussion proceeds in this section, it only relates to πρωτότοκος of *men* (i.e. from the dead), and is equivalent to the 'beginning of ways.'

137   Ibid. (p. 381)

138   Bp. Bull considers συγκατάβασις as equivalent to a figurative γέννησις, an idea which (vid. *supr.* p. 346 *sq.*) seems quite foreign from Athan.'s meaning. In Bull's sense of the word, Athan. could not have said that the senses of Only-begotten and First-born were contrary to each other, Or. i. 28. Συγκαταβῆναι occurs *supr.* 51 fin. of the Incarnation. What is meant by it will be found *infr.* 78–81. viz. that our Lord came "to implant in the creatures a type and semblance of His Image;" which is just what is here maintained against Bull. The whole passage referred to is a comment on the word συγκατάβασις, and begins and ends with an introduction of that word. Vid. also *c. Gent.* 47.

139   Ibid. (p. 382)

140   Cf. Heb 4:15

141   Cf. 1 Jn 3:1

142   Cyril of Alexandria. (2013). *Festal Letters, 13–30.* (J. J. O'Keefe & D. G. Hunter, Eds., P. R. Amidon, Trans.) (Vol. 127, p. 117). Washington, DC: The Catholic University of America Press.

143   Ibid. (p. 123)

144   Cyril of Alexandria. (1859). *A Commentary upon the Gospel according to S. Luke.* (R. P. Smith, Trans.) (p. 96). Oxford: Oxford University Press.

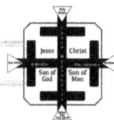

Son."[145]

h. "Christ, Who calls us to the adoption of sons and brotherhood with Him."[146]

i. "From His infinite love to mankind, is not ashamed to call us brethren, thus saying; 'I will preach Thy name to My brethren.'[147] For because He became like unto us, we thereby have gained brotherhood with Him."[148]

j. "He calls us his brothers."[149]

5. Drink

a. "But when we drink of the Spirit, we drink of Christ. . . . "[150]

6. The Face of the Father

a. "What then is the face of God the Father... Surely it is none other than the only begotten Son of God."[151]

b. "God the Father's face (i.e., the Son)."[152]

c. "The Son, then, is the true face of the God and Father."[153]

---

145   Ibid. (p. 142)

146   Ibid. (p. 147)

147   Ps 22:22

148   Cyril of Alexandria. (1859). *A Commentary upon the Gospel according to S. Luke*. (R. P. Smith, Trans.) (p. 327). Oxford: Oxford University Press.

149   Cyril of Alexandria. (2013–2015). *Commentary on John*. (J. C. Elowsky, T. C. Oden, & G. L. Bray, Eds., D. R. Maxwell, Trans.) (Vol. 2, p. 363). Downers Grove, IL: IVP Academic: An Imprint of InterVarsity Press.

150   Athanasius and Didymus. (2011). *Works on the Spirit: Athanasius's Letters to Serapion on the Holy Spirit, and, Didymus's on the Holy Spirit*. (J. Behr, Ed., M. DelCogliano, A. Radde-Gallwitz, & L. Ayres, Trans.) (Vol. 43, p. 82). Yonkers, NY: St Vladimir's Seminary Press.

151   Cyril of Alexandria. (2013–2015). *Commentary on John*. (J. C. Elowsky, T. C. Oden, & G. L. Bray, Eds., D. R. Maxwell, Trans.) (Vol. 1, p. 46). Downers Grove, IL: IVP Academic: An Imprint of InterVarsity Press.

152   Ibid. (p. 47)

153   Cyril of Alexandria. (2007). *Commentary on the Twelve Prophets*. (T. P. Halton, Ed., R. C. Hill, Trans.) (Vol. 115, p. 137). Washington, DC: The Catholic University of America Press.

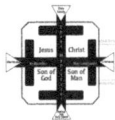

7. Fountain of Life

   a. "Christ is the fountain of life . . ."[154]

8. Fountain of Living Water

   a. "The fountain of living water, that is, Christ. . . ."[155]

9. Fruit of the Father

   a. "And to sum all up, He is the wholly perfect Fruit of the Father, and is alone the Son, and unchanging Image of the Father."[156]

   b. "He is, rather, the fruit of his [the Father's] substance and a genuine offspring. . . . God the Word . . . is the fruit of the Father's Substance."[157]

10. Garment of Joy

    a. "The garment of joy, which is Christ."[158]

    b. "Therefore, Christ is the most fitting garment for every holy person; he is the robe of spiritual joy that provides us with strength and glory."[159]

---

154   Cyril of Alexandria. (2018). *Glaphyra on the Pentateuch, Volume 1 Genesis*. (N. P. Lunn, Trans.) (Vol. 137, p. 152). Washington, DC: The Catholic University of America Press.

155   Ibid.

156   Athanasius of Alexandria. (1892). <u>Against the Heathen</u>. In P. Schaff & H. Wace (Eds.), A. T. Robertson (Trans.), St. Athanasius: Select Works and Letters (Vol. 4, p. 29). New York: Christian Literature Company.

157   Cyril of Alexandria. (2013–2015). *Commentary on John*. (J. C. Elowsky, T. C. Oden, & G. L. Bray, Eds., D. R. Maxwell, Trans.) (Vol. 1, p. 15). Downers Grove, IL: IVP Academic: An Imprint of InterVarsity Press.

158   Cyril of Alexandria. (2013). *Festal Letters, 13–30*. (J. J. O'Keefe & D. G. Hunter, Eds., P. R. Amidon, Trans.) (Vol. 127, p. 144). Washington, DC: The Catholic University of America Press.

159   Wilken, R. L., Christman, A. R., & Hollerich, M. J. (Eds.). (2007). *Isaiah: Interpreted by Early Christian and Medieval Commentators*. (R. L. Wilken, A. R. Christman, & M. J. Hollerich, Trans.) (p. 402). Grand Rapids, MI; Cambridge, UK: William B. Eerdmans Publishing Company.

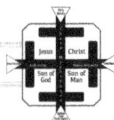

11. Hand of the Father[160]

   a. "Who uses His [the Father's] proper Word as a Hand."[161]

   b. "The Hand and the Wisdom and the Word was nothing else than the Son."[162]

   c. "The Son cannot be a work, but He is the Hand of God."[163]

   d. "As the right hand of God our Savior is invincible."[164]

   e. "He is the almighty right hand of the Father, since the Father does everything through him. . . . In many places in the Scripture, Christ is called the 'hand' or the 'right hand' of the Father, which means his power. The almighty power and activity of God is called simply his 'hand.'"[165]

   f. "The hand of the Father through which all things exist (that is, the Son)."[166]

12. Image of the Father

   a. "Hence the Word is suitably and appropriately confessed not to be a creature, since he is the Image of the Father."[167]

---

160   This does not mean that He is a portion of the Father

161   Athanasius of Alexandria. (1892). De Decretis or Defence of the Nicene Definition. In P. Schaff & H. Wace (Eds.), J. H. Newman & A. T. Robertson (Trans.), St. Athanasius: Select Works and Letters (Vol. 4, p. 155). New York: Christian Literature Company.

162   Ibid. (p. 161)

163   Athanasius of Alexandria. (1892). Four Discourses against the Arians. In P. Schaff & H. Wace (Eds.), J. H. Newman & A. T. Robertson (Trans.), St. Athanasius: Select Works and Letters (Vol. 4, p. 387). New York: Christian Literature Company.

164   Cyril of Alexandria. (1859). A Commentary upon the Gospel according to S. Luke. (R. P. Smith, Trans.) (p. 165). Oxford: Oxford University Press.

165   Cyril of Alexandria. (2013–2015). Commentary on John. (J. C. Elowsky, T. C. Oden, & G. L. Bray, Eds., D. R. Maxwell, Trans.) (Vol. 2, p. 77). Downers Grove, IL: IVP Academic: An Imprint of InterVarsity Press.

166   Ibid. (p. 220)

167   Athanasius and Didymus. (2011). Works on the Spirit: Athanasius's Letters to Serapion on the Holy Spirit, and, Didymus's on the Holy Spirit. (J. Behr, Ed., M. DelCogliano, A. Radde-Gallwitz, & L. Ayres, Trans.) (Vol. 43, p. 91). Yonkers, NY: St Vladimir's Seminary Press.

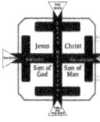

13. Light

a. "By saying 'the light,' with the article, he [Jesus] signified himself, since he alone is the true light."[168]

14. Our Nephew

a. "Christ the Savior of all, who is also our nephew, being born of our sister, as it were, the holy virgin."[169]

15. A Paraclete

a. "The Son also is and is called a Paraclete."[170]

b. "In that he is human, he is now understood to be the high priest of our souls and the Paraclete and the propitiation for our sins."[171]

c. "In his capacity as mediator, high priest and Paraclete, he brings supplications to the Father on our behalf."[172]

d. "The Son in his capacity as Paraclete and mediator."[173]

16. Peace

a. "'Peace be with you,' he says, referring to himself as 'peace.'... the peace of all people, that is, Christ. 'For he is

168 Cyril of Alexandria. (2013–2015). *Commentary on John*. (J. C. Elowsky, T. C. Oden, & G. L. Bray, Eds., D. R. Maxwell, Trans.) (Vol. 2, p. 110). Downers Grove, IL: IVP Academic: An Imprint of InterVarsity Press.

169 Cyril of Alexandria. (2007). *Commentary on the Twelve Prophets*. (T. P. Halton, Ed., R. C. Hill, Trans.) (Vol. 115, p. 268). Washington, DC: The Catholic University of America Press.

170 Cyril of Alexandria. (2013–2015). *Commentary on John*. (J. C. Elowsky, T. C. Oden, & G. L. Bray, Eds., D. R. Maxwell, Trans.) (Vol. 2, p. 178). Downers Grove, IL: IVP Academic: An Imprint of InterVarsity Press.

171 Ibid. (p. 252)

172 Ibid. (p. 263)

173 Ibid. (p. 264)

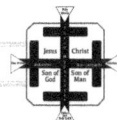

our peace,' according to the Scriptures."[174]

17. Pearl of Great Value

a. "That one pearl of great value, which is Christ."[175]

18. Physician

a. "Jesus is the Physician of souls and spirits."[176]

19. Radiance

a. "But the Son, as if in reference to the Fountain, is called River. . . . And in reference to the Light, he is called Radiance. . . . Thus the Father is Light and his Radiance is the Son."[177]

20. River

a. "But the Son, as if in reference to the Fountain, is called River . . . the Father is the Fountain and the Son is called the River."[178]

21. Seal of the Father

a. "The Son being the seal of the God and Father, . . . By him

---

174   Ibid. (p. 366)

175   Cyril of Alexandria. (2018). *Glaphyra on the Pentateuch, Volume 1 Genesis*. (N. P. Lunn, Trans.) (Vol. 137, p. 196). Washington, DC: The Catholic University of America Press.

176   Cyril of Alexandria. (1859). *A Commentary upon the Gospel according to S. Luke*. (R. P. Smith, Trans.) (p. 154). Oxford: Oxford University Press.

177   Athanasius and Didymus. (2011). *Works on the Spirit: Athanasius's Letters to Serapion on the Holy Spirit, and, Didymus's on the Holy Spirit*. (J. Behr, Ed., M. DelCogliano, A. Radde-Gallwitz, & L. Ayres, Trans.) (Vol. 43, p. 82). Yonkers, NY: St Vladimir's Seminary Press.

178   Ibid.

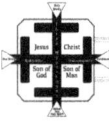

God also sets the seal of his peculiar likeness on us as well; by being conformed to Christ, we acquire the image of God, as it were. The Son is therefore the precise stamp of the God and Father."[179]

22. Sun of Righteousness

a. "Our Lord Jesus Christ is the Sun of Righteousness."[180]

23. Tree of Life

a. "The tree of life, that is to say, Christ."[181]

24. Understanding

a. "The Will of God is Wisdom and Understanding, and the Son is Wisdom."[182]

25. Will of the Father

a. "He [the Word] is the Father's Will."[183, 184]

---

179   Cyril of Alexandria. (2012). *Commentary on the Twelve Prophets*. (D. G. Hunter, Ed., R. C. Hill, Trans.) (Vol. 124, p. 88). Washington, DC: The Catholic University of America Press.

180   Cyril of Alexandria. (1859). *A Commentary upon the Gospel according to S. Luke*. (R. P. Smith, Trans.) (p. 154). Oxford: Oxford University Press.

181   Cyril of Alexandria. (2018). *Glaphyra on the Pentateuch, Volume 1 Genesis*. (N. P. Lunn, Trans.) (Vol. 137, p. 344). Washington, DC: The Catholic University of America Press.

182   Athanasius of Alexandria. (1892). Four Discourses against the Arians. In P. Schaff & H. Wace (Eds.), J. H. Newman & A. T. Robertson (Trans.), *St. Athanasius: Select Works and Letters* (Vol. 4, p. 429). New York: Christian Literature Company.

183   βουλή. And so βούλησις presently; and ζῶσα βουλή, *supr.* 2. and *Orat.* iii. 63. fin. and so Cyril *Thes.* p. 54, who uses it expressly (as it is always used by implication), in contrast to the κατὰ βούλησιν of the Arians, though Athan. uses κατὰ τὸ βούλημα, e.g. *Orat.* iii. 31. where vid. note; αὐτὸς τοῦ πατρὸς θέλημα. Nyss. *contr. Eunom.* xii. p. 345. The principle to be observed in the use of such words is this; that we must ever speak of the Father's will, command, &c., and the Son's fulfilment, assent, &c., as one act. vid. notes on *Orat.* iii. 11 and 15. *infr.*

184   Athanasius of Alexandria. (1892). Four Discourses against the Arians. In P. Schaff & H. Wace (Eds.), J. H. Newman & A. T. Robertson (Trans.), *St. Athanasius: Select Works and Letters* (Vol. 4, p. 365). New York:

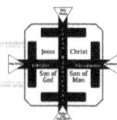

b. "He himself is the living and hypostatic counsel and will of the one who begat him."[185]

C. Never called

1. Father

    a. "In their case the Father's name has always been 'Father' and the Son's name always 'Son.' And just as the Father could never have been a son, so too the Son could never become a father. And just as the Father will never cease to be only a father, so too the Son will never cease to be only a son."[186]

    b. "Our faith is in the Father and the Son and the Holy Spirit: the Father who cannot be called grandfather, the Son who cannot be called father, and the Holy Spirit who is given no other name than the one he has. It is not permitted to exchange the names of this faith: the Father is always Father, and the Son always Son, and the Holy Spirit is and is said to be always Holy Spirit."[187]

    c. "And the Son is a son and not a father."[188]

2. Father of the Holy Spirit

    a. "It is not otherwise than that the Father is Father and not grandfather, and the Son is the Son of God and not the

Christian Literature Company.

185   Cyril of Alexandria. (2013–2015). *Commentary on John*. (J. C. Elowsky, T. C. Oden, & G. L. Bray, Eds., D. R. Maxwell, Trans.) (Vol. 1, p. 347). Downers Grove, IL: IVP Academic: An Imprint of InterVarsity Press.

186   Athanasius and Didymus. (2011). *Works on the Spirit: Athanasius's Letters to Serapion on the Holy Spirit, and, Didymus's on the Holy Spirit*. (J. Behr, Ed., M. DelCogliano, A. Radde-Gallwitz, & L. Ayres, Trans.) (Vol. 43, p. 78-79). Yonkers, NY: St Vladimir's Seminary Press.

187   Ibid. (p. 135)

188   Cyril of Alexandria. (2013–2015). *Commentary on John*. (J. C. Elowsky, T. C. Oden, & G. L. Bray, Eds., D. R. Maxwell, Trans.) (Vol. 2, p. 179). Downers Grove, IL: IVP Academic: An Imprint of InterVarsity Press.

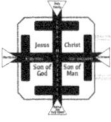

father of the Spirit, and the Holy Spirit is Holy Spirit and not grandson of the Father nor the brother of the Son."[189]

3. The Holy Spirit

   a. "In the Scriptures the Spirit is not called son but Holy Spirit and Spirit of God. Just as the Spirit is not called son, so too it is not written that the Son is the Holy Spirit . . . the Spirit is not called son, nor is it said that the Son is the Spirit. . ."[190,191]

D. The Son's Incarnation was accomplished by all three Divine Hypostases working together

1. "Thus also when the Word visited the holy virgin Mary,[192] the Spirit came to her with him, and the Word in the Spirit formed the body[193] and accommodated it to himself."[194]

2. "We believe that he overshadowed the holy Virgin (that is, the power of the Most High Father did) and formed for himself a body from her, albeit through the working of the Holy Spirit, and became a man and was called son of Abraham and of David."[195]

---

189 Athanasius and Didymus. (2011). *Works on the Spirit: Athanasius's Letters to Serapion on the Holy Spirit, and, Didymus's on the Holy Spirit*. (J. Behr, Ed., M. DelCogliano, A. Radde-Gallwitz, & L. Ayres, Trans.) (Vol. 43, p. 133). Yonkers, NY: St Vladimir's Seminary Press.

190 Here we prefer to read ὁ υἱός instead of υἱός (PG 26.641; AW I/1.570), following Shapland (183 n. 313).

191 Athanasius and Didymus. (2011). *Works on the Spirit: Athanasius's Letters to Serapion on the Holy Spirit, and, Didymus's on the Holy Spirit*. (J. Behr, Ed., M. DelCogliano, A. Radde-Gallwitz, & L. Ayres, Trans.) (Vol. 43, p. 131-132). Yonkers, NY: St Vladimir's Seminary Press.

192 Athanasius understands the "Power of the Most High" in Lk 1.35 as a reference to the Son; see Serap. 1.11.1 and 2.15.2.

193 I.e. of Jesus.

194 Athanasius and Didymus. (2011). *Works on the Spirit: Athanasius's Letters to Serapion on the Holy Spirit, and, Didymus's on the Holy Spirit*. (J. Behr, Ed., M. DelCogliano, A. Radde-Gallwitz, & L. Ayres, Trans.) (Vol. 43, p. 102). Yonkers, NY: St Vladimir's Seminary Press.

195 Cyril of Alexandria. (2014). *Three Christological Treatises*. (D. Hunter, Ed., D. King, Trans.) (Vol. 129, p. 139-40). Washington, DC: The Catholic University of America Press.

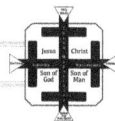

3. "He maintains that he has become flesh from the Father even though Solomon says, 'Wisdom has built herself a house,' and the blessed Gabriel attributes the creation of the divine body to the operation of the Spirit when he says to the holy virgin, 'The Holy Spirit will come upon you, and the power of the Most High will overshadow you.' The Son maintains this in order that you may understand that since the divinity is one in nature and is in the Father and the Son as well as in the Holy Spirit, none will act separately in any instance, but whatever may be said to happen through one, this is completely the work of the entire divine nature."[196]

4. His Body was complete, not lacking a soul.

   a. "He as I said, God in human shape, by taking not inanimate flesh (as some heretics have seen fit to imagine) but flesh endowed with mental life."[197]

   b. "As for the flesh united with him which became his own, we declare it was endowed with mental life."[198]

   c. "We say that the 'mediator between God and men,' as the Scripture expresses it, is composed of a manhood that is like our own, complete according to its proper definition."[199]

5. There was **never** a point in which His human nature ever existed as its own individual subject, distinct from Himself or Saint Mary.

   a. "And He became man, and did not come into man; for this it is necessary to know, lest perchance these irreligious men

---

196   Cyril of Alexandria. (2013–2015). *Commentary on John*. (J. C. Elowsky, T. C. Oden, & G. L. Bray, Eds., D. R. Maxwell, Trans.) (Vol. 1, p. 240). Downers Grove, IL: IVP Academic: An Imprint of InterVarsity Press.

197   "Mental life" in Greek: "ψυχῇ νοερᾷ"; quote taken from Cyril of Alexandria. (1983). On the Creed. L. Wickham (Trans.), *Cyril of Alexandria: Select letters* (p. 109). Oxford: Oxford University Press.

198   Ibid. ("Answer to Tiberius: #5", p. 155)

199   Cyril of Alexandria. (2014). *Three Christological Treatises*. (D. Hunter, Ed., D. King, Trans.) (Vol. 129, p. 51). Washington, DC: The Catholic University of America Press.

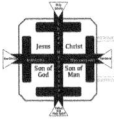

fall into this notion also, and beguile any into thinking, that, as in former times the Word was used to come into each of the Saints, so now He sojourned in a man, hallowing him also, and manifesting[200] Himself as in the others."[201]

b. "Or how can they wish to be called Christians who say that the Word has descended upon a holy man as upon one of the prophets, and has not Himself become man, taking the body from Mary; but that Christ is one person, while the Word of God, Who before Mary and before the ages was Son of the Father, is another?"[202]

c. "For Jesus was not a mere man prior to the communion and union of God with him, but the same Logos, having come into the blessed Virgin herself, took to Himself His own Temple from the essence of the Virgin.[203] He went forth from her as a man and was seen to be man externally, although internally, He existed truly as God."[204]

d. "For from Mary was the Holy Body, yet at the beginning of its formation or subsistence in the womb, was it holy as being the body of Christ, and there is not an instant in

---

200   τούτῳ χρώμενος ὀργάνῳ *infr.* 42. and ὄργανον πρὸς τὴν ἐνέργειαν καὶ τὴν ἔκλαμψιν τῆς θεότητος. 53. This was a word much used afterwards by the Apollinarians, who looked on our Lord's manhood as merely a *manifestation* of God. vid. *Or.* ii. 8, n. 3. vid. σχῆμα ὀργανικὸν in *Apoll.* i. 2, 15. vid. a parallel in Euseb. *Laud. Const.* p. 536. However, it is used freely by Athan. e.g. *infr.* 35, 53. *Incarn.* 8, 9, 41, 43, 44. This use of ὄργανον must not be confused with its heretical application to our Lord's Divine Nature, vid. Basil *de Sp. S.* n. 19 fin. of which *de Syn.* 27 (3). It may be added that φανέρωσις is a Nestorian as well as Eutychian idea; Facund. *Tr. Cap.* ix. 2, 3. and the Syrian use of *parsopa* Asseman. *B. O.* t. 4. p. 219. Thus both parties really denied the Atonement. vid. *supr. Or.* i. 60, n. 5; ii. 8, n. 4.

201   Athanasius of Alexandria. (1892). <u>Four Discourses against the Arians</u>. In P. Schaff & H. Wace (Eds.), J. H. Newman & A. T. Robertson (Trans.), *St. Athanasius: Select Works and Letters* (Vol. 4, p. 410). New York: Christian Literature Company.

202   Ibid. (p. 571)

203   Οὐσίας τῆς Παρθένου

204   Saint Cyril of Alexandria. (2004). <u>4</u>. Protopresbyter G. Dragas (Ed. & Trans.), *Against Those Who Are Unwilling to Confess that the Holy Virgin Is Theotokos* (p. 11). Rollinsford: Orthodox Research Institute.

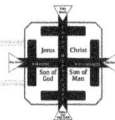

which it was not His."[205, 206]

e. "From his very conception he united to himself a temple taken from her."[207]

f. "God the Word was made flesh and became man, and by the act of conception united to Himself the temple that He received from her."[208]

g. "Christ is not to be thought of as a man who later proceeded to become God; the Word who is God has become man, so that we recognize him as being at once God and man."[209]

h. "We say, therefore, that the body came to belong to the Word rather than to some man individually and separately, someone thought of as being another besides Christ the Son."[210]

E. The Incarnation of the Son of God was a union of:

1. Divinity and humanity

a. "So then, we affirm that the union occurred 'naturally' out of two unequal elements, divinity and humanity, without thereby either confusing or blending the natures together, despite what our opponents might say. We also consistently

205   Card. Mai citing this from Severus' Philalethes ends it differently, *no one will admit so much as an instant of time in which that (flesh) will be common and like other flesh as you say and not rather be the Flesh of the Word* (n. 18 in Migne).

206   Cyril of Alexandria. (1881). *Five Tomes against Nestorius; Scholia on the Incarnation; Christ Is One; Fragments against Diodore of Tarsus, Theodore of Mopsuestia, the Synousiasts* (pp. 327–328). London; Oxford; Cambridge: James Parker and Co.; Rivingtons.

207   Cyril of Alexandria. (1987). *Letters, 1–50*. (T. P. Halton, Ed., J. I. McEnerney, Trans.) (Vol. 76, p. 145). Washington, DC: The Catholic University of America Press.

208   Cyril of Alexandria. (1859). *A Commentary upon the Gospel according to S. Luke*. (R. P. Smith, Trans.) (p. 8). Oxford: Oxford University Press.

209   Cyril of Alexandria. (1983). On the Creed. L. Wickham (Trans.), *Cyril of Alexandria: Select letters* (p. 109-111). Oxford: Oxford University Press.

210   Cyril of Alexandria. (2014). *Three Christological Treatises*. (D. Hunter, Ed., D. King, Trans.) (Vol. 129, p. 173). Washington, DC: The Catholic University of America Press.

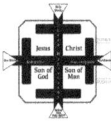

insist that there is a single Christ, Son, and Lord."[211]

2. Godhead and manhood

a. "But even though the things named be conceived of as diverse and sundered in diverseness of nature, yet is Christ conceived of as One out of[212] both, the Godhead and manhood having come together one to another in true union."[213]

F. Divinity, Godhead, humanity and manhood can all be referred to as:

1. Essences

a. "For it is unattainable that any creature change into the essence or nature of divinity, and flesh is a creature."[214]

b. "Accordingly we confess that the only begotten Son of God is perfect God, consubstantial to the Father according to divinity, and that the same [Son] is consubstantial to us according to humanity. For there was a union of two natures."[215]

c. "Consubstantial with the Father according to the Godhead and Consubstantial with us according to the Manhood: for a Union hath taken place of two natures, wherefore we

---

211   Ibid. (p. 143)

212   ἐξ

213   Cyril of Alexandria. (1881). *Five Tomes against Nestorius; Scholia on the Incarnation; Christ Is One; Fragments against Diodore of Tarsus, Theodore of Mopsuestia, the Synousiasts* (p. 41). London; Oxford; Cambridge: James Parker and Co.; Rivingtons.

214   Cyril of Alexandria. (1987). *Letters, 1–50*. (T. P. Halton, Ed., J. I. McEnerney, Trans.) (Vol. 76, p. 196). Washington, DC: The Catholic University of America Press.

215   Cyril of Alexandria. (1987). *Letters, 51–110*. (T. P. Halton, Ed., J. I. McEnerney, Trans.) (Vol. 77, p. 154). Washington, DC: The Catholic University of America Press.

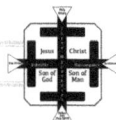

confess one Christ, One Son, One Lord."[216, 217]

d. "How could one posit an identity of essence in things which are so disparate in the rationale of their respective natures? Godhead is one thing, manhood quite another."[218]

e. "For they add, indicating who the perfect as God and perfect as man is: 'Who was begotten of the Father before the ages in respect of his Godhead and in the last days for us and for our salvation of Mary the holy Virgin in respect of his manhood, the same consubstantial with the Father in Godhead and consubstantial with us in manhood.'"[219, 220]

2. Natures

a. "How could anyone possibly think that way, when we all know that divinity, within the context of its own nature, is something quite different from humanity in the context of *its* own nature? Christ, though, is one individual comprised from both divinity and humanity, and this in the context of the union that brings salvation."[221]

b. "I know that the nature of God is impassible, unchangeable, and immutable, even though by the nature of his humanity Christ is one in both natures and from both natures."[222]

---

216 ὁμοούσιον τῷ Πατρὶ τὸν αὐτὸν κατὰ τὴν θεότητα, καὶ ὁμοούσιον ἡμῖν κατὰ τὴν ἀνθρωπότητα· δύο γὰρ φύσεων ἕνωσις γέγονε· διὸ ἕνα Χριστὸν, ἕνα Υἱὸν, ἕνα Κύριον ὁμολογοῦμεν.

217 Cyril of Alexandria. (1872). *The Three Epistles of S. Cyril, Archbishop of Alexandria: English Text.* (P. E. Pusey, Ed.) (p. 72). Oxford; London: James Parker and Co.

218 St Cyril of Alexandria. (1995). *On the Unity of Christ.* (J. Behr, Ed., J. A. McGuckin, Trans.) (Vol. 13, p. 77). Crestwood, NY: St Vladimir's Seminary Press.

219 ὁμοούσιον τῳ πατρὶ τὸν αὐτὸν κατὰ τὴν θεότητα καὶ ὁμοούσιον ἡμῖν κατὰ τὴν ἀνθρωπότητα

220 Cyril of Alexandria. (1983). To Acacius of Melitene. L. Wickham (Trans.), *Cyril of Alexandria: Select letters* (p. 47). Oxford: Oxford University Press.

221 St. Cyril of Alexandria. (2014). *Three Christological Treatises.* (D. King, Trans.) (Vol. 129, p. 111). Washington, D.C.: The Catholic University of America Press.

222 Cyril of Alexandria. (1987). *Letters, 51–110.* (T. P. Halton, Ed., J. I. McEnerney, Trans.) (Vol. 77, p. 11). Washington, DC: The Catholic University of America Press.

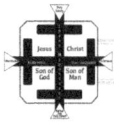

c. "Then he does not have two natures? that of God, and that of man? Well, Godhead is one thing, and manhood is another thing."[223]

d. "And as to the Gospel and Apostolic words concerning the Lord, we know that Divines make some common, as to One Person,[224] apportion others, as to two Natures,[225] and give the God-befitting to Christ according to His Godhead,[226] the lowly ones according to His Manhood."[227, 228]

e. "Though the natures joined together to form a real unity are different, it is one, Christ and Son coming from them- not implying that the difference between the natures[229] was abolished through their union but that instead Godhead and manhood[230] have given us the one Lord, Christ and Son by their mysterious and inexpressible unification."[231]

f. "This is the key to the holy fathers' thinking. This is why they dare to call the holy Virgin 'mother of God,' not because the Word's nature, his Godhead,[232] originated from the holy Virgin but because his holy body, endowed with life and reason was born from her and the Word was 'born' in flesh because united to this body substantially."[233]

223   St Cyril of Alexandria. (1995). *On the Unity of Christ*. (J. Behr, Ed., J. A. McGuckin, Trans.) (Vol. 13, p. 77). Crestwood, NY: St Vladimir's Seminary Press.

224   ἑνὸς προσώπου

225   δύο φύσεων

226   θεότητα

227   ἀνθρωπότητα

228   Cyril of Alexandria. (1872). *The Three Epistles of S. Cyril, Archbishop of Alexandria: English Text*. (P. E. Pusey, Ed.) (p. 72). Oxford; London: James Parker and Co.

229   τῶν φύσεων

230   Θεότητός τε καὶ ἀνθρωπότητος

231   Cyril of Alexandria. (1983). Second Letter to Nestrorius. L. Wickham (Trans.), *Cyril of Alexandria: Select letters* (p. 7). Oxford: Oxford University Press.

232   τῆς τοῦ λόγου φύσεως ἤτοι τῆς θεότητος αὐτοῦ

233   Cyril of Alexandria. (1983). Second Letter to Nestrorius. L. Wickham (Trans.), *Cyril of Alexandria: Select letters* (p. 11). Oxford: Oxford University Press.

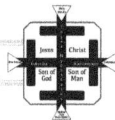

g. "But even though the things named be conceived of as diverse and sundered in diverseness of nature, yet is Christ conceived of as One out of[234] both, the Godhead and manhood having come together one to another in true union."[235]

h. "As far then as pertained to His being God by Nature, He was not with us; for incomparable is the difference between Godhead and manhood and exceeding great the difference of the natures."[236]

G. Thus, it can be said that the Incarnation was a union of:

1. Essences

a. "And in another Psalm, we find him preserving no less the principle of the indivisibility of the union and attributing again the things, which are proper to the humanity to the very Logos of God. This is not the result of confusion of their essences,[237] but rather of clearly perceiving the reason of the union of the essences."[238, 239]

2. Natures

a. "It is precisely because Nestorius constantly denied that God the Word's birth happened according to flesh, and instead introduced a mere unity of dignities, and it is

---

234 ἐξ

235 Cyril of Alexandria. (1881). *Five Tomes against Nestorius; Scholia on the Incarnation; Christ Is One; Fragments against Diodore of Tarsus, Theodore of Mopsuestia, the Synousiasts* (p. 41). London; Oxford; Cambridge: James Parker and Co.; Rivingtons.

236 Ibid. (p. 187)

237 Οὐσιῶν

238 ἑνώσεως τῶν οὐσιῶν

239 Cyril of Alexandria, *Against Those who are Unwilling to Confess that the Holy Virgin is Theotokos*, trans. Fr, George Dragas, vol. 1, Patristic and Ecclesiastical Texts and Translations (Rollinsford, NH: The Orthodox Research Institute, 2004), 17.

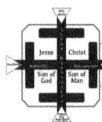

because he said that a man, honored by sharing the title of Sonship, was connected to God, that we were forced to battle against these notions of his and to assert instead that the union was 'at the level of concrete existence,' meaning by this simply that the Word's nature, that is, his concrete existence, which is the Word himself, was genuinely united to a human nature, quite apart from any change or confusion, as we have said often enough. He is reckoned to be, and actually is, a single Christ; the same individual is both God and man."[240]

b. "Furthermore, looked at from a different point of view, there would be nothing contradictory in thinking that, at the level of nature, the flesh is something quite different from the Word that was begotten of God the Father. In fact it would be perfectly reasonable to think so, and could not be gainsaid. And of course the Only-Begotten is, in turn, something different at the level of his own nature. But to acknowledge this is not the same as separating the natures after they have been united. . . . What the Word (being God) took to himself was not his own nature but Abraham's seed. . . . Even though, however, the body and the Word of God the Father belong to different natures, there is still only a single Christ and Son, God and Lord, despite his becoming flesh. This idea of dissolving the means by which a genuine union occurred by keeping the concrete existences apart is very damaging. They end up each as a separate individual, connected by nothing but an external relationship based on degrees of honor."[241]

c. "Though the natures joined together to form a real unity are different, it is one, Christ and Son coming from them—

---

240   Cyril of Alexandria. (2014). *Three Christological Treatises*. (D. King, Trans.) (Vol. 129, p. 93). Washington, D.C.: The Catholic University of America Press.

241   Ibid. (p. 142)

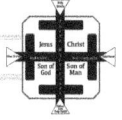

not implying that the difference between the natures[242] was abolished through their union but that instead Godhead and manhood[243] have given us the one Lord, Christ and Son by their mysterious and inexpressible unification."[244]

d. "In this way, when we have the idea of the elements of the one and unique Son and Lord Jesus Christ, we speak of two natures being united; but after the union, the duality has been abolished and we believe the Son's nature[245] to be one,[246] since he is one Son, yet become man and incarnate."[247]

e. "Accordingly we confess that the only begotten Son of God is perfect God, consubstantial to the Father according to divinity, and that the same [Son] is consubstantial to us according to humanity. For there was a union of two natures."[248]

f. "Consubstantial with the Father according to the Godhead and Consubstantial with us according to the Manhood: for a Union hath taken place of two natures, wherefore we confess one Christ, One Son, One Lord.[249, 250]

g. "This, my friend, is the definition of human nature which is also called a substance, that it is a rational animal, mortal,

---

242   τῶν φύσεων

243   Θεότητός τε καὶ ἀνθρωπότητος

244   Cyril of Alexandria. (1983). Second Letter to Nestrorius. L. Wickham (Trans.), *Cyril of Alexandria: Select letters* (p. 7). Oxford: Oxford University Press.

245   φύσιν

246   μίαν

247   Cyril of Alexandria. (1983). To Acacius of Melitene. L. Wickham (Trans.), *Cyril of Alexandria: Select letters* (p. 49). Oxford: Oxford University Press.

248   Cyril of Alexandria. (1987). *Letters, 51–110*. (T. P. Halton, Ed., J. I. McEnerney, Trans.) (Vol. 77, p. 154). Washington, DC: The Catholic University of America Press.

249   ὁμοούσιον τῷ Πατρὶ τὸν αὐτὸν κατὰ τὴν θεότητα, καὶ ὁμοούσιον ἡμῖν κατὰ τὴν ἀνθρωπότητα· δύο γὰρ φύσεων ἕνωσις γέγονε· διὸ ἕνα Χριστὸν, ἕνα Υἱὸν, ἕνα Κύριον ὁμολογοῦμεν.

250   Cyril of Alexandria. (1872). *The Three Epistles of S. Cyril, Archbishop of Alexandria: English Text*. (P. E. Pusey, Ed.) (p. 72). Oxford; London: James Parker and Co.

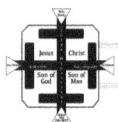

recipient of mind and learning. . . . We have already often said, when we were making our Defense of all the Chapters, that not because the natures came together unto union, must duality be admitted."[251]

3. Hypostases[252]

    a. "We know perfectly well that the divine, transcendent nature cannot experience any 'shadow of turning,'[253] nor did the Word of God give up being what he is to be transformed into a fleshly nature. Since he points out that God's form took upon himself the form of a servant, let him go on and explain whether it was just these 'forms' that came together by themselves, quite apart from their concrete existences. Well, I reckon that even he would shrink from saying that, for it was not mere resemblances and forms, things with no concrete existence, that conjoined together to bring about the saving union; rather, it was a convergence of the very things themselves, of two concrete existences."[254]

    b. "When he hears us say that the union is natural, that is, that it is genuine and free from change and that the convergence of the concrete existences is altogether unconfused. . . . The result is that we believe the concrete existences to have been united and the Word to have become man and

---

251   Cyril of Alexandria. (1881). *Five Tomes against Nestorius; Scholia on the Incarnation; Christ Is One; Fragments against Diodore of Tarsus, Theodore of Mopsuestia, the Synousiasts* (pp. 335–336). London; Oxford; Cambridge: James Parker and Co.; Rivingtons.

252   In the following three quotes, the author of the book *Three Christological Treatises*, notes that he chose to translate the word "hypostasis" as "concrete existence." It is crucial to bear in mind that the term "hypostasis" had an older definition which meant essence or substance; only later did it come to mean an individual subject *constituted of* an essence.

253   Jas 1:17

254   St. Cyril of Alexandria. (2014). *Three Christological Treatises*. (D. King, Trans.) (Vol. 129, pp. 89–90). Washington, D.C.: The Catholic University of America Press.

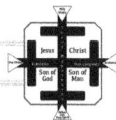

incarnate, and hence we appropriately refer to the union as 'natural.'"[255]

c. "Furthermore, looked at from a different point of view, there would be nothing contradictory in thinking that, at the level of nature, the flesh is something quite different from the Word that was begotten of God the Father. In fact it would be perfectly reasonable to think so, and could not be gainsaid. And of course the Only-Begotten is, in turn, something different at the level of his own nature. But to acknowledge this is not the same as separating the natures after they have been united. . . . What the Word (being God) took to himself was not his own nature but Abraham's seed. . . . Even though, however, the body and the Word of God the Father belong to different natures, there is still only a single Christ and Son, God and Lord, despite his becoming flesh. This idea of dissolving the means by which a genuine union occurred by keeping the concrete existences apart is very damaging. They end up each as a separate individual, connected by nothing but an external relationship based on degrees of honor."[256]

H. The union, in which the Word of God united human nature to His Divine Nature was:

1. Hypostatic

a. "It is precisely because Nestorius constantly denied that God the Word's birth happened according to flesh . . . that we were forced to battle against these notions of his and to assert instead that the union was 'at the level of concrete existence,'[257] meaning by this simply that the Word's nature,

---

255   Ibid. (p. 98)

256   Ibid. (p. 142)

257   Καθ᾽ ὑπόστασιν

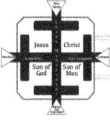

that is, his concrete existence,[258] which is the Word himself, was genuinely united to a human nature, quite apart from any change or confusion. . . ."[259]

2. Natural

   a. "We maintain that the Word was naturally, that is, genuinely, not contingently, united to the holy flesh, which possessed a rational soul . . . but he fails to comprehend what this 'natural union' means, namely, that it is genuine, one that neither confuses nor mixes the natures together such that each would need to be in a different state from what it actually is."[260]

   b. "If we were to refer to the union as 'natural,' we would be speaking accurately. . . . The expression 'by nature' here simply means 'in truth.'"[261]

3. Without confusion, fusion, merging or mingling: A + B → C

   a. "Though we affirm that the Word is God on becoming incarnate and made man, any suspicion of change is to be repudiated entirely because he remained what he was, and we are to acknowledge the union as totally free from merger."[262]

   b. "He has become flesh not by . . . undergoing mingling,[263]

---

258 ὑποστάσις

259 Cyril of Alexandria. (2014). *Three Christological Treatises*. (D. Hunter, Ed., D. King, Trans.) (Vol. 129, p. 93). Washington, DC: The Catholic University of America Press.

260 Ibid. (p. 97)

261 Ibid. (p. 143)

262 Cyril of Alexandria. (1983). To Acacius of Melitene. L. Wickham (Trans.), *Cyril of Alexandria: Select letters* (p. 49). Oxford: Oxford University Press.

263 σύγκρασιν

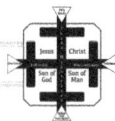

mixture or the 'consubstantiation'[264] some people prate about."[265]

c. "It is therefore idle for them to claim that if there is one incarnate nature of the Word[266] it follows there must have been a mingling and merger, with the human nature being diminished by its removal."[267]

d. Definition

   1) "But if the two natures have been brought into one mingling, because they happen to be of different substances, neither one is preserved, but both have disappeared after they have been blended."[268]

4. Without Alteration or Change: A + B → A or A + B → B

a. "For I am the Lord your God; I have not changed."[269]

b. "He did not become other than Himself on taking the flesh."[270]

c. "Even when made man, 'Jesus Christ' is 'the same yesterday, and to-day, and for ever'[271] is unchangeable."[272]

d. "What lower region has vomited the statement that ...

---

264 συνουσίωσιν

265 Cyril of Alexandria. (1983). On the Creed. L. Wickham (Trans.), *Cyril of Alexandria: Select letters* (p. 109-111). Oxford: Oxford University Press.

266 μία φύσις του λόγου σεσαρκωμένη

267 Cyril of Alexandria. (1983). Second Letter to Succensus. L. Wickham (Trans.), *Cyril of Alexandria: Select letters* (p. 87-89). Oxford: Oxford University Press.

268 Cyril of Alexandria. (1987). *Letters, 51–110.* (T. P. Halton, Ed., J. I. McEnerney, Trans.) (Vol. 77, p. 155). Washington, DC: The Catholic University of America Press.

269 Mal 3:6

270 Athanasius of Alexandria. (1892). Four Discourses against the Arians. In P. Schaff & H. Wace (Eds.), J. H. Newman & A. T. Robertson (Trans.), *St. Athanasius: Select Works and Letters* (Vol. 4, p. 352). New York: Christian Literature Company.

271 Heb 13:8

272 Ibid. (p. 353)

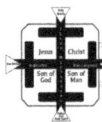

the Word has been changed into flesh, bones, hair, and the whole body, and altered from its own nature? . . . Or whoever went so far in impiety as to say and hold, that this Godhead, which is coessential with the Father, was circumcised and became imperfect instead of perfect."[273]

e. "The Word Himself was not, changed into bones and flesh, but came in the flesh."[274]

f. "The Word's Nature has not transferred to the nature of the flesh or that of the flesh to that of the Word."[275]

g. "He has become flesh not by changing into the nature of flesh by way of transference, variation or alteration." [276]

h. "The Word from God the Father united to himself in some inscrutable and ineffable manner, a body endowed with mental life and that he came forth, man from woman, become what we are, not by change of nature but in gracious fulfilment of God's plan. . . . So we unite the Word from God the Father without merger, alteration or changes to holy flesh owning mental life in a manner inexpressible and surpassing understanding, and confess one Son, Christ and Lord, the self-same God and man, not a diverse pair but one and the same, being and being seen to be both things. . . . So if we consider, as I said, the mode of his becoming man we see that two natures[277] have met without merger and without alteration in unbreakable mutual union[278]—the point being that flesh is flesh and not Godhead even though it has become God's flesh and equally

---

273 Ibid. (p. 570)

274 Ibid. (p. 573)

275 Cyril of Alexandria. (1983). Second Letter to Succensus. L. Wickham (Trans.), *Cyril of Alexandria: Select letters* (p. 87-89). Oxford: Oxford University Press.

276 Cyril of Alexandria. (1983). On the Creed. L. Wickham (Trans.), *Cyril of Alexandria: Select letters* (p. 109-111). Oxford: Oxford University Press.

277 δύο φύσεις

278 ἕνωσιν

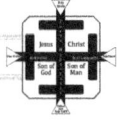

the Word is God and not flesh even though in fulfillment of God's plan he made the flesh his own. Whenever we take this point into consideration, therefore, we do not damage the concurrence into unity by declaring it was effected out of two natures."[279, 280]

   i. "Indeed talk of the body's being changed into Godhead's nature is equally as absurd as talk of the Word's being changed into the nature of the flesh. Just as the latter is impossible (for the Word is unchanging and unalterable) so is the former—that a creature could transfer to Godhead's substance or nature[281] does not come within the realm of possibilities, and the flesh is a created thing."[282]

5. Without Division or Separation A + B → AB → A + B

   a. "This Body it was that was laid in a grave, when the Word had left it, yet was not parted from it, to preach, as Peter says, also to the spirits in prison."[283, 284]

   b. "Not dividing the Son and the Word, but knowing that the Son is the Word Himself."[285]

   c. "However, after the union we do not divide the natures from each other and do not sever the one and indivisible into two sons."[286]

279 δύο φύσεων

280 Cyril of Alexandria. (1983). First Letter to Succensus. L. Wickham (Trans.), *Cyril of Alexandria: Select letters* (p. 75-77). Oxford: Oxford University Press.

281 Θεότητος οὐσίαν ἤτοι φύσιν

282 Cyril of Alexandria. (1983). First Letter to Succensus. L. Wickham (Trans.), *Cyril of Alexandria: Select letters* (p. 81). Oxford: Oxford University Press.

283 1 Pet 3:19

284 Athanasius of Alexandria. (1892). Personal Letters. In P. Schaff & H. Wace (Eds.), A. T. Robertson (Trans.), *St. Athanasius: Select Works and Letters* (Vol. 4, p. 572). New York: Christian Literature Company.

285 Ibid. (p. 574)

286 Cyril of Alexandria. (1983). First Letter to Succensus. L. Wickham (Trans.), *Cyril of Alexandria: Select letters* (p. 75-77). Oxford: Oxford University Press.

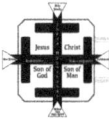

d. "It seems to me that one cannot reproach or upbraid this desire not to separate after the union what has been joined or to push them apart from each other."[287]

e. "Once they [the natures] have been united, though, it is dangerous to split them up again."[288]

f. "To divide the single Son into two, and thereby to dissolve the genuineness of the union by splitting it up into bits, putting the man over here and the god over there, separate from each other, is an offense of the very highest sacrilege."[289]

g. "There is also no way that we are going to allow these worldly and unspiritual types to think in terms of two sons as a result of dividing up the concrete existences after the unfathomable union, or even to speak in such a way."[290]

h. "We came to appreciate that to divide up the concrete existences after union is not some harmless activity but actually entails completely reversing the holy mystery of the Incarnation."[291]

6. Division of the natures would necessitate two individual subjects

a. "This idea of dissolving the means by which a genuine union occurred by keeping the concrete existences apart is very damaging. They end up each as a separate individual, connected by nothing but an external relationship based on degrees of honor."[292]

---

287 Cyril of Alexandria. (2014). *Three Christological Treatises*. (D. Hunter, Ed., D. King, Trans.) (Vol. 129, p. 98). Washington, DC: The Catholic University of America Press.

288 Ibid. (p. 99)

289 Ibid. (p. 140)

290 Ibid. (p. 149)

291 Ibid. (p. 151)

292 Ibid. (p. 142)

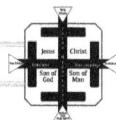

I. After the union, Jesus Christ is said to have:

1. *One nature, on the plane of reality or truth*[293]

   a. ". . . the reality is one incarnate nature of the Word."[294, 295]

   b. "In this way, when we have the idea of the elements of the one and unique Son and Lord Jesus Christ, we speak of two natures being united; but after the union, the duality has been abolished and we believe the Son's nature[296] to be one,[297] since he is one Son, yet become man and incarnate."[298]

   c. "But say 'one Son' and, as the fathers[299] have put it, one incarnate nature of the Word."[300, 301]

   d. "We unite these, acknowledging one Christ, one Son, the same one Lord and, further, one[302] incarnate nature[303] of the Son in the same way that the phrase can be used of ordinary man."[304]

2. On the plane of mental contemplation, two united:

293   ἀλήθειάν; Liddell, H. G. (1996). *A lexicon: Abridged from Liddell and Scott's Greek-English lexicon* (p. 34). Oak Harbor, WA: Logos Research Systems, Inc.

294   ἀλήθειάν ἐστι μία φύσις του λόγον σεσαρκωμένη

295   Cyril of Alexandria. (1983). Second Letter to Succensus. L. Wickham (Trans.), *Cyril of Alexandria: Select letters* (p. 87-89). Oxford: Oxford University Press.

296   φύσιν

297   μίαν

298   Cyril of Alexandria. (1983). To Acacius of Melitene. L. Wickham (Trans.), *Cyril of Alexandria: Select letters* (p. 49). Oxford: Oxford University Press.

299   πατέρες

300   μία φύσιν τον λόγου σεσαρκωμένην

301   Cyril of Alexandria. (1983). First Letter to Succensus. L. Wickham (Trans.), *Cyril of Alexandria: Select letters* (p. 75-77). Oxford: Oxford University Press.

302   μίαν

303   φύσιν

304   Cyril of Alexandria. (1983). To Eulogius. L. Wickham (Trans.), *Cyril of Alexandria: Select letters* (p. 63-65). Oxford: Oxford University Press.

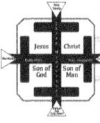

a. Essences

   1) "For, just as the Logos was God before the advent, so also in becoming man and mediating in the human nature,[305] he is again one. This is why he has been called Mediator between God and man, because he is one out of both essences.[306] For what mediates between some [essences] of necessity possess both. He is, then, a Mediator of God, because he is of the same essence with the Father,[307] and again, he is a mediator of man, because he has partaken of human nature perfectly[308] but without sin."[309]

b. Natures

   1) "So far, then, as the question of the manner of the Only-begotten's becoming man appears for purely mental consideration by the mind's eye,[310] our view is that there are two united natures[311] but one Christ, Son and Lord, the Word of God become man and incarnate."[312]

   2) "The Antiochene brethren, on the other hand, taking the recognized elements of Christ at the level only of mere ideas, have mentioned a difference of natures,[313] because, as I have said, Godhead[314] and manhood[315]

---

305 τῇ ἀνθρώπου φύσει

306 τῶν οὐσιῶν ἕνα

307 τῆς αὐτῆς οὐσίας τω Πατρί

308 τῆς ἀνθρωπείας μετεσχηκέναι φύσεως τελείως

309 Cyril of Alexandria, *Against Those who are Unwilling to Confess that the Holy Virgin is Theotokos*, trans. Fr, George Dragas, Vol. 1, Patristic and Ecclesiastical Texts and Translations (Rollinsford, NH: The Orthodox Research Institute, 2004), 31.

310 οὐκοῦν οσον μὲν ηκεν εἰς ἔννοιαν καὶ εἰς μόνον τὸ ὁρᾶν τοῖς τῆς ψυχῆς ομμασι'

311 δύο τὰς φύσεις

312 Cyril of Alexandria. (1983). <u>First Letter to Successus</u>. L. Wickham (Trans.), *Cyril of Alexandria: Select letters* (p. 75-77). Oxford: Oxford University Press.

313 φύσεων

314 Θεότης

315 ἀνθρωπότης

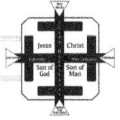

are not the same thing in quality of nature,[316] yet they do declare there is one Son and Christ and Lord, and, since he is actually one in reality, that his person too is one."[317]

3. **After** the union, two natures should **not** be spoken of beyond in thought alone

    a. "So if we speak of a 'union' we are affirming that it is a union of flesh, endowed with mental life and reason, and Word and this is how those who say 'two natures' understand it; yet, with the acknowledgement of union the united elements no longer stand apart from each other but from then on [after the Incarnation] there is one Son, one nature of him,[318] the Word incarnate."[319]

    b. Any individual nature must exist as an individual subject

        1) "For if they pretend to say there is one person of Christ, while there are two *hypostaseis* separate and distinct, by all means there will be two persons also."[320]

            A) To speak of two natures, beyond in thought alone, is to *attack* Miaphysitism

                i. "I am given to understand that a further query has been raised. Anyone, surely, who states that the Lord suffered exclusively in the flesh renders the

---

316   φυσικη

317   Cyril of Alexandria. (1983). To Acacius of Melitene. L. Wickham (Trans.), *Cyril of Alexandria: Select letters* (p. 53). Oxford: Oxford University Press.

318   Μία φύσις αὐτου

319   Cyril of Alexandria. (1983). To Eulogius. L. Wickham (Trans.), *Cyril of Alexandria: Select letters* (p. 65). Oxford: Oxford University Press.

320   Cyril of Alexandria. (1987). *Letters, 1–50.* (T. P. Halton, Ed., J. I. McEnerney, Trans.) (Vol. 76, p. 226). Washington, DC: The Catholic University of America Press.

suffering irrational and involuntary, but if you say he suffered with his soul and mind, to make the suffering voluntary, there is no bar to saying that he suffered in the manhood's nature.[321] If that is true, must we not be conceding that two natures exist[322] inseparably after the union?[323] With the result that if you quote 'Christ therefore having suffered for us in flesh' your meaning is the same as if you had said 'Christ having suffered for us in our nature.' The objection is just one more attack upon those who affirm one incarnate nature of the Son;[324] apparently aiming to prove the affirmation idle, they obstinately argue always for the existence of two natures."[325, 326]

B) The Alexandrian preference is to say that Christ has one incarnate nature, not two, to avoid worship of two subjects

i. "So, our father and bishop Athanasius, who is held in such very high regard, wrote as follows on the subject of our universal Savior Christ: . . . We do not confess that this single Son is two natures, one to be worshiped and one not to be worshiped. He is rather one incarnate nature of the Word, and is to be worshiped, with his flesh, with a single worship."[327]

---

321 φύσει της άνθρωπότητος

322 δύο φύσεις ὑφεστάναι

323 ἕνωσιν

324 μίαν υἱου φύσιν σεσαρκωμένην

325 δύο φύσεις ὑφεστώσας

326 Cyril of Alexandria. (1983). Second Letter to Successus. L. Wickham (Trans.), *Cyril of Alexandria: Select letters* (p. 91-93). Oxford: Oxford University Press.

327 Cyril of Alexandria. (2014). *Three Christological Treatises.* (D. Hunter, Ed., D. King, Trans.) (Vol. 129, p. 156). Washington, DC: The Catholic University of America Press.

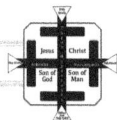

J. Before *and* after the Incarnation, the same Son is *one* individual Subject

1. "Or who have been so venturesome as to say that Christ Who suffered in the flesh and was crucified is not Lord, Saviour, God, and Son of the Father? Or how can they wish to be called Christians who say that the Word has descended upon a holy man as upon one of the prophets, and has not Himself become man, taking the body from Mary; but that Christ is one person, while the Word of God, Who before Mary and before the ages was Son of the Father, is another? Or how can they be Christians who say that the Son is one, and the Word of God another?"[328]

2. "Again it was consistent that when He went about in the body, He should not hide what belonged to the Godhead, lest he of Samosata should find an excuse to call Him man, as distinct in person from God the Word."[329]

3. "But as he was perfect in his deity, so also in his humanity, while existing as a single being in a way that is ineffable and beyond understanding."[330]

4. "He is reckoned to be, and actually is, a single Christ; the same individual is both God and man."[331]

5. "Even though, however, the body and the Word of God the Father belong to different natures, there is still only a single Christ and Son, God and Lord, despite his becoming flesh."[332]

6. After the Incarnation, this single Subject is a composition of two natures

---

328   Athanasius of Alexandria. (1892). Personal Letters. In P. Schaff & H. Wace (Eds.), A. T. Robertson (Trans.), *St. Athanasius: Select Works and Letters* (Vol. 4, p. 571). New York: Christian Literature Company.

329   Ibid. (p. 579)

330   Cyril of Alexandria. (2018). *Glaphyra on the Pentateuch, Volume 1 Genesis.* (N. P. Lunn, Trans.) (Vol. 137, p. 283). Washington, DC: The Catholic University of America Press.

331   St. Cyril of Alexandria. (2014). *Three Christological Treatises.* (D. King, Trans.) (Vol. 129, p. 93). Washington, D.C.: The Catholic University of America Press.

332   Ibid. (p. 142)

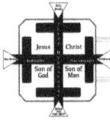

a. "Emmanuel consisted of one Christ and Son, composed of two perfections—of both deity and humanity. For we do not accept the opinion of some who consider that the divine temple, which the divine Logos possessed from the holy Virgin, was void of a rational soul. But as he was perfect in his deity, so also in his humanity, while existing as a single being in a way that is ineffable and beyond understanding."[333]

K. It is *not* wrong to analyze the Incarnation

1. "The way the Incarnation works is profound and cannot be expressed or even grasped by our minds, though that does not mean it is inappropriate to analyze it."[334]

L. Humans also have one nature formed from a union of two natures, namely soul and body

1. "The point is that man results from two natures[335]—body and soul, I mean—and intellectual perception recognizes the difference; but we unite[336] them and then get one[337] nature[338] of man. So, recognizing the difference of natures is not dividing the one Christ into two."[339]

M. Saying "one" by itself can be misunderstood; "one" can refer

---

333   Cyril of Alexandria. (2018). *Glaphyra on the Pentateuch, Volume 1 Genesis*. (N. P. Lunn, Trans.) (Vol. 137, p. 283). Washington, DC: The Catholic University of America Press.

334   St. Cyril of Alexandria. (2014). *Three Christological Treatises*. (D. King, Trans.) (Vol. 129, p. 58). Washington, D.C.: The Catholic University of America Press.

335   φύσεων

336   ἐνώσαντες

337   μίαν

338   φύσιν

339   Cyril of Alexandria. (1983). To Eulogius. L. Wickham (Trans.), *Cyril of Alexandria: Select letters* (p. 63-65). Oxford: Oxford University Press.

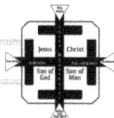

to a single object that is basic and alone, or compounded and composite

1. "While each element was seen to persist in its particular natural character for the reason just given, mysteriously and inexpressibly unified he displayed to us one nature[340] (but as I said, *incarnate*[341] nature) of the Son. 'One'[342] is a term applied properly not only to basic single elements[343] but to such composite[344] entities as man compounded of soul and body.[345] Soul and body are different kinds of things and are not mutually consubstantial;[346] yet united[347] they constitute man's single nature[348] despite the fact that the difference in nature of the elements brought into unity is present in the composite[349] condition."[350]

2. Ex: 1 is a single uncompounded number. 33 is a single composite number; in truth 33 is one number, although the mind understands that this single composite number is two number 3's united together.

N. Monophysitism[351] is to say that Jesus Christ has one nature that is either His Divine Nature *alone*, or His human nature *alone*. This is *not* synonymous with Miaphysitism and the Oriental orthodox Churches **reject** monophysitism

---

340 μίαν φύσιν
341 σεσαρκωμένη
342 μόνων
343 φύσιν
344 σύνθεσιν
345 ψυχῆς καὶ σώματος
346 ὁμοούσια
347 ἑνωθέντα
348 μίαν ἀνθρώπου φύσιν
349 συνθέσεως
350 Cyril of Alexandria. (1983). Second Letter to Succensus. L. Wickham (Trans.), *Cyril of Alexandria: Select letters* (p. 87-89). Oxford: Oxford University Press.
351 μονος, alone, only; Liddell, H. G. (1996). *A lexicon: Abridged from Liddell and Scott's Greek-English lexicon* (p. 518). Oak Harbor, WA: Logos Research Systems, Inc.

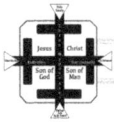

1. "If the self-same is seen as fully God and fully man, as consubstantial in Godhead with the Father and consubstantial with us in manhood,[352] what about the fulness if the manhood no longer exists? What about the consubstantiality with us, if our substance[353] (nature)[354] no longer exists? ... If we had spoken of the one nature[355] of the Word without making the overt addition 'incarnate,' to the exclusion apparently of the divine plan, there might have been some plausibility to their pretended question about the complete humanity or the possibility of our substance's[356] continued existence. In view, though, of the fact that the introduction of the word 'incarnate' expresses completeness in manhood and our nature,[357] they should cease leaning on that broken reed."[358]

2. "We too must stoutly refuse to range Christ purely and simply in the nature that is ours, but must preserve the union inseparable, the union, that is, which human nature has with the Word from God the Father."[359]

O. The human nature that the Son of God took from Saint Mary, for His incarnation:

1. Had *sinless* corruption, or passions

   a. "When He had fasted forty days and forty nights, afterward He was hungry."[360]

---

352 ὁμοούσιος μὲν τω πατρὶ κατὰ τὴν Θεότητα, κατὰ δὲ τὴν ἀνθρωπότητα ὁμοούσιος

353 οὐσία

354 φύσις

355 μίαν φύσιν

356 ἡμᾶς οὐσία

357 ἀνθρωπότητι τελειότης καὶ τῆς καθ᾽ἡμᾶς οὐσίας

358 Cyril of Alexandria. (1983). Second Letter to Succensus. L. Wickham (Trans.), *Cyril of Alexandria: Select letters* (p. 89-91). Oxford: Oxford University Press.

359 Cyril of Alexandria. (2013). *Festal Letters, 13–30*. (J. J. O'Keefe & D. G. Hunter, Eds., P. R. Amidon, Trans.) (Vol. 127, p. 70). Washington, DC: The Catholic University of America Press.

360 Mt 4:2

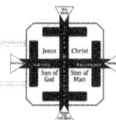

b. "And this being so, no heretic shall object, 'Wherefore rises the flesh, being by nature mortal? And if it rises, why not hunger too and thirst, and suffer, and remain mortal? For it came from the earth, and how can its natural condition pass from it?' since the flesh is able now to make answer to this so contentious heretic: 'I am from earth, being by nature mortal, but afterwards I have become the Word's flesh, and He 'carried' my affections, though He is without them; and so I became free from them, being no more abandoned to their service because of the Lord who has made me free from them. For if you object to my being rid of that corruption which is by nature, see that you object not to God's Word having taken my form of servitude; for as the Lord, putting on the body, became man, so we men are deified by the Word as being taken to Him through His flesh, and henceforward inherit life everlasting."[361]

c. "But if the flesh is the Word's (for 'the Word became flesh'), of necessity then the affections also of the flesh are ascribed to Him, whose the flesh is. And to whom the affections are ascribed, such namely as to be condemned, to be scourged, to thirst, and the cross, and death, and the other infirmities of the body, of Him too is the triumph and the grace."[362]

d. "For in the incorporeal, the properties of body had not been, unless He had taken a body corruptible and mortal;[363] for mortal was Holy Mary, from whom was His body. Wherefore of necessity when He was in a body suffering, and weeping, and toiling, these things which are proper to the flesh, are ascribed to Him together with the body."[364]

---

361 Athanasius of Alexandria. (1892). Four Discourses against the Arians. In P. Schaff & H. Wace (Eds.), J. H. Newman & A. T. Robertson (Trans.), *St. Athanasius: Select Works and Letters* (Vol. 4, pp. 412–413). New York: Christian Literature Company.

362 Ibid. (p. 411)

363 *Or.* i. 43, 44, notes; ii. 66, n. 7. *Serm. Maj. de Fid.* 9. Tertull. *de Carn. Chr.* 6.

364 Athanasius of Alexandria. (1892). Four Discourses against the Arians. In P. Schaff & H. Wace (Eds.), J.

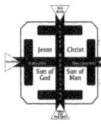

e. "And like as the Body was His own, so too the natural and blameless passions of the body and the things which by the frowardness of some were put upon Him."[365]

f. "He showed his garment stained with blood and the wounds in his hands, not because he had wounds incapable of being cast aside, for, when he rose from the dead, he put off corruption and with it all that is from it."[366]

g. "He made use of his own body, like an instrument, for carrying out bodily activities and its physical infirmities, at least such only as are not immoral, while his own soul experienced what is peculiarly human but not open to condemnation. We are told that he suffered hunger, that he bore with the trials of extensive travel, that he experienced violence and fear, grief and agony, and even death on the cross."[367]

h. "'If it is possible, let this chalice pass from me,'[368] fearful as he was and, as it were, depressed."[369]

i. "Yet, it says, we no longer know him according to the flesh, that is, no longer in flesh subject to passions, by which I mean the natural passions which are innocent of sin.[370] For before the precious cross, he is said to have hungered, to have grown weary from journeys, to have experienced

H. Newman & A. T. Robertson (Trans.), *St. Athanasius: Select Works and Letters* (Vol. 4, p. 424). New York: Christian Literature Company.

365   Cyril of Alexandria. (1881). *Five Tomes against Nestorius; Scholia on the Incarnation; Christ Is One; Fragments against Diodore of Tarsus, Theodore of Mopsuestia, the Synousiasts* (p. 232). London; Oxford; Cambridge: James Parker and Co.; Rivingtons.

366   Cyril of Alexandria. (1987). *Letters, 1–50*. (T. P. Halton, Ed., J. I. McEnerney, Trans.) (Vol. 76, p. 178). Washington, DC: The Catholic University of America Press.

367   Cyril of Alexandria. (2014). *Three Christological Treatises*. (D. Hunter, Ed., D. King, Trans.) (Vol. 129, p. 56). Washington, DC: The Catholic University of America Press.

368   Mt 26:39

369   Cyril of Alexandria. (2008). *Commentary on the Twelve Prophets*. (T. P. Halton, Ed., R. C. Hill, Trans.) (Vol. 116, p. 166). Washington, DC: The Catholic University of America Press.

370   Anenkletois, "blameless," "without reproach."

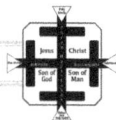

sorrow, and then to have endured death itself upon a tree on our account."[371]

j. "He had to—had to—show himself through these to be a man born of a woman, not in appearance and fantasy but naturally and truly, experiencing the full human condition except for sin. Fear and cowardice are natural passions among us, but they escape being classified as sins. Furthermore, human emotions were profitably stirred up in Christ, not that the emotions should prevail and go forward, as they do in our case, but that once stirred up, they should be cut short by the power of the Word. Our nature is thus transformed, first in Christ, into a better and more divine condition. It was in this way and no other that the process of healing passed also to us. . . . From these things it is clear that he had a rational soul. Just as being hungry, for example, or undergoing some other such experience is a passion that belongs to the flesh, so also being troubled at the thought of terrible experiences would be a passion of the rational soul, through which alone a thought can enter us through our thought processes. Christ is not yet on the cross, but he experiences mental anguish ahead of time as he looks ahead to what is going to happen and endures by his rational faculty the thought of future events. We should say that the passion of fear belongs neither to the impassible divinity nor to flesh. That passion belongs to the thought processes of the soul, not to the flesh. Even though an irrational animal, which has a soul, is distressed and troubled, it does not arrive at its fear by anticipating future suffering through its thoughts and reasoning.[372] When it is seized by the evils themselves, then it basically takes in the perception of the present danger. But in this case, the Lord

---

371   Cyril of Alexandria. (2019). *Glaphyra on the Pentateuch, Volume 2 Genesis*. (N. P. Lunn, Trans.) (Vol. 138, p. 76). Washington, DC: The Catholic University of America Press.

372   For Cyril, animals and humans both have souls since they are both alive. Animal souls, however, are nonrational, while human souls are rational.

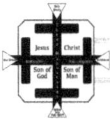

is troubled not by what he sees but by what he thinks and what he anticipates."[373]

k. "The law of sin was suppressed in the holy and chaste flesh of Christ. We assert that the excesses of human passion were never aroused in him, leaving in him only those not rooted in sin, such as hunger, thirst, fatigue, and whatever the law of nature itself does in us without any guilt. If then the law of sin was not active in Christ because it was restrained by the power and the action of the indwelling Word, then we can conclude that the nature of the flesh itself was no different in Christ than it is in us."[374]

l. He appropriated these to Himself in order to free us of them; humanity could not be freed from anything that Christ did not appropriate to Himself

1) "Suffering Himself, He gave us rest, hungering Himself, He nourished us."[375]

2) "Had not the properties of the flesh been ascribed to the Word, man had not been thoroughly delivered from them."[376, 377]

3) "Just as death was destroyed in no other way than the Savior dying, so it is with each of the passions of the flesh. If he had not been afraid, our nature would not have been freed from fear. If he had not grieved, there

---

373   Cyril of Alexandria. (2013–2015). *Commentary on John.* (J. C. Elowsky, T. C. Oden, & G. L. Bray, Eds., D. R. Maxwell, Trans.) (Vol. 2, p. 105). Downers Grove, IL: IVP Academic: An Imprint of InterVarsity Press.

374   Burns, J. P., Jr., Newman, C., & Wilken, R. L. (Eds.). (2012). *Romans: Interpreted by Early Christian Commentators.* (J. P. Burns Jr. & C. Newman, Trans.) (pp. 139–140). Grand Rapids, MI; Cambridge, UK: William B. Eerdmans Publishing Company.

375   Athanasius of Alexandria. (1892). On Luke 10:22 (Mt 11:27). In P. Schaff & H. Wace (Eds.), A. T. Robertson (Trans.), *St. Athanasius: Select Works and Letters* (Vol. 4, p. 88). New York: Christian Literature Company.

376   *Or.* i. 5 n. 5, ii. 56, n. 5, 68, n. 1, *infr.* note 6.

377   Athanasius of Alexandria. (1892). Four Discourses against the Arians. In P. Schaff & H. Wace (Eds.), J. H. Newman & A. T. Robertson (Trans.), *St. Athanasius: Select Works and Letters* (Vol. 4, p. 411). New York: Christian Literature Company.

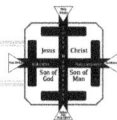

could never have been any deliverance from grief. If he had not been troubled and alarmed, there would have been no escape from these conditions. For every human experience, you will find the same corresponding experience in Christ. The passions of his flesh are stirred up, however, not to overcome him as they do us, but so that once they are stirred up they may be destroyed by the power of the Word who dwells in the flesh, transforming our nature to a better condition."[378]

2. Did *not* have *sinful* corruption, or passions, nor did He commit any sin; thus, He alone was born and is sinless

   a. "We do not have a High Priest who cannot sympathize with our weaknesses, but was in all points tempted as we are, yet without sin."[379]

   b. "He became sin for us and a curse, though not having sinned Himself, but because He Himself bare our sins and our curse."[380]

   c. "For from Mary was the Holy Body, yet at the beginning of its formation or subsistence in the womb, was it holy as being the body of Christ. . . . Holy and without sin is the body of Christ our God and Savior, and in this respect is incorruptible from the womb, and herein He hath ever no participation or likeness with us."[381]

---

378   Cyril of Alexandria. (2013–2015). *Commentary on John*. (J. C. Elowsky, T. C. Oden, & G. L. Bray, Eds., D. R. Maxwell, Trans.) (Vol. 2, p. 106-107). Downers Grove, IL: IVP Academic: An Imprint of InterVarsity Press.

379   Heb 4:15

380   Athanasius of Alexandria. (1892). Four Discourses against the Arians. In P. Schaff & H. Wace (Eds.), J. H. Newman & A. T. Robertson (Trans.), *St. Athanasius: Select Works and Letters* (Vol. 4, p. 378). New York: Christian Literature Company.

381   Cyril of Alexandria. (1881). *Five Tomes against Nestorius; Scholia on the Incarnation; Christ Is One; Fragments against Diodore of Tarsus, Theodore of Mopsuestia, the Synousiasts* (p. 327). London; Oxford; Cambridge: James Parker and Co.; Rivingtons.

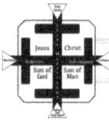

d. "For God the Word united from the very womb to His own flesh was One Son and thus also *spotless*, the Holy of holies."[382]

e. "Our Lord Jesus Christ committed no sin. . ."[383]

f. "He in fact gave his only-begotten Son, in order that, having become a human being like us and taken a body from holy Mary, the Mother of God,[384] he might put to death sin in the flesh. For he at once freed the body, which had become the Word's own, from the passions that afflict us, removed the goad of the movements toward wickedness, and transformed it, as it were, unto a purity ineffable and befitting God, once sin was put to death in it and pleasure shaken down to its very foundations, so to speak. For just as it [Christ's body] was superior to death, because it became the flesh of that life which is such by nature, in the same way, I think, it trod upon the power of sin. For it belonged to the One who did not know sin."[385]

g. "For Christ, since he was God, was eminently sinless in his own nature."[386]

h. "The law of sin lies hidden in our fleshly members, together with the shameful stirring of the natural lusts: but when the Word of God became flesh, that is man, and assumed our likeness, His flesh was holy and perfectly pure; so that He was indeed in the likeness of our flesh, but not according to its standard. For He was entirely free from the stains and

---

382   Ibid. (p. 359)

383   Cyril of Alexandria. (1983). <u>On the Creed</u>. L. Wickham (Trans.), *Cyril of Alexandria: Select letters* (p. 117). Oxford: Oxford University Press.

384   *Theotokos.* See note 34 in *Letter* 17, p. 64.

385   Cyril of Alexandria. (2013). *Festal Letters, 13–30.* (J. J. O'Keefe & D. G. Hunter, Eds., P. R. Amidon, Trans.) (Vol. 127, p. 93). Washington, DC: The Catholic University of America Press.

386   Cyril of Alexandria. (2019). *Glaphyra on the Pentateuch, Volume 2 Genesis.* (N. P. Lunn, Trans.) (Vol. 138, p. 163). Washington, DC: The Catholic University of America Press.

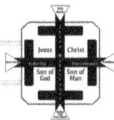

emotions natural to our bodies,[387] and from that inclination which leads us to what is not lawful."[388]

i. "Moreover, the saints indeed fast that they may quell the passions of the body by exhausting it: but Christ needed not to fast for the perfecting of virtue, because, as being God, He was free from all passion."[389]

j. "Therefore, the Word, being by nature God, condemned sin in his own flesh by commanding his flesh to be still and reforming it so that it moved toward what pleases God instead of toward its own will. In this way, though the body was 'natural,' he made it 'spiritual.'"[390]

k. "He was holy as an embryo in the womb."[391]

l. "The law of sin was suppressed in the holy and chaste flesh of Christ. We assert that the excesses of human passion were never aroused in him, leaving in him only those not rooted in sin, such as hunger, thirst, fatigue, and whatever the law of nature itself does in us without any guilt. If then the law of sin was not active in Christ because it was restrained by the power and the action of the indwelling Word, then we can conclude that the nature of the flesh itself was no different in Christ than it is in us."[392]

---

387 The Syriac translator has here misinterpreted S. Cyril, who does not say that our Lord was free from the emotions natural to bodies, but κινήματος καὶ ῥοπῆς τῆς ἡμᾶς ἀποφερούσης ἐφ' ἃ μὴ θέμις, that is, from that corruption of our nature which suggests sin to us, and inclines us to seek it (Jas 1:14). S. Cyril's main argument here is used by him with great force in his treatise De Incarnat. Dom. c. xi., wherein he shews, that our Lord took the flesh holy and perfectly pure, "to convict sin of injustice, and to destroy the power of death. For as long as sin sentenced only the guilty to death, no interference with it was possible, seeing that it had justice on its side. But when it subjected to the same punishment Him Who was innocent, and guiltless, and worthy of crowns of honour and hymns of praise, being convicted of injustice, it was by necessary consequence stripped of its power."

388 Cyril of Alexandria. (1859). *A Commentary upon the Gospel according to S. Luke*. (R. P. Smith, Trans.) (p. 14). Oxford: Oxford University Press.

389 Ibid. (p. 88)

390 Cyril of Alexandria. (2013–2015). *Commentary on John*. (J. C. Elowsky, T. C. Oden, & G. L. Bray, Eds., D. R. Maxwell, Trans.) (Vol. 2, p. 186). Downers Grove, IL: IVP Academic: An Imprint of InterVarsity Press.

391 Ibid. (p.300)

392 Burns, J. P., Jr., Newman, C., & Wilken, R. L. (Eds.). (2012). *Romans: Interpreted by Early Christian*

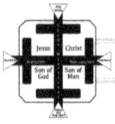

m. "The *body of sin* was destroyed in him—though in our own flesh this is not yet completely accomplished. The inborn wildness of passion in our flesh constantly draws our minds toward shameful deeds and incites us to earthy pleasures, as though our minds were mired in mud and filth. How could anyone doubt that in Christ this flaw of human nature has been corrected? For Paul states clearly: God has done what the law, weakened by the flesh, could not do: by sending God's own Son in the likeness of sinful flesh, and to deal with sin, God condemned sin in the flesh (Rom 8:3). Do you understand how the body of sin was destroyed? The urge for sin was condemned in the flesh; sin died first in Christ, then from him and through him grace has passed into us."[393]

n. "The difference was that everyone else's body could be called sinful flesh, made sick by the desire for disordered pleasure. Now no one would say that Christ's body is sinful flesh (may it not be so!), but is instead in the likeness of sinful flesh; it resembled our bodies, but it was not sickened by the impurities of the flesh. That divine temple was holy from his mother's womb. Everyone recognizes that because he was flesh, he had the natural movements by which he thought and reasoned as a human being. Since the Logos who sanctifies all creation took up his dwelling in that flesh, however, the power of sin was condemned in it, so that this restored nature could be transmitted to us as well."[394]

o. "For the Word became flesh, only not sinful flesh."[395]

p. Christ is *not* capable of sinning

Commentators. (J. P. Burns Jr. & C. Newman, Trans.) (pp. 139–140). Grand Rapids, MI; Cambridge, UK: William B. Eerdmans Publishing Company.

393   Ibid. (p. 140)

394   Ibid. (p. 185)

395   Heen, E. M., & Krey, P. D. W. (Eds.). (2005). *Hebrews* (p. 45). Downers Grove, IL: InterVarsity Press.

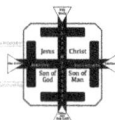

1) "It is utterly foolish for people to imagine somehow or other that because Christ came to exist in our shape for the divine plan, took slave's form and had dealings with men on earth, he could have sinned."[396]

2) "He was and is far removed from all sin, and incapable of iniquity."[397]

3) "But the glory of God, in addition to other things, is to be utterly unable to fall into sin, which of course is reserved for Christ alone. For he alone has become 'free among the dead' since he committed no sin, even though he came to be among the dead, that is, he was classified with human beings, over whom the death of sin once had mastery."[398]

4) "He [Christ] cannot fall into sin."[399]

5) "He is not capable of and neither can he endure falling into sin, but he is the source of all virtue and of the glory that is found in sanctification."[400]

P. Christ can be said to *simultaneously* will and not will something

1. "For He willed[401] what He deprecated, for therefore had He come; but His was the willing (for for it He came), but the terror belonged to the flesh. Wherefore as man He utters this speech also, and yet both were said by the Same, to shew that He was

---

396   Cyril of Alexandria. (1983). Answers to Tiberias: #13. L. Wickham (Trans.), *Cyril of Alexandria: Select letters* (p. 173). Oxford: Oxford University Press.

397   Cyril of Alexandria. (1859). *A Commentary upon the Gospel according to S. Luke*. (R. P. Smith, Trans.) (p. 399). Oxford: Oxford University Press.

398   Cyril of Alexandria. (2013–2015). *Commentary on John*. (J. C. Elowsky, T. C. Oden, & G. L. Bray, Eds., D. R. Maxwell, Trans.) (Vol. 1, p. 355). Downers Grove, IL: IVP Academic: An Imprint of InterVarsity Press.

399   Ibid. (Vol. 2, p.8)

400   Ibid. (Vol. 2, p.294)

401   [The human will of the Saviour is in absolute harmony with the Divine, though psychologically distinct.] Cf. Anast. *Hodeg.* i. p. 12.

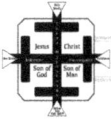

God, willing in Himself, but when He had become man, having a flesh that was in terror."[402]

2. "The divine plan, namely, death for the sake of us all, which he willingly underwent by surrendering his own body to the cross."[403]

3. "And was the necessity for Him to suffer, or rather the violence of those who plotted against Him, stronger than His own will?"[404]

4. "His passion did not happen to Him without His own will, nor could they have seized Him, had He not consented to be taken."[405]

5. "The suffering on the cross is both unwilled in a sense by Christ our Savior and willed because of us and the good pleasure of God the Father. . . . Do you see how death was not willed by Christ both because of the flesh and because of the ignominy of the suffering, but at the same time it was willed until he brings the whole world to its fitting consummation intended by the good pleasure of the Father, that is, salvation and life for all?"[406]

6. "The suffering on the cross is seen to be truly unwilled and at the same time willed by the Only Begotten, as we said before."[407]

7. "He [Christ] says these words to teach that he considers dying for all to be willed on the one hand because the divine nature has willed it but unwilled on the other because of the suffering on the cross—and this insofar as the flesh is concerned, which

402   Athanasius of Alexandria. (1892). <u>Four Discourses against the Arians</u>. In P. Schaff & H. Wace (Eds.), J. H. Newman & A. T. Robertson (Trans.), *St. Athanasius: Select Works and Letters* (Vol. 4, p. 424). New York: Christian Literature Company.

403   Cyril of Alexandria. (2012). *Commentary on the Twelve Prophets*. (D. G. Hunter, Ed., R. C. Hill, Trans.) (Vol. 124, p. 123). Washington, DC: The Catholic University of America Press.

404   Cyril of Alexandria. (1859). *A Commentary upon the Gospel according to S. Luke*. (R. P. Smith, Trans.) (p. 690). Oxford: Oxford University Press.

405   Ibid. (p. 695)

406   Cyril of Alexandria. (2013–2015). *Commentary on John*. (J. C. Elowsky, T. C. Oden, & G. L. Bray, Eds., D. R. Maxwell, Trans.) (Vol. 1, p. 217). Downers Grove, IL: IVP Academic: An Imprint of InterVarsity Press.

407   Ibid. (p.218)

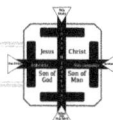

seeks to avoid death . . . suffering on the cross is clearly unwilled, in a sense, by Christ our Savior in that he is a human being. . . . Since there was no other way to raise what had fallen into death back to life except for the only begotten Word of God to become human (and once he became human he certainly had to suffer), he made what was unwilled into something willed, and the divine nature accepted this because of its love for us."[408]

8. "The Son 'came down from heaven' to undergo death for all, willingly and at the same time unwillingly."[409]

9. "One should attribute to Christ the Savior the will to suffer for all in order that he may rescue all."[410]

10. "Christ endured death for us and in our place, he did so not against his will, but he came to it willingly, even though he could easily have escaped it if he did not want to suffer."[411]

Q. Through the reality of the union, attributes possessed by either nature can be manifested through the one Subject of Jesus Christ; this is called communication of properties

1. Divine Attributes:

   a. "The natural properties of the Word who came forth from the Father were maintained even when he became flesh."[412]

   b. Divine Glory (this was present but hidden upon Incarnation)

      1) 'God who has appeared in humanity, the Son, who has neither departed from the glory of his own dignities because of what is human, nor disdained being like us

408   Ibid. (p.221)
409   Ibid. (p.222)
410   Ibid. (p.327)
411   Ibid. (Vol. 2, p.68)
412   Heen, E. M., & Krey, P. D. W. (Eds.). (2005). *Hebrews* (p. 233). Downers Grove, IL: InterVarsity Press.

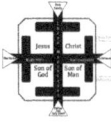

according to the economy."[413]

2) "He did not lose the dignities naturally his, but assumed flesh and blood, in order that we in turn might become sharers in the divine nature, gaining spiritually by being joined to him. For we are joined to him through faith, sanctification, and the virtuous deeds that make for piety."[414]

3) "For even if he came to be like unto us and shared in like manner in blood and flesh,[415] still he did not therefore abandon being God nor did it make him cast aside being what he was, for he remained adorable in the glory of God the Father."[416]

4) "He made the human characteristics his very own, albeit continuing to enjoy the full possession of his own nature's virtues, retaining without confusion the state in which he was, is, and ever shall be."[417]

5) "Although he was not bereft of God-befitting glory (especially since he was begotten as God from God the Father), nevertheless, since he diminished that glory somewhat at the time of his *oikonomia* for us by taking on this body that has no glory, there is good reason for him to ask as one who truly has no glory. When he says this he is speaking as a human being."[418]

---

413   Cyril of Alexandria. (2013). *Festal Letters, 13–30*. (J. J. O'Keefe & D. G. Hunter, Eds., P. R. Amidon, Trans.) (Vol. 127, p. 70). Washington, DC: The Catholic University of America Press.

414   Cyril of Alexandria. (2013). *Festal Letters, 13–30*. (J. J. O'Keefe & D. G. Hunter, Eds., P. R. Amidon, Trans.) (Vol. 127, p. 146). Washington, DC: The Catholic University of America Press.

415   Heb 2:14

416   Cyril of Alexandria. (1987). *Letters, 1–50*. (T. P. Halton, Ed., J. I. McEnerney, Trans.) (Vol. 76, p. 223). Washington, DC: The Catholic University of America Press.

417   Cyril of Alexandria. (2014). *Three Christological Treatises*. (D. Hunter, Ed., D. King, Trans.) (Vol. 129, p. 104). Washington, DC: The Catholic University of America Press.

418   Cyril of Alexandria. (2013–2015). *Commentary on John*. (J. C. Elowsky, T. C. Oden, & G. L. Bray, Eds., D. R. Maxwell, Trans.) (Vol. 2, p. 277). Downers Grove, IL: IVP Academic: An Imprint of InterVarsity Press.

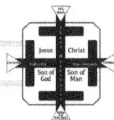

6) "He is surely not bereft of his glory, even if he were to ask without receiving, since the Word, being true God, was never excluded from his own honors. Rather, he is raising his own temple to the glory that he always had. . . . The Son was never excluded from the glory of the Father."[419]

c. God-like power

1) "The holy flesh, which He had made His own, and endowed with godlike power, possessed the active presence of the might of the Word."[420]

2) "The holy flesh which He had made His own was endowed with the activity of the power of the Word by His having implanted in it a godlike might."[421]

d. Life-giving power

1) "Unless you eat the flesh of the Son of Man and drink His blood, you have no life in you."[422]

2) "Hence we affirm Christ's body to be divine, seeing that it is God's body, adorned with ineffable glory, incorruptible, holy and life-giving. . . ."[423]

3) "Christ's holy body and blood are life-giving. For the body, as I said, does not belong to some human participant in Life but is personally owned by Life himself, that is the

---

419 Ibid. (p.278)

420 Cyril of Alexandria. (1859). *A Commentary upon the Gospel according to S. Luke*. (R. P. Smith, Trans.) (p. 70). Oxford: Oxford University Press.

421 Ibid. (p. 71)

422 Jn 6:53

423 Cyril of Alexandria. (1983). First Letter to Succensus. L. Wickham (Trans.), *Cyril of Alexandria: Select letters* (p. 81). Oxford: Oxford University Press.

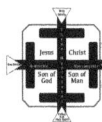

Only-begotten."[424]

4) "Because it became the flesh of the Word, Who gives life to all, it therefore also has the power of giving life, and annihilates the influence of death and corruption."[425, 426]

2. Human attributes:

a. "So likewise, we know that he became human, and so we do not deny whatever is said about him that reflects his humanity, for example, that he was hungry, that he was thirsty, that he was slapped, that he wept, that he slept, and finally, that he accepted death on a cross for our sake . . . for we human beings have been created and made. But just as, when we hear that he was hungry, slept, and was slapped, we do not deny his divinity, so too, when we hear the phrase, 'he created,' it would be consistent to remember that, though he is God, he was created a human being."[427]

b. "The incorporeal Word made His own the properties of the Body, as being His own Body."[428]

c. "Just as the body has been made his own possession, so

---

424   Ibid.("On the Creed", p. 129)

425   Two passages follow in Mai, not recognised by the Syriac. The first from Cod. A. is as follows: "for we believe that the body of Christ makes alive, because It is both the temple and dwelling-place of the living Word, and possesses all Its activity. It was not enough therefore for Him only to command, though accustomed by a word to accomplish whatsoever He wished, but He laid also His hands on the bier, shewing that His body also possesses the power of making alive." The second from Codd. A and C. is referred also by Aquinas and Cramer's MS. to Cyril: "That fear fell upon all, and they glorified God, was indeed a great thing on the part of the senseless and ungrateful people (Cr. reads λόγῳ for λαῷ): for shortly afterwards they regard Him neither as a prophet, nor as having appeared for the good of the people: yea they deliver up to death Him Who destroys death, not knowing that at that very time He destroyed death, when in His own person He wrought the resurrection."

426   Cyril of Alexandria. (1859). *A Commentary upon the Gospel according to S. Luke.* (R. P. Smith, Trans.) (p. 135). Oxford: Oxford University Press.

427   Athanasius and Didymus. (2011). *Works on the Spirit: Athanasius's Letters to Serapion on the Holy Spirit, and, Didymus's on the Holy Spirit.* (J. Behr, Ed., M. DelCogliano, A. Radde-Gallwitz, & L. Ayres, Trans.) (Vol. 43, p. 115-116). Yonkers, NY: St Vladimir's Seminary Press.

428   Athanasius of Alexandria. (1892). Personal Letters. In P. Schaff & H. Wace (Eds.), A. T. Robertson (Trans.), *St. Athanasius: Select Works and Letters* (Vol. 4, p. 572). New York: Christian Literature Company.

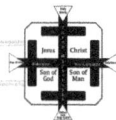

all features of the body (with the sale exception of sin) are to be attributed to him in accordance with God's plan of appropriation."[429]

d. "He made the properties[430] of the flesh his own, for the flesh united in expressibly mysterious fashion with him was his and no other's."[431]

e. "He made the properties of the flesh his own . . ."[432]

f. "The shared properties of our human nature were taken up into his person."[433]

g. "The Son, who is God and a human being in the same person, and so you will not think that human properties must be rejected, even though they are imported to the only one who is Son by nature, I mean Christ."[434]

h. Being created

   1) "For when he says he created, he signifies his humanity, that he became human and was created."[435]

   2) "It is true to say that the Son was created too, but this took place when He became man."[436]

---

429   Cyril of Alexandria. (1983). Second Letter to Succensus. L. Wickham (Trans.), *Cyril of Alexandria: Select letters* (p. 87-89). Oxford: Oxford University Press.

430   ἴδια

431   Cyril of Alexandria. (1983). On the Creed. L. Wickham (Trans.), *Cyril of Alexandria: Select letters* (p. 109-111). Oxford: Oxford University Press.

432   Cyril of Alexandria. (2014). *Three Christological Treatises*. (D. Hunter, Ed., D. King, Trans.) (Vol. 129, p. 150). Washington, DC: The Catholic University of America Press.

433   Cyril of Alexandria. (2013–2015). *Commentary on John*. (J. C. Elowsky, T. C. Oden, & G. L. Bray, Eds., D. R. Maxwell, Trans.) (Vol. 1, p. 64). Downers Grove, IL: IVP Academic: An Imprint of InterVarsity Press.

434   Ibid. (Vol. 2, p.300)

435   Athanasius and Didymus. (2011). *Works on the Spirit: Athanasius's Letters to Serapion on the Holy Spirit, and, Didymus's on the Holy Spirit*. (J. Behr, Ed., M. DelCogliano, A. Radde-Gallwitz, & L. Ayres, Trans.) (Vol. 43, p. 115-116). Yonkers, NY: St Vladimir's Seminary Press.

436   Athanasius of Alexandria. (1892). De Decretis or Defence of the Nicene Definition. In P. Schaff & H. Wace (Eds.), J. H. Newman & A. T. Robertson (Trans.), *St. Athanasius: Select Works and Letters* (Vol. 4, p. 158). New York: Christian Literature Company.

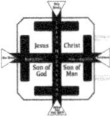

3) "For when He had taken that which He had to offer on our behalf, namely His body of the Virgin Mary, then it is written of Him that He had been created, and formed, and made."[437]

4) "It was the Son, not the Father, who had put on the originated, formed, created body; for which reason the Son also is said to have been originated, created, and formed."[438]

5) "We have been ordered to adore Christ, let him be regarded as above created nature as God, even if he is regarded as having been created because of what is human."[439]

i. Ignorance

1) "For just as, when he said: He created me [Prov 8.22], he meant it as a reference to his humanity, so too, when he said: nor the Son, he meant it as a reference to his humanity.[440] And there is a good reason why he spoke in this way. For he became human, as it is written, and being ignorant is proper to human beings, just like being hungry and all the rest, since they do not know something unless they hear and learn it. Therefore, when he became human, he indicated his human ignorance for two reasons: first, so that he could show that he really has a human body; second, since he had human ignorance in his body, so that he could redeem his humanity from all and cleanse it and so offer it perfect and holy to the Father. . . . Likewise, when he says 'No one knows, not even the Son [Mk 13.32],' he

---

437   Ibid. (On the Opinion of Dionysius, p. 180)

438   Ibid. (On the Opinion of Dionysius, p. 183)

439   Cyril of Alexandria. (2013). *Festal Letters, 13–30*. (J. J. O'Keefe & D. G. Hunter, Eds., P. R. Amidon, Trans.) (Vol. 127, p. 71). Washington, DC: The Catholic University of America Press.

440   In both cases, "he meant it as a reference to his humanity" translates ἀνθρωπίνως εἴρηκεν.

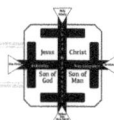

again speaks as a human being. For being ignorant is proper to human beings. . . . So then, in the Gospel according to John the disciples said to the Lord: Now we know that you know all things [Jn 16.30]. Thus it is clear that there is nothing of which he is ignorant, seeing that he is the Word through whom all things were made [Jn 1.3]." [441]

2) "If the one who is omniscient is not identical with the one who has limited knowledge—the one perfect in wisdom, who knows all that the Father knows, not identical with the one who receives only a partial revelation—then certainly there would indeed be two subjects. And if be-cause of the fact of there being a genuine union he is actually one and the same individual, not two separate things, each on its own, then knowing and also not knowing can both be reasonably predicated of him. He has divine knowledge because he is the Father's wisdom, but since for salvation's sake he has subjected himself to the boundaries of human knowledge, then this boundary he has made his very own along with the other characteristics, even though, as I just mentioned, there is nothing he does not know—in fact, he has complete knowledge like the Father." [442]

3) "So the Lord saying what precedes that day and that hour, knows exactly, nor is ignorant, when the hour and the day are at hand . . . but why, though He knew, He said, 'no, not the Son knows,' this I think none of the faithful is ignorant, viz. that He made this as those other declarations as man by reason of the flesh. For this as

441 Athanasius and Didymus. (2011). *Works on the Spirit: Athanasius's Letters to Serapion on the Holy Spirit, and, Didymus's on the Holy Spirit.* (J. Behr, Ed., M. DelCogliano, A. Radde-Gallwitz, & L. Ayres, Trans.) (Vol. 43, p. 115-116). Yonkers, NY: St Vladimir's Seminary Press.

442 Cyril of Alexandria. (2014). *Three Christological Treatises.* (D. Hunter, Ed., D. King, Trans.) (Vol. 129, p. 104). Washington, DC: The Catholic University of America Press.

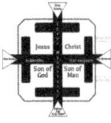

before is not the Word's deficiency,[443] but of that human nature[444] whose property it is to be ignorant. . . . For it is proper to the Word to know what was made, nor be ignorant either of the beginning or of the end of these (for the works are His), and He knows how many things He wrought, and the limit of their consistence. And knowing of each the beginning and the end, He knows surely the general and common end of all. Certainly when He says in the Gospel concerning Himself in His human character, 'Father, the hour is come, glorify Thy Son,'[445] it is plain that He knows also the hour of the end of all things, as the Word, though as man He is ignorant of it, for ignorance is proper to man,[446] and especially ignorance of these things. Moreover this is proper to the Savior's love of man; for since He was made man, He is not ashamed, because of the flesh which is ignorant, to say 'I know not,' that He may shew that knowing as

---

443   *Or.* i. 45.

444   Cf. ii. 45, n. 2.

445   Jn 17:1

446   Though our Lord, as having two natures, had a human as well as a divine knowledge, and though that human knowledge was not only limited because human, but liable to ignorance in matters in which greater knowledge was possible; yet it is the doctrine of the [later] Church, that *in fact* He was not ignorant even in His human nature, according to its capacity, since it was from the first taken out of its original and natural condition, and 'deified' by its union with the Word. As then (*supr.* ii. 45, note 1) His manhood was created, yet He may not be called a creature even in His manhood, and as (*supr.* ii. 14, note 5) His flesh was in its abstract nature a servant, yet He is not a servant in fact, even as regards the flesh; so, though He took on Him a soul which left to itself had been partially ignorant, as other human souls, yet as ever enjoying the beatific vision from its oneness with the Word, it never was ignorant really, but knew all things which human soul can know. vid. *Eulog. ap. Phot.* 230. p. 884. As Pope Gregory expresses it, 'Novit in natura, non ex natura humanitatis.' *Epp.* x. 39. However, this view of the sacred subject was received by the Church only after S. Athanasius's day, and it cannot be denied that others of the most eminent Fathers seem to impute ignorance to our Lord as man, as Athan. in this passage. Of course it is not meant that our Lord's soul has the same perfect knowledge as He has as God. This was the assertion of a General of the Hermits of S. Austin at the time of the Council of Basel, when the proposition was formally condemned, animam Christi Deum videre tam clare et intense quam clare et intense Deus videt seipsum. vid. Berti *Opp.* t. 3. P. 42. Yet Fulgentius had said, 'I think that in no respect was full knowledge of the Godhead wanting to that Soul, whose Person is one with the Word: whom Wisdom so assumed that it is itself that same Wisdom.' *ad Ferrand.* iii. p. 223. ed. 1639. Yet, *ad Trasmund.* i. 7. he speaks of ignorance attaching to our Lord's human nature.

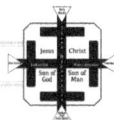

God, He is but ignorant according to the flesh."[447, 448]

4) "When He had spoken humanly[449] 'no, not the Son knows,' He yet shews that divinely He knew all things."[450]

5) "The Word, not as ignorant, considered as Word, has said 'I know not,' for He knows, but as shewing His manhood,[451] in that to be ignorant is proper to man,

---

447   And so Athan. *ad Serap.* ii. 9. S. Basil on the question being asked him by S. Amphilochius, says that he shall give him the answer he had 'heard from a boy from the fathers,' but which was more fitted for pious Christians than for cavillers, and that is, that 'our Lord says many things to men in His human aspect; as "Give me to drink," … yet He who asked was not flesh without a soul, but Godhead using flesh which had one.' *Ep.* 236, 1. He goes on to suggest another explanation which has been mentioned § 42, note 1. Cf. Cyril *Trin.* pp. 623, 4. vid. also *Thes.* p. 220. 'As he submitted as man to hunger and thirst, so…. to be ignorant." p. 221. vid. also Greg. Naz. *Orat.* 30, 15. Theodoret expresses the same opinion very strongly, speaking of a gradual revelation to the manhood from the Godhead, but in an argument where it was to his point to do so; in *Anath.* 4. t. v. p. 23. ed. Schulze. Theodore of Mopsuestia also speaks of a revelation made by the Word. ap. Leont. *c. Nest* (Canis. i. p. 579.)

448   Athanasius of Alexandria. (1892). <u>Four Discourses against the Arians</u>. In P. Schaff & H. Wace (Eds.), J. H. Newman & A. T. Robertson (Trans.), *St. Athanasius: Select Works and Letters* (Vol. 4, p. 417). New York: Christian Literature Company.

449   Leporius, in his Retractation, which S. Augustine subscribed, writes, 'That I may in this respect also leave nothing to be cause of suspicion to any one, I then said, nay I answered when it was put to me, that our Lord Jesus Christ was ignorant as He was man, (secundum hominem). But now not only do I not presume to say so, but I even anathematize my former opinion expressed on this point,' *ap. Sirm.* t. i. p. 210. A subdivision also of the Eutychians were called by the name of Agnoetæ from their holding that our Lord was ignorant of the day of judgment. 'They said,' says Leontius, 'that He was ignorant of it, as we say that He underwent toil.' *de Sect.* 5. circ. fin. Felix of Urgela held the same doctrine according to Agobard's testimony, see § 46, n. 2. Montfaucon observes on the text, that the assertion of our Lord's ignorance 'seems to have been condemned in no one in ancient times, unless joined to other error.' And Petavius, after drawing out the authorities for and against it, says, 'Of these two opinions, the latter, which is now received both by custom and by the agreement of divines, is deservedly preferred to the former. For it is more agreeable to Christ's dignity, and more befitting His character and office of Mediator and Head, that is, Fountain of all grace and wisdom, and moreover of Judge, who is concerned in knowing the time fixed for exercising that function. In consequence, the former opinion, though formerly it received the countenance of some men of high eminence, was afterwards marked as a heresy.' *Incarn.* xi. 1. § 15.

450   Athanasius of Alexandria. (1892). <u>Four Discourses against the Arians</u>. In P. Schaff & H. Wace (Eds.), J. H. Newman & A. T. Robertson (Trans.), *St. Athanasius: Select Works and Letters* (Vol. 4, pp. 417–418). New York: Christian Literature Company.

451   It is a question to be decided, whether our Lord speaks of actual ignorance in His human Mind, or of the natural ignorance of that Mind considered as human; ignorance *in* or *ex natura*; or, which comes to the same thing, whether He spoke of a real ignorance, or of an economical or professed ignorance, in a certain view of His incarnation or office, as when He asked, 'How many loaves have ye?' when 'He Himself knew what He would do,' or as He is called sin, though sinless. Thus it has been noticed, *supr.* ii. 55, n. 7, that Ath. seems to make His infirmities altogether only imputative, not real, as if shewing that the subject had not in his day been thoroughly worked out. In like manner S. Hilary, who, if the passage be genuine, states so clearly our Lord's ignorance, *de Trin.* ix. fin. yet, as Petavius observes, seems elsewhere to deny to Him those very affections of the flesh to which he has there paralleled it. And this view of Athan.'s meaning is favoured by the turn of his expressions. He says such a defect belongs to '*that human nature* whose prop-

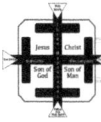

and that He had put on flesh that was ignorant, being in which, He said according to the flesh, 'I know not' . . . it belongs to man to be ignorant; for whose sake He too having a flesh like theirs and having become man, said 'no, not the Son knows,' for He knew not in flesh, though knowing as Word."[452]

6) "Suitably said He then, 'no, nor the Son,' according to the flesh because of the body; that He might shew that, as man, He knows not; for ignorance is proper to man. . . ."[453] For as, on becoming man, He hungers and thirsts and suffers with men, so with men as man He

---

erty it is to be ignorant;' § 43. that 'since He was made man, He is not *ashamed,* because of the flesh which is ignorant, *to say,* "I know not;" ' ibid. and, as here, that 'as *shewing* His manhood, in that to be ignorant is *proper* to man, and that He had *put on* a flesh *that was ignorant,* being in which, He *said* according to the flesh, "I know not;" ' 'that He might *shew* that as man He knows not;' § 46. that '*as* man' (i.e. on the *ground* of being man, not in the *capacity* of man), 'He knows not;' ibid. and that, 'He *asks* about Lazarus humanly,' even when 'He was *on His way* to raise him,' which implied surely knowledge in His human nature. The reference to the parallel of S. Paul's professed ignorance when he really knew, § 47. leads us to the same suspicion. And so 'for *our profit* as I think, did He this.' §§ 48–50. The natural want of precision on such questions in the early ages was shewn or fostered by such words as οικονομικως, which, in respect of this very text, is used by S. Basil to denote both our Lord's Incarnation, *Ep.* 236, 1 fin. and His gracious accommodation of Himself and His truth, *Ep.* 8, 6. and with the like variety of meaning, with reference to the same text, by Cyril. *Trin.* p. 623. and *Thesaur.* p. 224. (And the word *dispensatio* in like manner, Ben. note on *Hil.* x. 8.) In the latter *Ep.* S. Basil suggests that our Lord 'economizes by a reigned ignorance.' § 6. And S. Cyril. *Thesaur.* p. 224. And even in *de Trin.* vi. he seems to recognise the distinction laid down just now between the natural and actual state of our Lord's humanity; and so Hilary, *Trin.* ix. 62. And he gives reasons why He professed ignorance, n. 67. viz. as S. Austin words it, Christum se dixisse nescientem, in quo alios facit occultando nescientes. *Ep.* 180, 3. S. Austin follows him, saying, Hoc nescit quod nescienter facit. *Trin.* i. 23. Pope Gregory says that the text 'is most certainly to be referred to the Son not as He is Head, but as to His body which we are.' *Ep* x. 39. And S. Ambrose *de fid.* v. 222. And so Cæsarius, Qu. 20. and Photius *Epp.* p. 366. Chrysost. in Matt. *Hom.* 77, 3. Theodoret, however, but in controversy, is very severe on the principle of Economy. 'If He knew the day, and wishing to conceal it, said He was ignorant, see what a blasphemy is the result. Truth tells an untruth.' l. c, pp. 23, 4.

452   Athanasius of Alexandria. (1892). <u>Four Discourses against the Arians</u>. In P. Schaff & H. Wace (Eds.), J. H. Newman & A. T. Robertson (Trans.), *St. Athanasius: Select Works and Letters* (Vol. 4, p. 418). New York: Christian Literature Company.

453   The mode in which Athan. here expresses himself, is as if he did not ascribe ignorance literally, but apparent ignorance, to our Lord's soul, vid. *supr.* 45. n. 2; not certainly in the broad sense in which heretics have done so. As Leontius, e.g. reports of Theodore of Mopsuestia, that he considered Christ 'to be ignorant so far, as not to know, when He was tempted, who tempted Him;' *contr. Nest.* iii. (Canis. t. i. p. 579.) and Agobard of Felix the Adoptionist that he held 'Our Lord Jesus Christ according to the flesh *truly* to have been ignorant of the sepulchre of Lazarus, when He said to his sisters, 'Where have ye laid him?' and was *truly* ignorant of the day of judgment; and was *truly* ignorant what the two disciples were saying, as they walked by the way, of what had been done at Jerusalem; and was *truly* ignorant whether He was more loved by Peter than by the other disciples, when He said, 'Simon Peter, Lovest thou Me more than these?' *B. P.* t. 9. p. 1177. [Cf. *Prolegg.* ch. iv. § 5.]

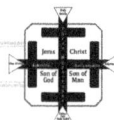

knows not; though divinely, being in the Father Word and Wisdom, He knows, and there is nothing which He knows not."[454]

7) "God's only-begotten Word took on along with his humanity all its attributes save sin alone. Ignorance of future events properly belongs to the limitations of humanity and so, in so far as he is viewed as God, he knows all the Father knows; in so far, though, as the same Son is man, he does not repudiate the appearance of ignorance because it is an attribute of humanity. Just as he who is personally the Life and Power of all took bodily nourishment out of respect for the measure of his self-emptying is recorded as having slept and been weary, so, though knowing all things, he is not ashamed to allot himself the ignorance which belongs to humanity; because his were all the attributes of humanity save sin alone. But seeing that the disciples wanted to learn things beyond them, he helped them by claiming not to know as man, and tells them that not even the angels in heaven know, in order that they might not be disappointed at not being entrusted with the mystery."[455]

8) "For as far as the law of humanity is concerned, the time had not yet allowed the baby to be able to distinguish the natures of things. He was also, however, as I said, God in humanity, letting the nature which is as ours proceed by its own laws, while preserving with this the purity of the divinity."[456]

454   Athanasius of Alexandria. (1892). Four Discourses against the Arians. In P. Schaff & H. Wace (Eds.), J. H. Newman & A. T. Robertson (Trans.), *St. Athanasius: Select Works and Letters* (Vol. 4, p. 419). New York: Christian Literature Company.

455   Cyril of Alexandria. (1983). Answers to Tiberius: #4. L. Wickham (Trans.), *Cyril of Alexandria: Select letters* (p. 153). Oxford: Oxford University Press.

456   Cyril of Alexandria. (2013). *Festal Letters, 13–30*. (J. J. O'Keefe & D. G. Hunter, Eds., P. R. Amidon, Trans.) (Vol. 127, p. 64). Washington, DC: The Catholic University of America Press.

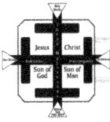

j. Suffering

1) "And verily it is strange that He it was Who suffered and yet suffered not. Suffered, because His own Body suffered, and He was in it, which thus suffered; suffered not, because the Word, being by Nature God, is impassible."[457]

2) "And that the Lord suffered in flesh we affirm."[458]

3) "God's Word is, of course, undoubtedly impassible in his own nature and nobody is so mad as to imagine the all-transcending nature capable of suffering; but by very reason of the fact that he has become man making flesh from the holy Virgin his own, we adhere to the principles of the divine plan and maintain that he, who as God transcends suffering, suffered humanly in his own flesh."[459]

4) "God the Word is the Savior who remains impassible in his divine nature while also suffering in the flesh."[460]

5) "Christ suffering indeed in the flesh according to the Scriptures, but remaining also beyond the power of suffering."[461]

6) "For he was impassible even as he was suffering."[462]

457   Athanasius of Alexandria. (1892). Personal Letters. In P. Schaff & H. Wace (Eds.), A. T. Robertson (Trans.), *St. Athanasius: Select Works and Letters* (Vol. 4, p. 572). New York: Christian Literature Company.

458   Cyril of Alexandria. (1983). Second Letter to Succensus. L. Wickham (Trans.), *Cyril of Alexandria: Select letters* (p. 92-93). Oxford: Oxford University Press.

459   Ibid. ("On the Creed", p. 123)

460   Cyril of Alexandria. (2014). *Three Christological Treatises*. (D. Hunter, Ed., D. King, Trans.) (Vol. 129, p. 130). Washington, DC: The Catholic University of America Press.

461   Cyril of Alexandria. (1859). *A Commentary upon the Gospel according to S. Luke*. (R. P. Smith, Trans.) (p. 77). Oxford: Oxford University Press.

462   Cyril of Alexandria. (2013–2015). *Commentary on John*. (J. C. Elowsky, T. C. Oden, & G. L. Bray, Eds., D. R. Maxwell, Trans.) (Vol. 2, p. 348). Downers Grove, IL: IVP Academic: An Imprint of InterVarsity Press.

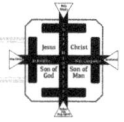

R. <u>Christ can have words, or actions, assigned to Him as God or a human</u>

1. "Anyone who reads the Scripture must examine and judge where it speaks of the divinity of the Word and where is speaks of his human acts. . . . So likewise, we know that he became human, and so we do not deny whatever is said about him that reflects his humanity, for example, that he was hungry, that he was thirsty, that he was slapped, that he wept, that he slept, and finally, that he accepted death on a cross for our sake. . . . For we human beings have been created and made. But just as, when we hear that he was hungry, slept, and was slapped, we do not deny his divinity, so too, when we hear the phrase, 'he created,' it would be consistent to remember that, though he is God, he was created a human being . . . when he said: nor the Son, he meant it as a reference to his humanity."[463, 464]

2. "But the expressions used about His Godhead, and His becoming man, are to be interpreted with discrimination and suitably to the particular context. And he that writes of the human attributes of the Word knows also what concerns His Godhead: and he who expounds concerning His Godhead is not ignorant of what belongs to His coming in the flesh: but discerning each as a skilled and 'approved money-changer,' he will walk in the straight way of piety; when therefore he speaks of His weeping, he knows that the Lord, having become man, while he exhibits his human character in weeping, as God raises up Lazarus; and He knows that He used to hunger and thirst physically, while divinely He fed five thousand persons from five loaves; and knows that while a human body lay in the tomb, it was raised as God's body by the Word Himself."[465]

---

463   In both cases, "he meant it as a reference to his humanity" translates ἀνθρωπίνως εἴρηκεν.

464   Athanasius and Didymus. (2011). *Works on the Spirit: Athanasius's Letters to Serapion on the Holy Spirit, and, Didymus's on the Holy Spirit.* (J. Behr, Ed., M. DelCogliano, A. Radde-Gallwitz, & L. Ayres, Trans.) (Vol. 43, p. 115-116). Yonkers, NY: St Vladimir's Seminary Press.

465   Athanasius of Alexandria. (1892). <u>On the Opinion of Dionysius</u>. In P. Schaff & H. Wace (Eds.), A. T. Robertson (Trans.), *St. Athanasius: Select Works and Letters* (Vol. 4, p. 179). New York: Christian Literature

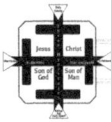

3. "For whatever is written concerning our Savior in His human nature."[466]

4. "For had they known the person, and the subject, and the season of the Apostle's words, they would not have expounded of Christ's divinity what belongs to His manhood."[467]

5. "For the passage in the Proverbs, as I have said before, signifies, not the Essence, but the manhood of the Word."[468]

6. "Though human things are ascribed to the Savior in the Gospel, let us, considering the nature of what is said and that they are foreign to God, not impute them to the Word's Godhead, but to His manhood."[469]

7. "To say that the child grew, and waxed strong in spirit, being filled with wisdom, and the grace of God was upon Him, must be taken as referring to His human nature."[470]

8. "You see, when someone says something about him that is especially fitting for a god, we say that it is absolutely correct, since we know that he is God, and if what is said is something more appropriate to a human, we would also assent."[471]

9. "For since the same is both God and man, he speaks both in human and divine terms and effects human and divine things alike."[472]

10. "And as to the Gospel and Apostolic words concerning the Lord,

Company.

466   Ibid. (Defence of His Flight, p. 259)

467   Ibid. (Four Discourses against the Arians, p. 338)

468   Ibid. (Four Discourses against the Arians, p. 376)

469   Ibid. (Four Discourses against the Arians, p. 416)

470   Cyril of Alexandria. (1859). *A Commentary upon the Gospel according to S. Luke*. (R. P. Smith, Trans.) (p. 29). Oxford: Oxford University Press.

471   Cyril of Alexandria. (2014). *Three Christological Treatises*. (D. Hunter, Ed., D. King, Trans.) (Vol. 129, p. 169). Washington, DC: The Catholic University of America Press.

472   Cyril of Alexandria. (1983). Answers to Tiberius: #5. L. Wickham (Trans.), *Cyril of Alexandria: Select letters* (p. 115). Oxford: Oxford University Press.

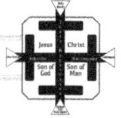

we know that Divines make some common, as to One Person,[473] apportion others, as to two Natures,[474] and give the God-befitting to Christ according to His Godhead,[475] the lowly ones according to His Manhood."[476, 477]

III. The Holy Spirit

A. Is always referred to in Holy Scripture using "the," or some adjective, so as to distinguish Him alone as the one eternal Holy Spirit

1. "Tell me: have you found any passage in the Divine Scriptures where the Holy Spirit is called 'spirit' without qualification, without being modified with either 'of God,' or 'of the Father,' or 'my,' or 'his,' or 'of Christ' and 'of the Son,' or 'from me,' that is, from God, or with the definite article[478] (such that he is not called 'spirit' without qualification but 'the Spirit'), or the very term 'the Holy Spirit,' or 'Paraclete,' or 'of Truth' (that is, of the Son, who says: I am the Truth [Jn 14:6])—any passage in which, when you hear 'spirit' without any qualification, you assume that it is the Holy Spirit?"[479]

2. "In general, if 'spirit' is said without the definite article or

---

473 ἑνὸς προσώπου

474 δύο φύσεων

475 θεότητα

476 ἀνθρωπότητα

477 Cyril of Alexandria. (1872). *The Three Epistles of S. Cyril, Archbishop of Alexandria: English Text*. (P. E. Pusey, Ed.) (p. 72). Oxford; London: James Parker and Co.

478 See Didymus, *Spir.* 8, 73, and 246.

479 Athanasius and Didymus. (2011). *Works on the Spirit: Athanasius's Letters to Serapion on the Holy Spirit, and, Didymus's on the Holy Spirit*. (J. Behr, Ed., M. DelCogliano, A. Radde-Gallwitz, & L. Ayres, Trans.) (Vol. 43, p. 57). Yonkers, NY: St Vladimir's Seminary Press.

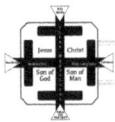

without one of the aforementioned modifiers, it cannot be the Holy Spirit who is signified."[480]

3. "This is why Paul also speaks of him using the definite article, attesting that he is unique and one."[481]

4. "So too is the Spirit, who is given and sent from the Son, also one and not many, nor one of many, but the only Spirit."[482]

B. Is called:

1. An Anointing, Seal and Unction

   a. "You were sealed with the Holy Spirit."[483]

   b. "The Spirit is said to be an anointing and is a seal, . . . the Spirit is the anointing and the seal by whom and in whom the Word anoints and seals all things . . ."[484]

   c. "The holy anointing from God the Father, that is, the Spirit."[485]

      1) Believers, when sealed, partake of the Divine Nature

         A) "And the seal has the form of Christ who seals, and those who are sealed participate in him, being formed into him, as the Apostle says: My children, with whom I am again in labor until Christ be formed in you! [Gal 4.19]. Thus sealed, it is proper that we also become, as Peter said, sharers of the divine

---

480   Ibid. (p. 58)

481   Ibid. (p. 145)

482   Ibid. (p. 85)

483   Eph 1:13

484   Athanasius and Didymus. (2011). *Works on the Spirit: Athanasius's Letters to Serapion on the Holy Spirit, and, Didymus's on the Holy Spirit.* (J. Behr, Ed., M. DelCogliano, A. Radde-Gallwitz, & L. Ayres, Trans.) (Vol. 43, p. 89). Yonkers, NY: St Vladimir's Seminary Press.

485   Cyril of Alexandria. (2013–2015). *Commentary on John.* (J. C. Elowsky, T. C. Oden, & G. L. Bray, Eds., D. R. Maxwell, Trans.) (Vol. 1, p. 310). Downers Grove, IL: IVP Academic: An Imprint of InterVarsity Press.

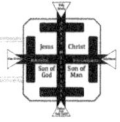

nature [2 Pet 1.4]."[486]

2) Thus, the Holy Spirit is a means by which believers partake of God

A) "It is through the Spirit that all of us are said to be partakers of God . . . we become sharers of the Divine Nature (2 Pet 1:4) by partaking of the Spirit."[487]

2. Another Paraclete

a. "Since the Son knows that he himself is also truly a Paraclete and is called that in the divine Scriptures, he calls the Spirit 'another Paraclete.'"[488]

3. Breath of the Son

a. "So it is creatures who are anointed by him and sealed in him. But if it is creatures who are anointed by him and sealed in him, then the Spirit cannot be a creature. For that which anoints is unlike that which is anointed. Indeed, this anointing is the breath of the Son, so that whoever has the Spirit can say: We are the good odor of Christ [2 Cor 2.15]. The seal makes an imprint of the Son, so that whoever has been sealed has the form of Christ, as the Apostle says: My little children, with whom I am again in travail until Christ is formed in you! [Gal 4.19]. But if the Spirit is the good odor and form of the Son, then it is perfectly clear that the Spirit

486   Athanasius and Didymus. (2011). *Works on the Spirit: Athanasius's Letters to Serapion on the Holy Spirit, and, Didymus's on the Holy Spirit*. (J. Behr, Ed., M. DelCogliano, A. Radde-Gallwitz, & L. Ayres, Trans.) (Vol. 43, p. 90). Yonkers, NY: St Vladimir's Seminary Press.

487   Ibid.

488   Cyril of Alexandria. (2013–2015). *Commentary on John*. (J. C. Elowsky, T. C. Oden, & G. L. Bray, Eds., D. R. Maxwell, Trans.) (Vol. 2, p. 178). Downers Grove, IL: IVP Academic: An Imprint of InterVarsity Press.

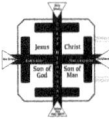

cannot be a creature."[489]

4. Breath of Life

   a. "And what is the breath of life but plainly the Spirit of Christ."[490]

   b. "'God breathed into his face the breath of life,'[491] that is, the Spirit of the Son, since he is life along with the Father, holding all things in existence. . . . The creator fixed upon it the Holy Spirit, that is, the breath of life, through which he shaped it into its archetypal beauty."[492]

   c. ". . . the breath of life. This is the Spirit furnished through the Son to rational creation."[493]

5. Drink

   a. ". . . we are said to drink of the Spirit . . ."[494]

6. Finger of God[495]

489 Athanasius and Didymus. (2011). *Works on the Spirit: Athanasius's Letters to Serapion on the Holy Spirit, and, Didymus's on the Holy Spirit*. (J. Behr, Ed., M. DelCogliano, A. Radde-Gallwitz, & L. Ayres, Trans.) (Vol. 43, p. 121). Yonkers, NY: St Vladimir's Seminary Press.

490 Cyril of Alexandria. (2013–2015). *Commentary on John*. (J. C. Elowsky, T. C. Oden, & G. L. Bray, Eds., D. R. Maxwell, Trans.) (Vol. 1, p. 311). Downers Grove, IL: IVP Academic: An Imprint of InterVarsity Press.

491 Gen 2:7

492 Cyril of Alexandria. (2013–2015). *Commentary on John*. (J. C. Elowsky, T. C. Oden, & G. L. Bray, Eds., D. R. Maxwell, Trans.) (Vol. 2, p. 187-188). Downers Grove, IL: IVP Academic: An Imprint of InterVarsity Press.

493 Cyril of Alexandria. (1983). Doctrinal Questions and Answers: #2. L. Wickham (Trans.), *Cyril of Alexandria: Select letters* (p. 189-191). Oxford: Oxford University Press.

494 Athanasius and Didymus. (2011). *Works on the Spirit: Athanasius's Letters to Serapion on the Holy Spirit, and, Didymus's on the Holy Spirit*. (J. Behr, Ed., M. DelCogliano, A. Radde-Gallwitz, & L. Ayres, Trans.) (Vol. 43, p. 82). Yonkers, NY: St Vladimir's Seminary Press.

495 This does not mean that He is a portion of the Father

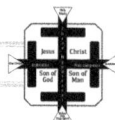

    a. "By the 'finger of God' He means the Holy Ghost."[496]

7. Fragrance of the Divine Essence

    a. "The Spirit is like a living and distinct fragrance of his [the Father's] essence."[497]

8. Image of the Son

    a. "The Son is in the Spirit as in his own Image."[498]

    b. "The Spirit is said to be and is the Image of the Son."[499]

    c. "He [the Spirit] is the Image of the Word."[500]

    d. "The Spirit is the Image of the Son."[501]

    e. "The Image of the Son, that is, the Spirit . . . He [the Holy Spirit] is in every respect the Image of the Son of God."[502]

9. Mind of Christ

    a. "That is why the Spirit is also called his mind. For example, Paul, referring to the same Spirit, says, 'But we have the

496   Cyril of Alexandria. (1859). *A Commentary upon the Gospel according to S. Luke*. (R. P. Smith, Trans.) (p. 370). Oxford: Oxford University Press.

497   Cyril of Alexandria. (2013–2015). *Commentary on John*. (J. C. Elowsky, T. C. Oden, & G. L. Bray, Eds., D. R. Maxwell, Trans.) (Vol. 2, p. 260). Downers Grove, IL: IVP Academic: An Imprint of InterVarsity Press.

498   Athanasius and Didymus. (2011). *Works on the Spirit: Athanasius's Letters to Serapion on the Holy Spirit, and, Didymus's on the Holy Spirit*. (J. Behr, Ed., M. DelCogliano, A. Radde-Gallwitz, & L. Ayres, Trans.) (Vol. 43, p. 84). Yonkers, NY: St Vladimir's Seminary Press.

499   Ibid. (p. 91)

500   Ibid. (p. 94-5)

501   Ibid. (p. 131-2)

502   Jurgens, W. A. (Trans.). (1970–1979). *The Faith of the Early Fathers* (Vol. 3, p. 212). Collegeville, MN: The Liturgical Press.

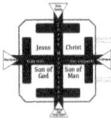

mind of Christ.'"[503]

b. "'But we have the mind of Christ,' referring to his Spirit as his 'mind.'"[504]

c. "'We have the mind of Christ.' By the 'mind' of the Savior, they mean nothing other than the Holy Spirit."[505]

10. Peace of Christ

a. "The peace of Christ is his Spirit . . . If Christ himself is peace in heaven and on earth, how could it not be clear to everyone that, as we said, his peace is surely his Spirit? . . . Therefore, the peace that is beyond principalities, beyond authorities, beyond thrones and dominions, and beyond every mind is the Spirit of Christ."[506]

b. "By the peace of Christ beyond all understanding he is referring to none other than his Spirit."[507]

11. Peace of God

a. "In his own self the Spirit is the peace of God."[508]

12. Shield

a. "By 'shield of favor,' he means nothing other than the Holy Spirit who shields us and embraces us with unexpected

---

503   Cyril of Alexandria. (2013–2015). *Commentary on John*. (J. C. Elowsky, T. C. Oden, & G. L. Bray, Eds., D. R. Maxwell, Trans.) (Vol. 2, p. 180). Downers Grove, IL: IVP Academic: An Imprint of InterVarsity Press.

504   Ibid. (p.191)

505   Ibid. (p.256)

506   Ibid. (p.199)

507   Ibid. (p.366)

508   Cyril of Alexandria. (2018). *Glaphyra on the Pentateuch, Volume 1 Genesis*. (N. P. Lunn, Trans.) (Vol. 137, p. 109). Washington, DC: The Catholic University of America Press.

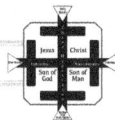

strength to do what pleases God."[509]

13. Truth

   a. "He has just called the Father 'holy' and asked that the disciples be protected by the truth, that is, by his own Spirit (since 'the Spirit is the truth,' as John says, and he is 'the Spirit of the truth,' that is, of the Only Begotten himself)."[510]

   b. "Truth, in his statement, is none other than his own Spirit."[511]

C. Is never called:

1. A "Son"

   a. "In the Scriptures the Spirit is not called son but Holy Spirit and Spirit of God. Just as the Spirit is not called son, so too it is not written that the Son is the Holy Spirit. . . . The Spirit is not called son, nor is it said that the Son is the Spirit."[512,513]

   b. "The Spirit is not the Son."[514]

   c. "The Spirit, after all, is the Spirit, not the Son."[515]

---

509 Cyril of Alexandria. (2013–2015). *Commentary on John*. (J. C. Elowsky, T. C. Oden, & G. L. Bray, Eds., D. R. Maxwell, Trans.) (Vol. 2, p. 181). Downers Grove, IL: IVP Academic: An Imprint of InterVarsity Press.

510 Ibid. (p.295)

511 Ibid. (p.309)

512 Here we prefer to read ὁ υἱός instead of υἱός (PG 26.641; AW I/1.570), following Shapland (183 n. 313).

513 Athanasius and Didymus. (2011). *Works on the Spirit: Athanasius's Letters to Serapion on the Holy Spirit, and, Didymus's on the Holy Spirit*. (J. Behr, Ed., M. DelCogliano, A. Radde-Gallwitz, & L. Ayres, Trans.) (Vol. 43, p. 131-132). Yonkers, NY: St Vladimir's Seminary Press.

514 Cyril of Alexandria. (2013–2015). *Commentary on John*. (J. C. Elowsky, T. C. Oden, & G. L. Bray, Eds., D. R. Maxwell, Trans.) (Vol. 2, p. 178). Downers Grove, IL: IVP Academic: An Imprint of InterVarsity Press.

515 Ibid. (p.260)

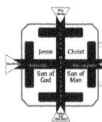

d. He is not a "brother" to the Son

1) "It is impossible to say that the Son has a brother."[516]

2) "In the Scriptures the Spirit is never called a son, lest he be considered a brother. Nor is he called a son of the Son, lest the Father be thought of as a grandfather. Instead, the Son is called the Son of the Father, and the Spirit is called the Spirit of the Father, and thus in the Holy Trinity there is one divinity and one faith."[517]

e. He is not a "Son" of the Son, nor "Grandson" of the Father

1) "It is not otherwise than that the Father is Father and not grandfather, and the Son is the Son of God and not the father of the Spirit, and the Holy Spirit is Holy Spirit and not grandson of the Father nor the brother of the Son."[518]

2. The soul of Adam or of any human[519]

a. "Let none of us catechize falsely on this point, thinking that we said that the divine breath has become the soul of the living creature. We deny this, guided to the truth of the matter by an argument like the following. If any think that the divine breath has become a soul, let them tell us whether it at that time turned aside from its own nature and became a soul, or it remained in the identity of its own nature. If they say that it has in any way changed and transgressed the law of its own nature, they will be convicted of blasphemy, since they will obviously be

---

516   Athanasius and Didymus. (2011). *Works on the Spirit: Athanasius's Letters to Serapion on the Holy Spirit, and, Didymus's on the Holy Spirit*. (J. Behr, Ed., M. DelCogliano, A. Radde-Gallwitz, & L. Ayres, Trans.) (Vol. 43, p. 77). Yonkers, NY: St Vladimir's Seminary Press.

517   Ibid. (p. 78-79)

518   Ibid. (p. 133)

519   This is the Alexandrian tradition on this topic; there are other schools of thought which reference other Patristic Fathers that _seem_ to hold the tradition that the Breath of Life is, or became Adam's soul

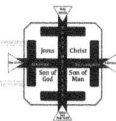

claiming that the nature that is immutable and always the same is actually mutable."[520]

b. "'God breathed into his face the breath of life,'[521] that is, the Spirit of the Son, since he is life along with the Father, holding all things in existence. . . . I do not think that any right-minded person would think that the divine breath, which proceeds from the divine nature, became the soul of the living creature."[522]

c. "Thus we can see that the in-breathed spirit did not become man's soul or his mind, as some imagine. For in the first place the in-breather is understood to be God, and what he breathed out must *also* belong to him, his substance. How in that case could the Spirit of God have changed into the of a soul or become mind? The Spirit is incapable of change. Were anyone to concede that the Spirit is the soul or mind and has become such by a process of change (which is impossible) he can still see the following point: if the divine Spirit became man's soul, soul and mind would have remained incapable of sin. But if the Spirit of God transformed into soul fell victim to sins, a two-fold charge is preferred against him by us: first that he underwent change into what he had not been and then, besides this, we are declaring him to have been made capable of sin... But seeing that God the Father was pleased to sum up all things in Christ (meaning bring them to the primal state by re-establishing in us the Holy Spirit who had taken flight and quitted us) he breathed it into the holy apostles with the words 'Receive the Holy Spirit.' Christ's act was a renewal of that primal gift and of the in-breathing bestowed on us, bringing us back to the form of initial hallowing and carrying

---

520 Cyril of Alexandria. (2013–2015). *Commentary on John*. (J. C. Elowsky, T. C. Oden, & G. L. Bray, Eds., D. R. Maxwell, Trans.) (Vol. 2, p. 187). Downers Grove, IL: IVP Academic: An Imprint of InterVarsity Press.

521 Gen 2:7

522 Ibid. (p. 187-188)

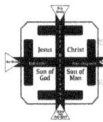

man's nature up, as a kind of first-fruits amongst the holy apostles, into the hallowing bestowed on us initially at the first creation."[523]

D. Is only "given" to believers

1. "The Holy Spirit, who is given to those who believe and are reborn [1 Pet 1:23] through the washing of regeneration [Titus 3:5]."[524]

E. Belongs to and is possessed by the Father *and* Son:

1. "So too is the Holy Spirit, who is said to be the Son's, also the Father's."[525]

2. "The Holy Spirit, who knows all things accurately, is not only the Spirit of the Father but also of the Son."[526]

3. "He is the Spirit of the Father and of the Son."[527]

4. ". . . his [the Word of God] Spirit . . ."[528]

5. ". . . the Spirit of the Son . . ."[529]

6. "After all, the Spirit of Christ is also the Spirit of the Father himself. For example, the divinely inspired Paul says in one place

---

523 Cyril of Alexandria. (1983). Doctrinal Questions and Answers: #2. L. Wickham (Trans.), *Cyril of Alexandria: Select letters* (p. 191-193). Oxford: Oxford University Press.

524 Athanasius and Didymus. (2011). *Works on the Spirit: Athanasius's Letters to Serapion on the Holy Spirit, and, Didymus's on the Holy Spirit*. (J. Behr, Ed., M. DelCogliano, A. Radde-Gallwitz, & L. Ayres, Trans.) (Vol. 43, p. 58). Yonkers, NY: St Vladimir's Seminary Press.

525 Ibid. (p. 119)

526 Cyril of Alexandria. (2013–2015). *Commentary on John*. (J. C. Elowsky, T. C. Oden, & G. L. Bray, Eds., D. R. Maxwell, Trans.) (Vol. 1, p. 27). Downers Grove, IL: IVP Academic: An Imprint of InterVarsity Press.

527 Ibid. (Vol. 2, p.178)

528 Athanasius and Didymus. (2011). *Works on the Spirit: Athanasius's Letters to Serapion on the Holy Spirit, and, Didymus's on the Holy Spirit*. (J. Behr, Ed., M. DelCogliano, A. Radde-Gallwitz, & L. Ayres, Trans.) (Vol. 43, p. 54). Yonkers, NY: St Vladimir's Seminary Press.

529 Ibid. (p. 55)

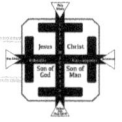

that the Spirit belongs to the Father but in another that the Spirit belongs to the Son."[530]

7. However, the Holy Spirit is sent:

    a. From the Father

        1) "The Holy Spirit, whom the Father will send."[531]

        2) "Indeed, when the Father sends the Spirit, it is the Son who breathes upon His disciples and gives the Spirit to them."[532]

        3) "He is poured out from the Father and supplied to creation through his Son."[533]

    b. Through the Son

        1) "For if I do not go away, the Helper will not come to you; but if I depart, I will send Him to you."[534]

        2) "The Paraclete will be sent from the Father to the saints. . . . God the Father has given the Paraclete, that is, the Holy Spirit, through the Son, since all things are from the Father through him."[535]

        3) "It was necessary that the Son be seen to cooperate with the Father in giving the Spirit."[536]

---

530   Cyril of Alexandria. (2013–2015). *Commentary on John*. (J. C. Elowsky, T. C. Oden, & G. L. Bray, Eds., D. R. Maxwell, Trans.) (Vol. 2, p. 193). Downers Grove, IL: IVP Academic: An Imprint of InterVarsity Press.

531   Jn 14:26

532   Athanasius and Didymus. (2011). *Works on the Spirit: Athanasius's Letters to Serapion on the Holy Spirit, and, Didymus's on the Holy Spirit*. (J. Behr, Ed., M. DelCogliano, A. Radde-Gallwitz, & L. Ayres, Trans.) (Vol. 43, p. 132). Yonkers, NY: St Vladimir's Seminary Press.

533   Cyril of Alexandria. (2013–2015). *Commentary on John*. (J. C. Elowsky, T. C. Oden, & G. L. Bray, Eds., D. R. Maxwell, Trans.) (Vol. 2, p. 296). Downers Grove, IL: IVP Academic: An Imprint of InterVarsity Press.

534   Jn 16:7

535   Cyril of Alexandria. (2013–2015). *Commentary on John*. (J. C. Elowsky, T. C. Oden, & G. L. Bray, Eds., D. R. Maxwell, Trans.) (Vol. 2, p. 181). Downers Grove, IL: IVP Academic: An Imprint of InterVarsity Press.

536   Ibid. (p. 369)

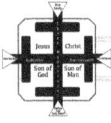

4) "The Spirit, who proceeds from the Father (Jn 15:26) and, being proper to the Son, is given by Him."[537]

5) "After completing their account of Christ the thrice-blessed fathers call to mind the Holy Ghost, declaring their belief in him just as in the case of the Father and the Son. He is consubstantial[538] with them; he pours out (or proceeds[539]) from,[540] as it were, the fount of God the Father and is bestowed[541] on creation through[542] the Son."[543]

F. Divinizes those in whom He dwells

1. "Those in whom the Spirit dwells are divinized."[544]

---

537   Athanasius and Didymus. (2011). *Works on the Spirit: Athanasius's Letters to Serapion on the Holy Spirit, and, Didymus's on the Holy Spirit*. (J. Behr, Ed., M. DelCogliano, A. Radde-Gallwitz, & L. Ayres, Trans.) (Vol. 43, p. 55). Yonkers, NY: St Vladimir's Seminary Press.

538   ὁμοούσιον

539   προχεῖται

540   ἀπό

541   χορηγεῖται

542   διά

543   Cyril of Alexandria. (1983). On the Creed. L. Wickham (Trans.), *Cyril of Alexandria: Select letters* (p. 129). Oxford: Oxford University Press.

544   Athanasius and Didymus. (2011). *Works on the Spirit: Athanasius's Letters to Serapion on the Holy Spirit, and, Didymus's on the Holy Spirit*. (J. Behr, Ed., M. DelCogliano, A. Radde-Gallwitz, & L. Ayres, Trans.) (Vol. 43, p. 90). Yonkers, NY: St Vladimir's Seminary Press.

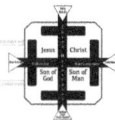

The Divine Hypostases Are All:

I. Consubstantial, coessential or connatural, being constituted of the same Divine Essence

A. "On the other hand, if we confess that He is not a work but the genuine offspring of the Father's essence, it would follow that He is inseparable from the Father, being connatural, because He is begotten from Him."[545]

B. "For what is it to be thus connatural with the Father, but to be one in essence with Him?"[546]

C. "For on this account it was that the Fathers, after declaring that the Son was begotten from the Father's essence, and Coessential with Him."[547]

D. "Why do they reject that of Nicæa, at which their Fathers signed the confession that the Son is of the Father's Essence and coessential with Him?"[548]

E. "He [the Holy Spirit] is proper to the one Word and proper to and the same as the one God in substance."[549, 550]

F. "And we believe in like manner too of the Holy Spirit, not cataloging[551] Him as foreign to the divine nature; for He is by nature of the Father, poured out upon creation through the Son;

---

545 Athanasius of Alexandria. (1892). Councils of Ariminum and Seleucia. In P. Schaff & H. Wace (Eds.), J. H. Newman & A. T. Robertson (Trans.), *St. Athanasius: Select Works and Letters* (Vol. 4, p. 475). New York: Christian Literature Company.

546 Ibid. (p. 478)

547 Ibid. (p. 471)

548 Ibid. (To the Bishops of Africa, p. 492)

549 This is the only passage in Serap. where Athanasius applies the term homoousios to the Holy Spirit.

550 Athanasius and Didymus. (2011). *Works on the Spirit: Athanasius's Letters to Serapion on the Holy Spirit, and, Didymus's on the Holy Spirit*. (J. Behr, Ed., M. DelCogliano, A. Radde-Gallwitz, & L. Ayres, Trans.) (Vol. 43, p. 96). Yonkers, NY: St Vladimir's Seminary Press.

551 καταλογιζόμενοι.

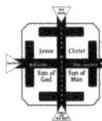

for thus the Holy and Adorable Trinity is understood to be one and consubstantial."[552, 553]

G. "The divine and consubstantial Trinity[554] ... The Spirit is consubstantial with Father and Son."[555, 556]

H. "The fullness of the divine and ineffable nature[557] exists in three hypostases."[558, 559]

I. "And we hold that the Father, in turn, is in the Son *connaturally*, as in an offspring of the same substance, and *separately* only because of the difference in what he is and is understood to be."[560]

J. "There is one divine nature in the Father and in the Son and in the Holy Spirit."[561]

II. Each united to, and thus indivisible from the other two Divine Hypostases

A. <u>Father</u> ← → <u>Son</u>

  1. "The Holy Spirit, who has the same unity with the Son as the Son has with the Father."[562]

---

552 ὁμοούσιος.

553 Jurgens, W. A. (Trans.). (1970–1979). *The Faith of the Early Fathers* (Vol. 3, p. 227). Collegeville, MN: The Liturgical Press.

554 Θεία τε καὶ ὁμοούσιος Τριάς

555 ὁμοούσιον τω πατρὶ καὶ υἱω

556 Cyril of Alexandria. (1983). <u>Answers to Tiberius: #2</u>. L. Wickham (Trans.), *Cyril of Alexandria: Select letters* (p. 143). Oxford: Oxford University Press.

557 θείας φύσεως

558 τρισὶν ὑποστάσεσιν

559 Cyril of Alexandria. (1983). <u>Doctrinal Questions and Answers: #4</u>. L. Wickham (Trans.), *Cyril of Alexandria: Select letters* (p. 197-199). Oxford: Oxford University Press.

560 Cyril of Alexandria. (2013–2015). *Commentary on John*. (J. C. Elowsky, T. C. Oden, & G. L. Bray, Eds., D. R. Maxwell, Trans.) (Vol. 1, p. 30). Downers Grove, IL: IVP Academic: An Imprint of InterVarsity Press.

561 Ibid. (p.158)

562 Athanasius and Didymus. (2011). *Works on the Spirit: Athanasius's Letters to Serapion on the Holy Spirit, and, Didymus's on the Holy Spirit.* (J. Behr, Ed., M. DelCogliano, A. Radde-Gallwitz, & L. Ayres, Trans.) (Vol. 43, p. 55). Yonkers, NY: St Vladimir's Seminary Press.

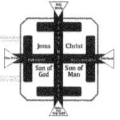

2. "The indivisible and holy Trinity . . . the Holy Trinity is indivisible
   . . . joining the Son with the Father and not dividing the Spirit
   from the Son, so as to preserve the truth of the Holy Trinity's
   indivisibility and sameness of nature."[563]

B. Father ← → Holy Spirit

1. "The Holy Spirit is united to the Son and the Father."[564]

C. Son ← → Holy Spirit

1. ". . . the Spirit who is . . . united to the Son as the Son is united
   to the Father . . ."[565]

D. Division from one another would cause:

1. The Godhead, or Divine Essence, to be multiple

   a. "By dividing the Spirit from the Word they no longer
      preserve the divinity in the Trinity as one, but rupture it,
      and mix with it a nature that is foreign to it and different
      in kind, and reduce it to the level of creatures? This in turn
      renders the Trinity no longer one but compounded of two
      distinct natures, because the Spirit, as they imagine among
      themselves, is different in substance."[566]

2. The Holy Trinity to be imperfect

   a. 'So too it is incorrect for the Spirit, who is in the Son and the
      Son in him, to be ranked with creatures or to be separated

---

563   Ibid. (p. 80)
564   Ibid. (p. 72)
565   Ibid. (p. 99-101)
566   Ibid. (p. 55)

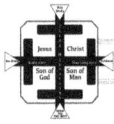

from the Word, thereby destroying the perfection of the Trinity."[567]

    b. "In this way, since the Holy Spirit is numbered with them [Father and Son] and also counted as God, the holy Trinity will have the proper fullness."[568]

3. Destruction of the unity of God

    a. "By not dividing the Son from the Father they preserve the unity of God."[569]

4. One to lose eternal life

    a. "They should not divide the Trinity lest they be divided from life."[570]

III. Each completely in the other two Divine Hypostasis (perichoresis/coinherence)

A. Father → Son

1. "If the Son is named, the Father is in the Son."[571]

2. ". . . the Son, who is in the Father and the Father in him . . ."[572]

---

567   Ibid. (p. 86)

568   Cyril of Alexandria. (2013–2015). *Commentary on John*. (J. C. Elowsky, T. C. Oden, & G. L. Bray, Eds., D. R. Maxwell, Trans.) (Vol. 1, p. 10). Downers Grove, IL: IVP Academic: An Imprint of InterVarsity Press.

569   Athanasius and Didymus. (2011). *Works on the Spirit: Athanasius's Letters to Serapion on the Holy Spirit, and, Didymus's on the Holy Spirit*. (J. Behr, Ed., M. DelCogliano, A. Radde-Gallwitz, & L. Ayres, Trans.) (Vol. 43, p. 55). Yonkers, NY: St Vladimir's Seminary Press.

570   Ibid (p. 105)

571   Ibid. (p. 75)

572   Ibid. (p. 86)

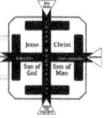

3. "I have within myself the one who begat me . . ."[573]

B. Son → Father

1. ". . . the Son is in the Father . . ."[574]

2. "Whoever believes in the Father knows the Son in the Father."[575]

3. ". . . the Son, who is in the Father and the Father in him . . ."[576]

4. "The Son has the one who begat him in himself since he is of one essence with him, and he himself is in the Father by nature."[577]

C. Father → Holy Spirit

1. "For as the Son is in the Spirit as in his own Image, so too is the Father in the Son."[578]

D. Son → Holy Spirit

1. ". . . the Spirit, who is in the Son and the Son in him . . ."[579]

2. "The Son is seen in the consubstantial Spirit."[580]

---

573   Cyril of Alexandria. (2013–2015). *Commentary on John*. (J. C. Elowsky, T. C. Oden, & G. L. Bray, Eds., D. R. Maxwell, Trans.) (Vol. 2, p. 112). Downers Grove, IL: IVP Academic: An Imprint of InterVarsity Press.

574   Athanasius and Didymus. (2011). *Works on the Spirit: Athanasius's Letters to Serapion on the Holy Spirit, and, Didymus's on the Holy Spirit*. (J. Behr, Ed., M. DelCogliano, A. Radde-Gallwitz, & L. Ayres, Trans.) (Vol. 43, p. 75). Yonkers, NY: St Vladimir's Seminary Press.

575   Ibid. (p. 126)

576   Ibid. (p. 86)

577   Cyril of Alexandria. (2013–2015). *Commentary on John*. (J. C. Elowsky, T. C. Oden, & G. L. Bray, Eds., D. R. Maxwell, Trans.) (Vol. 2, p. 193). Downers Grove, IL: IVP Academic: An Imprint of InterVarsity Press.

578   Athanasius and Didymus. (2011). *Works on the Spirit: Athanasius's Letters to Serapion on the Holy Spirit, and, Didymus's on the Holy Spirit*. (J. Behr, Ed., M. DelCogliano, A. Radde-Gallwitz, & L. Ayres, Trans.) (Vol. 43, p. 84). Yonkers, NY: St Vladimir's Seminary Press.

579   Ibid. (p. 86)

580   Cyril of Alexandria. (1983). Doctrinal Questions and Answers: #4. L. Wickham (Trans.), *Cyril of Alexandria: Select letters* (p. 197). Oxford: Oxford University Press.

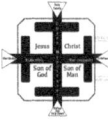

E. Holy Spirit → Father

1. "Since the Spirit was in the Word, it should be clear that through the Word the Spirit was also in God."[581]

2. "The divine nature is comprehended completely in the person of God the Father, since he has the Son and the Spirit in himself."[582]

3. "God the Father, then, has his own Spirit, that is, the Holy Spirit, from himself and in himself."[583]

F. Holy Spirit → Son

1. ". . . the Spirit who is in the Son . . . the Spirit is not external to the Word."[584]

2. "He was very much aware that the Spirit was in the Word . . . the Spirit was in the Word."[585]

3. "We are also permitted to see in the Son the Spirit in whom we are enlightened."[586]

4. "He would not foretell the future like I do unless he were surely in me and proceeded through me and were of the same substance as I am."[587]

5. "He [the Son] is referring to the Spirit, who is through him and

---

581   Athanasius and Didymus. (2011). *Works on the Spirit: Athanasius's Letters to Serapion on the Holy Spirit, and, Didymus's on the Holy Spirit*. (J. Behr, Ed., M. DelCogliano, A. Radde-Gallwitz, & L. Ayres, Trans.) (Vol. 43, p. 125). Yonkers, NY: St Vladimir's Seminary Press.

582   Cyril of Alexandria. (2013–2015). *Commentary on John*. (J. C. Elowsky, T. C. Oden, & G. L. Bray, Eds., D. R. Maxwell, Trans.) (Vol. 2, p. 112). Downers Grove, IL: IVP Academic: An Imprint of InterVarsity Press.

583   Ibid. (p. 259)

584   Athanasius and Didymus. (2011). *Works on the Spirit: Athanasius's Letters to Serapion on the Holy Spirit, and, Didymus's on the Holy Spirit*. (J. Behr, Ed., M. DelCogliano, A. Radde-Gallwitz, & L. Ayres, Trans.) (Vol. 43, p. 75). Yonkers, NY: St Vladimir's Seminary Press.

585   Ibid. (p. 125)

586   Ibid. (p. 82)

587   Cyril of Alexandria. (2013–2015). *Commentary on John*. (J. C. Elowsky, T. C. Oden, & G. L. Bray, Eds., D. R. Maxwell, Trans.) (Vol. 2, p. 256). Downers Grove, IL: IVP Academic: An Imprint of InterVarsity Press.

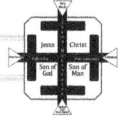

in him."[588]

G. They are *not* in each Other as if compensating for incompleteness

1. "They are not therefore, as these suppose, discharged into Each Other, filling the One the Other, as in the case of empty vessels, so that the Son fills the emptiness of the Father and the Father that of the Son,[589] and Each of Them by Himself is not complete and perfect (for this is proper to bodies, and therefore the mere assertion of it is full of irreligion), for the Father is full and perfect, and the Son is the Fulness of Godhead."[590]

IV. Equal in power (substantial Attributes)

A. "Where, indeed, can one see inferiority or superiority in the selfsame substance? . . . Accordingly, having shown us the Son, consubstantial, equal in renown, equal in operation to the Father."[591]

B. "Where does inferiority manifest itself in him, since he perfectly

---

588   Ibid. (p. 260)

589   This is not inconsistent with S. Jerome as quoted in the foregoing note. Athan. merely means that such illustrations cannot be taken literally, as if spoken of natural subjects. The Father is the τόπος or locus of the Son, because when we contemplate the Son in His fulness as ὅλος θεός, we merely view the Father as that Person in whom God the Son is; our mind abstracts His Essence which is the Son for the moment from Him, and regards Him merely as Father. Thus *in Illud. Omn.* 4, *supr.* p. 89. It is, however, but an operation of the mind, and not a real emptying of Godhead from the Father, if such words may be used. Father and Son are both the same God, though really and eternally distinct from each other; and Each is full of the Other, that is, their Essence is one and the same. This is insisted on by S. Cyril, *in Joan.* p. 28. And by S. Hilary, *Trin.* vii. fin. vid. also iii. 23. Cf. the quotation from S. Anselm made by Petavius, *de Trin.* iv. 16 fin. [Cf. D.C.B. *s.v.* METANGISMONITAE.]

590   Athanasius of Alexandria. (1892). Four Discourses against the Arians. In P. Schaff & H. Wace (Eds.), J. H. Newman & A. T. Robertson (Trans.), *St. Athanasius: Select Works and Letters* (Vol. 4, p. 394). New York: Christian Literature Company.

591   Cyril of Alexandria. (1983). On the Creed. L. Wickham (Trans.), *Cyril of Alexandria: Select letters* (p. 107). Oxford: Oxford University Press.

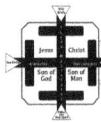

possesses all that belongs to his progenitor and has God-befitting power to the fullest extent?"[592]

C. "So he calls the Spirit 'another Paraclete,' willing him to be conceived of in his own hypostasis, but having such likeness to the Son and having such power to do exactly the same things as the Son himself might do, that he seems to be none other than the Son."[593]

D. There was never a time in which any One of the Divine Hypostases possessed substantial Attributes that the Others did not

1. "For He has not said 'all things whatsoever the Father hath, He hath given to Me,' lest He should appear at one time not to have possessed these things; but 'are Mine.' For these things, being in the Father's power, are equally in that of the Son."[594]

E. All work together on any given task; however, each has a unique role

1. All things are "from" the Father, "through" the Son & "in" the Holy Spirit[595]

   a. "The Father does all things through the Word in the Holy Spirit."[596]

   b. "'The Father himself through the Word in the Spirit works

592   Cyril of Alexandria. (2013–2015). *Commentary on John*. (J. C. Elowsky, T. C. Oden, & G. L. Bray, Eds., D. R. Maxwell, Trans.) (Vol. 1, p. 366). Downers Grove, IL: IVP Academic: An Imprint of InterVarsity Press.

593   Ibid. (Vol. 2, p. 179)

594   Athanasius of Alexandria. (1892). <u>On Luke 10:22 (Mt 11:27)</u>. In P. Schaff & H. Wace (Eds.), A. T. Robertson (Trans.), *St. Athanasius: Select Works and Letters* (Vol. 4, p. 88). New York: Christian Literature Company.

595   Varying prepositions are used by different Fathers. The point is that each Divine Hypostasis has a different preposition

596   Athanasius and Didymus. (2011). *Works on the Spirit: Athanasius's Letters to Serapion on the Holy Spirit, and, Didymus's on the Holy Spirit*. (J. Behr, Ed., M. DelCogliano, A. Radde-Gallwitz, & L. Ayres, Trans.) (Vol. 43, p. 97). Yonkers, NY: St Vladimir's Seminary Press.

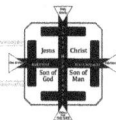

and gives all things."[597]

c. "Whatsoever is said to be done by God the Father, this necessarily is by the Son in the Spirit."[598]

d. "All things are from the Father, through the Son, in the Holy Spirit."[599]

e. "Where one finds members with identical definitions of an identical nature, their activity is not separate, even though it may perhaps be understood to be carried out in various different ways. Since there is one essence of the true and natural divinity understood in three hypostases (I mean in the Father and the Son and the Holy Spirit), how is it not indisputably clear that when we speak of an activity of one of them, this is a work of the one whole divine nature, according to the principle of natural power?"[600]

2. Examples:

a. Creating

1) "The Father creates all things through the Word in the Spirit."[601]

b. Giving Grace/gifts

1) "The gifts which the Spirit distributes to each are bestowed by the Father through the Word. For all that

597   Ibid. (p. 125)

598   Cyril of Alexandria. (1859). *A Commentary upon the Gospel according to S. Luke*. (R. P. Smith, Trans.) (p. 371). Oxford: Oxford University Press.

599   Cyril of Alexandria. (2013–2015). *Commentary on John*. (J. C. Elowsky, T. C. Oden, & G. L. Bray, Eds., D. R. Maxwell, Trans.) (Vol. 1, p. 58). Downers Grove, IL: IVP Academic: An Imprint of InterVarsity Press.

600   Ibid. (Vol. 2, p. 212)

601   Athanasius and Didymus. (2011). *Works on the Spirit: Athanasius's Letters to Serapion on the Holy Spirit, and, Didymus's on the Holy Spirit*. (J. Behr, Ed., M. DelCogliano, A. Radde-Gallwitz, & L. Ayres, Trans.) (Vol. 43, p. 123-124). Yonkers, NY: St Vladimir's Seminary Press.

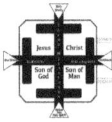

the Father has is the Son's. Thus what is given by the Son in the Spirit is a gift of the Father. And when the Spirit is in us, the Word who gives the Spirit is in us, and the Father is in the Word. . . . For this grace and gift given in the Trinity is given by the Father through the Son in the Holy Spirit. . . . The Apostle does not mean that the gifts given by each are different and distinct, but that whatever gift is given is given in the Trinity, and that all the gifts are from the one God."[602]

3. Each Hypostasis is capable of Itself to complete *any* work

   a. "Know too that the Father is sufficient for every strength and need, and so is the Son and the Holy Spirit as well."[603]

   b. "And we hold that the Father works with the Son, but not in the sense that the Father imports some other power of his own to the Son, who is perhaps weak, for the accomplishment of the works. If we think that, we might as well concede that both the power of the Father and that of the Son are surely imperfect, at least if it took both of them to accomplish any of the miracles, as though one were not sufficient for the need."[604]

4. To divide up work to Individual Hypostases would make separate gods

   a. "The Holy Trinity has therefore the same Operation, and whatsoever things the Father does and wills to accomplish, these things doth the Son too in equal manner, likewise the Spirit also. But the giving of the Operations severally

---

602   Ibid. (p. 99-101)

603   Cyril of Alexandria. (2013–2015). *Commentary on John.* (J. C. Elowsky, T. C. Oden, & G. L. Bray, Eds., D. R. Maxwell, Trans.) (Vol. 1, p. 223). Downers Grove, IL: IVP Academic: An Imprint of InterVarsity Press.

604   Ibid. (p. 323)

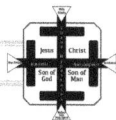

to Each of the Persons individually is nothing else than to set forth three gods severally and wholly distinct from one another."[605]

V. Able to be partaken of

A. "The Spirit is and is said to be the Spirit of sanctification and renewal . . . creatures are sanctified and renewed. . . . So, he [the Holy Spirit] who is not sanctified by another, nor participates in sanctification, but is himself the one who is participated in, the one in whom all creatures are sanctified."[606]

B. "The Holy Spirit is participated in but does not participate . . . angels and the other creatures participate in the Holy Spirit Himself."[607]

C. "For by partaking of Him, we partake of the Father."[608]

D. "A being that participates in life is not, strictly speaking, life, since life is clearly in that being as something other than it . . . originate beings participate in the Son as life."[609]

605   Cyril of Alexandria. (1881). *Five Tomes against Nestorius; Scholia on the Incarnation; Christ Is One; Fragments against Diodore of Tarsus, Theodore of Mopsuestia, the Synousiasts* (p. 134). London; Oxford; Cambridge: James Parker and Co.; Rivingtons.

606   Athanasius and Didymus. (2011). *Works on the Spirit: Athanasius's Letters to Serapion on the Holy Spirit, and, Didymus's on the Holy Spirit.* (J. Behr, Ed., M. DelCogliano, A. Radde-Gallwitz, & L. Ayres, Trans.) (Vol. 43, p. 88). Yonkers, NY: St Vladimir's Seminary Press.

607   Ibid. (p. 85)

608   Athanasius of Alexandria. (1892). Councils of Ariminum and Seleucia. In P. Schaff & H. Wace (Eds.), J. H. Newman & A. T. Robertson (Trans.), *St. Athanasius: Select Works and Letters* (Vol. 4, p. 477). New York: Christian Literature Company.

609   Cyril of Alexandria. (2013–2015). *Commentary on John.* (J. C. Elowsky, T. C. Oden, & G. L. Bray, Eds., D. R. Maxwell, Trans.) (Vol. 1, p. 34). Downers Grove, IL: IVP Academic: An Imprint of InterVarsity Press.

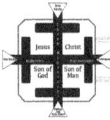

VI. Perfect

A. "The Three Subsistences[610] are perfect."[611]

B. "The faith of Christians acknowledges the blessed Triad as unalterable and perfect and ever what It was, neither adding to It what is more, nor imputing to It any loss (for both ideas are irreligious), and therefore it dissociates It from all things generated."[612]

C. "But the Father is all perfect, and is deficient of no good whatsoever that is suitable to Deity: therefore is the Son all perfect, as having all that the Father hath"[613]

D. "The Father is perfect because he has everything in himself perfectly. Therefore, it is clear that the Son . . . is also perfect."[614]

VII.   Able to 'dwell' within us

A. "We [The Father and Son] will come to him and make Our home with him."[615]

B. "When the Spirit is in us, the Word who gives the Spirit is in us, and the Father is in the Word . . . Indeed, when the Lord said: I

---

610   τρεῖς ὑποστάσεις. This expression is a link between this tract and the *Expositio* (§ 2), and is one of the indications it bears of an early date. At this time we see that Athanasius speaks of Three 'Hypostases,' but qualifies his language by the caveat (*Expos.* 2) that they are not μεμερισμέναι. In this he follows his Origenist predecessor Dionysius, and the language of the present passage is that of Basil or the Gregories. But it is not the language of Athan. himself in his later years. See above, Prolegg. ch. ii. § 3 (2) b, and Introd. to *Tom. ad Ant.* and to *Ad Afr.*

611   Athanasius of Alexandria. (1892). On Luke 10:22 (Mt 11:27). In P. Schaff & H. Wace (Eds.), A. T. Robertson (Trans.), *St. Athanasius: Select Works and Letters* (Vol. 4, p. 90). New York: Christian Literature Company.

612   Ibid. (Four Discourses against the Arians, p. 317)

613   Cyril of Alexandria. (1859). *A Commentary upon the Gospel according to S. Luke*. (R. P. Smith, Trans.) (p. 95). Oxford: Oxford University Press.

614   Cyril of Alexandria. (2013–2015). *Commentary on John*. (J. C. Elowsky, T. C. Oden, & G. L. Bray, Eds., D. R. Maxwell, Trans.) (Vol. 1, p. 13). Downers Grove, IL: IVP Academic: An Imprint of InterVarsity Press.

615   Jn 14:23

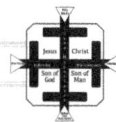

and the Father will come [Jn 14.23], the Spirit comes with them and dwells in us in a manner no different than the Son does. . . . And when the Son is in us, the Father is still there."[616]

C. This dwelling makes one a temple of God

1. "Anyone who has the Holy Spirit has the Son. When anyone has him, he is the temple of God."[617]

VIII. Able to be prayed to Individually or Collectively as the Holy Trinity

A. "Indeed, when Paul prayed for the Corinthians, he prayed in the Trinity."[618]

IX. Not:

A. <u>Created or originate, in a temporal sense, but have always existed eternally</u>

1. "The eternal Spirit . . ."[619]

2. "If the Spirit were a creature, he would not have ranked him together with the Father, lest the Trinity be inconsistent with itself[620] by being ranked together with something that is foreign and alien to it."[621]

616 Athanasius and Didymus. (2011). *Works on the Spirit: Athanasius's Letters to Serapion on the Holy Spirit, and, Didymus's on the Holy Spirit*. (J. Behr, Ed., M. DelCogliano, A. Radde-Gallwitz, & L. Ayres, Trans.) (Vol. 43, p. 99-101). Yonkers, NY: St Vladimir's Seminary Press.

617 Ibid. (p. 121)

618 Ibid. (p. 125)

619 Heb 9:14

620 Gk. ἀνόμοιος ἑαυτῇ, lit. "unlike itself."

621 Athanasius and Didymus. (2011). *Works on the Spirit: Athanasius's Letters to Serapion on the Holy*

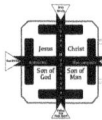

3. "So then, if the Trinity is eternal, the Spirit is not a creature since he exists eternally with the Word and is in him."[622]

4. "It is also insanity to call the Spirit a creature for the following reason: if he were a creature, he would not be ranked with the Trinity."[623]

5. "The Holy Trinity, which is identical with itself and united in itself, has nothing in it that belongs to things which have come into existence."[624]

6. "There is no creature in the Trinity because it is always a Trinity."[625]

7. "And so, the Father is eternal; the Son is eternal also."[626]

8. "The Son of God is neither creature or work, nor in the number of things originated,[627] but that the Word is an offspring from the substance of the Father."[628]

9. "Being an offspring of the essence of the Father, He is of consequence with Him eternally."[629]

10. "The Father then being eternal, the Son is eternal."[630]

11. "The Triad is not originated."[631]

12. "Further, Asterius, the unprincipled sophist, the patron too

Spirit, and, Didymus's on the Holy Spirit. (J. Behr, Ed., M. DelCogliano, A. Radde-Gallwitz, & L. Ayres, Trans.) (Vol. 43, p. 125). Yonkers, NY: St Vladimir's Seminary Press.

622   Ibid. (p. 126)
623   Ibid. (p. 79)
624   Ibid. (p. 98-99)
625   Ibid. (p. 127)
626   Ibid. (p. 107)
627   γενητῶν.
628   Athanasius of Alexandria. (1892). <u>De Decretis or Defence of the Nicene Definition</u>. In P. Schaff & H. Wace (Eds.), J. H. Newman & A. T. Robertson (Trans.), *St. Athanasius: Select Works and Letters* (Vol. 4, p. 152). New York: Christian Literature Company.
629   Ibid. (p. 170)
630   Ibid. (<u>On the Opinion of Dionysius</u>, p. 182)
631   Ibid. (<u>Four Discourses against the Arians</u>, p. 316)

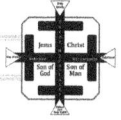

of this heresy, has added in his own treatise, that what is not made, but is ever, is 'unoriginate'. . . .[632] But if they ask according as Asterius ruled it, as if 'what is not a work but was always' were unoriginate, then they must constantly be told that the Son as well as the Father must in this sense be called unoriginate."[633]

13. "He is co-unoriginate and coeternal with His own Father."[634]

14. The Son and Holy Spirit are originate, not temporally, but as originating from the Father

    a. "Moreover, by 'unoriginate' is meant, what exists, but has not come into being from any, nor having a father at all."[635]

    b. "When then, after failing at every turn, they betake themselves to the other sense of the question, 'existing but not generated of any nor having a father,' we shall tell them that the unoriginate in this sense is only one, namely the Father."[636]

    c. "Some, for instance, call what is, but is neither generated, nor has any personal cause at all, unoriginate; and others, the uncreate. As then a person, having in view the former of these senses, viz. 'that which has no personal cause,' might say that the Son was not unoriginate, yet would not blame

632   The two first senses here given answer to the two first mentioned, de Decr. § 28. and, as he there says, are plainly irrelevant. The third in the de Decr. which, as he there observes, is ambiguous and used for a sophistical purpose, is here divided into third and fourth, answering to the two senses which alone are assigned in the de Syn. § 46 [where see note 5], and on them the question turns. This is an instance, of which many occur, how Athan. used his former writings and worked over again his former ground, and simplified or cleared what he had said. In the de Decr. after 350, we have three senses of ἀγένητον, two irrelevant and the third ambiguous; here in Orat. i. (358), he divides the third into two; in the de Syn. (359), he rejects and omits the two first, leaving the two last, which are the critical senses.

633   Athanasius of Alexandria. (1892). Four Discourses against the Arians. In P. Schaff & H. Wace (Eds.), J. H. Newman & A. T. Robertson (Trans.), St. Athanasius: Select Works and Letters (Vol. 4, p. 324). New York: Christian Literature Company.

634   Jurgens, W. A. (Trans.). (1970–1979). The Faith of the Early Fathers (Vol. 3, p. 227). Collegeville, MN: The Liturgical Press.

635   Athanasius of Alexandria. (1892). Four Discourses against the Arians. In P. Schaff & H. Wace (Eds.), J. H. Newman & A. T. Robertson (Trans.), St. Athanasius: Select Works and Letters (Vol. 4, p. 324). New York: Christian Literature Company.

636   Ibid. (p. 325)

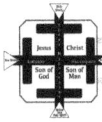

any one whom he perceived to have in view the other meaning, 'not a work or creature but an eternal offspring,' and to affirm accordingly that the Son was unoriginate, (for both speak suitably with a view to their own object)."[637]

d. "God is said to be the beginning of Christ since the Son is from him with regard to his nature. So he who is without beginning has the one who has begotten him as his beginning, while at the same time he coexists eternally with him."[638]

15. Christ *can* be considered originate through the Incarnation

a. "Christ is originate in that he became human, even though he is unoriginate by nature in that he came from God."[639]

B. Divided portions of each Other

1. "Nor does he have a nature that is divisible into parts. Hence he does not beget the Son by being divided into parts."[640]

2. "Nor is the Son a part of the Father."[641]

3. "The whole nature is understood in each [Divine Hypostasis]."[642]

4. "But he is of the substance of God the Father—not by cutting

637   Ibid. (Councils of Ariminum and Seleucia, p. 475)

638   Cyril of Alexandria. (2018). *Glaphyra on the Pentateuch, Volume 1 Genesis*. (N. P. Lunn, Trans.) (Vol. 137, p. 157). Washington, DC: The Catholic University of America Press.

639   Cyril of Alexandria. (2013–2015). *Commentary on John*. (J. C. Elowsky, T. C. Oden, & G. L. Bray, Eds., D. R. Maxwell, Trans.) (Vol. 2, p. 272). Downers Grove, IL: IVP Academic: An Imprint of InterVarsity Press.

640   Athanasius and Didymus. (2011). *Works on the Spirit: Athanasius's Letters to Serapion on the Holy Spirit, and, Didymus's on the Holy Spirit*. (J. Behr, Ed., M. DelCogliano, A. Radde-Gallwitz, & L. Ayres, Trans.) (Vol. 43, p. 78-79). Yonkers, NY: St Vladimir's Seminary Press.

641   Ibid. (p. 136)

642   Jurgens, W. A. (Trans.). (1970–1979). *The Faith of the Early Fathers* (Vol. 3, p. 215). Collegeville, MN: The Liturgical Press.

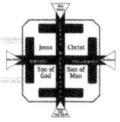

off or emanation or division or separation, for the divine nature is altogether impassible, but as one from one, always with him, coeternal, rooted in the one who begat him, both in him and proceeding from him indivisibly and without distance."[643]

C. Able to go:

1. Below three

   a. "And the Catholic Church does not entertain the thought of anything less than these [three] lest she fall to the level of Sabellius and today's Jews, who take after Caiaphas."[644]

2. Above three

   a. "Nor does she [the Catholic Church] conceive of anything more than these [three] lest she slip into Greek polytheism."[645]

---

643 Cyril of Alexandria. (2013–2015). *Commentary on John*. (J. C. Elowsky, T. C. Oden, & G. L. Bray, Eds., D. R. Maxwell, Trans.) (Vol. 1, p. 85). Downers Grove, IL: IVP Academic: An Imprint of InterVarsity Press.

644 Athanasius and Didymus. (2011). *Works on the Spirit: Athanasius's Letters to Serapion on the Holy Spirit, and, Didymus's on the Holy Spirit*. (J. Behr, Ed., M. DelCogliano, A. Radde-Gallwitz, & L. Ayres, Trans.) (Vol. 43, p. 97). Yonkers, NY: St Vladimir's Seminary Press.

645 Ibid.

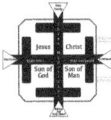

The Definition of Essence[646]

I. "You and I were formed out of the clay; thus; we have been formed out of the same substance."[647]

II. "Isaac does not make Jacob but begets him by nature, and Jacob is the same as him in substance . . . it is appropriate for someone to say that every son is the same as his father in substance."[648]

III. "For it is right, that they who have one nature, should have their name in common, though they differ from each other in point of time. For Adam was a man, and Paul a man, and he who is now born is a man, and time is not that which alters the nature of the race."[649, 650]

IV. "If anyone wants to compare a human with another human and examines the one common definition of their essence, that person would find no difference between them. A human will never differ from another human when it comes to being a rational animal, mortal, and capable of thought and reason. This is the one definition of essence that is in everyone. . . . It is clear that the definition of every essence is not perfect in some but

---

646   οὐσία

647   Job 33:6 LXX

648   Athanasius and Didymus. (2011). *Works on the Spirit: Athanasius's Letters to Serapion on the Holy Spirit, and, Didymus's on the Holy Spirit*. (J. Behr, Ed., M. DelCogliano, A. Radde-Gallwitz, & L. Ayres, Trans.) (Vol. 43, p. 113). Yonkers, NY: St Vladimir's Seminary Press.

649   *De Decr.* 10; *Or.* i. 26, n. 1.

650   Athanasius of Alexandria. (1892). Four Discourses against the Arians. In P. Schaff & H. Wace (Eds.), J. H. Newman & A. T. Robertson (Trans.), *St. Athanasius: Select Works and Letters* (Vol. 4, p. 404). New York: Christian Literature Company.

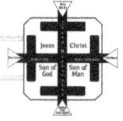

imperfect in others, but it is one and the same for all."[651]

Synonyms for the Divine Essence:

I. Divinity

A. "Instead, the Son is called the Son of the Father, and the Spirit is called the Spirit of the Father, and thus in the Holy Trinity there is one divinity and one faith."[652]

B. "In terms of nature and substance the Spirit has nothing in common with or proper to creatures. Rather, he is different from things that have come into existence, and he is proper to and not foreign to the substance and divinity of the Son."[653]

C. "Furthermore, how will the divinity which is holy by nature give birth to an offspring from itself that is devoid of holiness and produce fruit that is its own but which is stripped of the properties that belong to it?"[654]

D. "Divinity" can also refer to a substantial Attribute.

II. Godhead[655]

A. "In like manner when we hear the phrase 'one in essence,' let us not fall upon human senses, and imagine partitions and divisions

651   Cyril of Alexandria. (2013–2015). *Commentary on John*. (J. C. Elowsky, T. C. Oden, & G. L. Bray, Eds., D. R. Maxwell, Trans.) (Vol. 2, p. 205-206). Downers Grove, IL: IVP Academic: An Imprint of InterVarsity Press.

652   Athanasius and Didymus. (2011). *Works on the Spirit: Athanasius's Letters to Serapion on the Holy Spirit, and, Didymus's on the Holy Spirit*. (J. Behr, Ed., M. DelCogliano, A. Radde-Gallwitz, & L. Ayres, Trans.) (Vol. 43, p. 78-79). Yonkers, NY: St Vladimir's Seminary Press.

653   Ibid. (p. 96)

654   Cyril of Alexandria. (2013–2015). *Commentary on John*. (J. C. Elowsky, T. C. Oden, & G. L. Bray, Eds., D. R. Maxwell, Trans.) (Vol. 1, p. 79). Downers Grove, IL: IVP Academic: An Imprint of InterVarsity Press.

655   θεότητος

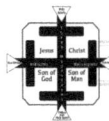

of the Godhead, but as having our thoughts directed to things immaterial, let us preserve undivided the oneness of nature."[656]

B. "Certain eloquent and distinguished bishops and writers even of ancient date used the word 'coessential' with reference to the Godhead of the Father and the Son."[657]

C. "The same [Jesus Christ] consubstantial with the Father in Godhead and consubstantial with us in manhood."[658, 659]

III. The Divine Nature[660]

A. "The body, then, as sharing the same nature with all, for it was a human body."[661]

B. "Let us consider the matter further with the following reasoning. The definition of an essence is not determined by knowing or not knowing but by what each item is by nature. Take, for example, Paul and Silvanus. Let Paul know and be instructed perfectly in the mystery of Christ, but let Silvanus be somewhat less so than Paul. Are they dissimilar, then, in nature? Will Paul surpass Silvanus as far as the principle of their nature is concerned since he knew the depth of the mystery to a greater degree than Silvanus did? No, I do not think anyone would be so foolish that they would ever imagine their natures to be different because of greater or lesser knowledge . . . therefore, matters of substance are carefully

---

656   Athanasius of Alexandria. (1892). De Decretis or Defence of the Nicene Definition. In P. Schaff & H. Wace (Eds.), J. H. Newman & A. T. Robertson (Trans.), *St. Athanasius: Select Works and Letters* (Vol. 4, p. 166). New York: Christian Literature Company.

657   Ibid. (To the Bishops of Africa, p. 492)

658   ὁμοούσιον τω πατρὶ τὸν αὐτὸν κατὰ τὴν Θεότητα καὶ ὁμοούσιον ἡμιν κατὰ τὴν ἀνθρωπότητα

659   Cyril of Alexandria. (1983). To Acacius of Melitene. L. Wickham (Trans.), *Cyril of Alexandria: Select letters* (p. 47). Oxford: Oxford University Press.

660   φύσις

661   Athanasius of Alexandria. (1892). On the Incarnation of the Word. In P. Schaff & H. Wace (Eds.), A. T. Robertson (Trans.), *St. Athanasius: Select Works and Letters* (Vol. 4, p. 47). New York: Christian Literature Company.

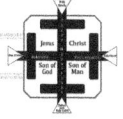

evaluated not on the basis of learning or teaching anything."[662]

C. "Nor is He like only outwardly, lest He seem in some respect or wholly to be other in essence, as brass shines like gold and silver like tin. For these are foreign and of other nature, are separated off from each other in nature and virtues, nor is brass proper to gold, nor is the pigeon born from the dove;[663] but though they are considered like, yet they differ in essence."[664]

D. "For from one were all made, and one is the nature of all men."[665]

E. "For what is it to be thus connatural with the Father, but to be one in essence with Him?"[666]

F. "This, my friend, is the definition of human nature which is also called a substance, that it is a rational animal, mortal, recipient of mind and learning."[667]

G. "When we consider the Father and the Son and the Holy Spirit, though we do truly assign them their own distinct subsistences, it is our habit to adorn them with a unity of nature. It is as though by means of this identity of essence we were raising up together[668] the length, the width, and the height by that one cubit, so completing the ark."[669]

H. "Peter is Peter and not Paul, and Paul is not Peter, but they remain without distinction according to their nature. The definition of

662   Cyril of Alexandria. (2013–2015). *Commentary on John*. (J. C. Elowsky, T. C. Oden, & G. L. Bray, Eds., D. R. Maxwell, Trans.) (Vol. 1, p. 348). Downers Grove, IL: IVP Academic: An Imprint of InterVarsity Press.

663   vid. *de Syn.* § 41.

664   Athanasius of Alexandria. (1892). De Decretis or Defence of the Nicene Definition. In P. Schaff & H. Wace (Eds.), J. H. Newman & A. T. Robertson (Trans.), *St. Athanasius: Select Works and Letters* (Vol. 4, pp. 165–166). New York: Christian Literature Company.

665   Ibid. (Four Discourses against the Arians, p. 405)

666   Ibid. (Councils of Ariminum and Seleucia, p. 478)

667   Cyril of Alexandria. (1881). *Five Tomes against Nestorius; Scholia on the Incarnation; Christ Is One; Fragments against Diodore of Tarsus, Theodore of Mopsuestia, the Synousiasts* (p. 335). London; Oxford; Cambridge: James Parker and Co.; Rivingtons.

668   Var. "we were closely connecting."

669   Cyril of Alexandria. (2018). *Glaphyra on the Pentateuch, Volume 1 Genesis*. (N. P. Lunn, Trans.) (Vol. 137, p. 95). Washington, DC: The Catholic University of America Press.

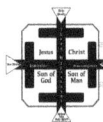

their substance is the same for both, and those who are joined in a natural unity have the exact same definition."[670]

I. Nature *can* also be used to refer to a set of properties belonging to a substance

J. Any "God is" verse is not defining what the Divine Essence is

   1. "'Our God is a consuming fire.' We should surely not claim that so wise a man was explaining the nature of God when he compared it with fire."[671]

IV. The Divine Substance

A. ". . . what is called in Latin 'Substantia,' but in Greek 'Usia' . . ."[672]

B. "Why hasn't it dawned on them that, just as by not dividing the Son from the Father they preserve the unity of God, so too, by dividing the Spirit from the Word they no longer preserve the divinity in the Trinity as one, but rupture it, and mix with it a nature that is foreign to it and different in kind, and reduce it to the level of creatures? This in turn renders the Trinity no longer one but compounded of two distinct natures, because the Spirit, as they imagine among themselves, is different in substance."[673]

C. "Who could be so audacious as to say that the Trinity is unlike itself and different in nature?[674] Or that the Son is foreign to the

---

670   Cyril of Alexandria. (2013–2015). *Commentary on John*. (J. C. Elowsky, T. C. Oden, & G. L. Bray, Eds., D. R. Maxwell, Trans.) (Vol. 2, p. 171). Downers Grove, IL: IVP Academic: An Imprint of InterVarsity Press.

671   Ibid. (p.159)

672   Athanasius of Alexandria. (1892). <u>Councils of Ariminum and Seleucia</u>. In P. Schaff & H. Wace (Eds.), J. H. Newman & A. T. Robertson (Trans.), *St. Athanasius: Select Works and Letters* (Vol. 4, p. 466). New York: Christian Literature Company.

673   Athanasius and Didymus. (2011). *Works on the Spirit: Athanasius's Letters to Serapion on the Holy Spirit, and, Didymus's on the Holy Spirit*. (J. Behr, Ed., M. DelCogliano, A. Radde-Gallwitz, & L. Ayres, Trans.) (Vol. 43, p. 55). Yonkers, NY: St Vladimir's Seminary Press.

674   ἀνόμοιον καὶ ἑτεροφυῆ.

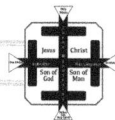

Father in substance?"[675, 676]

D. "But those who have come into existence and are creatures have a nature that is mutable, because it is external to the substance of God and comes into subsistence from nothing."[677]

E. "With those whom we are like and with whom we have identity we are the same in substance. For example, since we human beings are alike and have identity, we are the same as each other in substance."[678]

F. "Isaac does not make Jacob but begets him by nature, and Jacob is the same as him in substance . . . it is appropriate for someone to say that every son is the same as his own father in substance. So if there is Father and Son, then the Son must be Son by nature and in truth. But this is what it means to be the same as the Father in substance..."[679]

G. 'Seeing the substance of water changed and transformed into wine."[680]

675 ἀλλοτριοούσιον.

676 Athanasius and Didymus. (2011). *Works on the Spirit: Athanasius's Letters to Serapion on the Holy Spirit, and, Didymus's on the Holy Spirit*. (J. Behr, Ed., M. DelCogliano, A. Radde-Gallwitz, & L. Ayres, Trans.) (Vol. 43, p. 84). Yonkers, NY: St Vladimir's Seminary Press.

677 Ibid. (p. 92-93)

678 Ibid. (p. 108-109)

679 Ibid. (p. 113)

680 Athanasius of Alexandria. (1892). <u>On the Incarnation of the Word</u>. In P. Schaff & H. Wace (Eds.), A. T. Robertson (Trans.), *St. Athanasius: Select Works and Letters* (Vol. 4, p. 46). New York: Christian Literature Company.

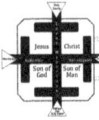

The Divine Essence is:

I.   Able to be partaken of by created beings

A. "But if we were joined to a creature, we would become strangers to the divine nature, inasmuch as we did not partake of it in any way. But if we become sharers of the divine nature [2 Pet 1.4] by partaking of the Spirit, someone would have to be insane to say that the Spirit has a created nature and not the nature of God."[681]

B. ". . . that we may become henceforth a holy race, and 'partakers of the Divine Nature,' as blessed Peter wrote."[682, 683]

C. "They were enriched with That Spirit Which makes free, even the Holy Ghost: they were made partakers of the divine nature."[684]

D. ". . . we become partakers of the divine nature . . ."[685]

E. ". . . it also makes us partakers in the divine nature . . ."[686]

II. Perceived by created beings, through faith and a godly use of reason, or logic

A. ". . . because what may be known of God is manifest in them, for God has shown it to them. For since the creation of the world

---

681   Athanasius and Didymus. (2011). *Works on the Spirit: Athanasius's Letters to Serapion on the Holy Spirit, and, Didymus's on the Holy Spirit*. (J. Behr, Ed., M. DelCogliano, A. Radde-Gallwitz, & L. Ayres, Trans.) (Vol. 43, p. 90). Yonkers, NY: St Vladimir's Seminary Press.

682   2 Pet 1:4

683   Athanasius of Alexandria. (1892). Personal Letters. In P. Schaff & H. Wace (Eds.), A. T. Robertson (Trans.), *St. Athanasius: Select Works and Letters* (Vol. 4, p. 576). New York: Christian Literature Company.

684   Cyril of Alexandria. (1859). *A Commentary upon the Gospel according to S. Luke*. (R. P. Smith, Trans.) (p. 27). Oxford: Oxford University Press.

685   Cyril of Alexandria. (2013–2015). *Commentary on John*. (J. C. Elowsky, T. C. Oden, & G. L. Bray, Eds., D. R. Maxwell, Trans.) (Vol. 1, p. 97). Downers Grove, IL: IVP Academic: An Imprint of InterVarsity Press.

686   Ibid. (p. 286)

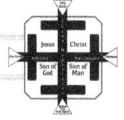

His invisible Attributes are clearly seen, being understood by the things that are made, even His eternal power and Godhead, so that they are without excuse . . ."[687]

B. "For the Divinity is not handed down through logical demonstration and arguments, as has been said, but by faith and by pious reasoning joined with reverence."[688]

C. It is able to be seen with the mind, but not with the physical eye

1. "Through whom and in whom they saw, intellectually, the nature of God and the Father."[689]

2. "We behold the varied beauty of the divine nature according to the subtlety of the mind and the precise movement in it."[690]

3. "I do not think anyone should suppose that the divine nature was manifested as it is in itself. Rather, it molded itself into an outward appearance that was suitable for the particular occasion. For example, the prophets saw him in different ways, and their description of God varies. Isaiah saw him one way, and Ezekiel saw him in a different way, not resembling the wonder in Isaiah. Philip, then, should have understood that it was completely impossible to be able to see the unincarnate divine essence by means of the flesh."[691]

4. "No one who has a brain would say that the nature of God is subject to fleshly seeing, nor could anyone see with the eyes of the flesh what can barely be grasped as in a mirror, since we see in an enigma."[692]

---

687   Rom 1:19-20

688   Athanasius and Didymus. (2011). *Works on the Spirit: Athanasius's Letters to Serapion on the Holy Spirit, and, Didymus's on the Holy Spirit*. (J. Behr, Ed., M. DelCogliano, A. Radde-Gallwitz, & L. Ayres, Trans.) (Vol. 43, p. 84). Yonkers, NY: St Vladimir's Seminary Press.

689   Simonetti, M. (Ed.). (2001). *Matthew 1–13* (p. 272). Downers Grove, IL: InterVarsity Press.

690   Cyril of Alexandria. (2013–2015). *Commentary on John*. (J. C. Elowsky, T. C. Oden, & G. L. Bray, Eds., D. R. Maxwell, Trans.) (Vol. 1, p. 51). Downers Grove, IL: IVP Academic: An Imprint of InterVarsity Press.

691   Ibid. (Vol. 2, p.154)

692   Ibid. (Vol. 2, p.156)

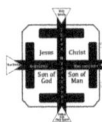

III. Not the same Thing as the Divine Hypostases

A. "Glory to the Father, with him and the Holy Spirit, the giver of life and of one substance, for ever and ever. Amen."[693]

B. "The nature that is simple and not composite is supreme,[694] broadened by different peculiarities of hypostases, of Persons and of names; and going into the Holy Trinity,[695] it still concurs in One by unity of nature and by an identity in every respect unalterable."[696]

C. "The ineffable Godhead's one nature exists in three distinct hypostases."[697, 698]

D. ". . . there is one divinity of the Trinity . . ."[699]

E. ". . . the true Godhead of the Subsistence . . ."[700]

F. "For whole the Holy Trinity opens out, as it were, into three distinct subsistences, or separate Persons, it is as though it contracts into the one nature of Deity."[701]

---

693 Athanasius of Alexandria. (1995) Fragments on the Moral Life. *Athanasius and Asceticism* (p. 319). Baltimore: The John Hopkins University Press.

694 παντός ἐστιν ἐπέκεινα. Literally, *is on the yonder side of everything*.

695 καὶ εἰς ἁγίαν ἰοῦσα τριάδα. This is not a happy expression. It too easily lends itself to a visualizing of the Godhead as Three Persons coming together into a unity rather than a simple Three and One.

696 Jurgens, W. A. (Trans.). (1970–1979). *The Faith of the Early Fathers* (Vol. 3, p. 215). Collegeville, MN: The Liturgical Press.

697 μία γὰρ φύσις ἐστὶ τῆς ἀρρήτου θεότητος ἐν ὑποστάσεσι τρισί

698 Cyril of Alexandria. (1983). Answer to Tiberius: #2. L. Wickham (Trans.), *Cyril of Alexandria: Select letters* (p. 145). Oxford: Oxford University Press.

699 Athanasius and Didymus. (2011). *Works on the Spirit: Athanasius's Letters to Serapion on the Holy Spirit, and, Didymus's on the Holy Spirit.* (J. Behr, Ed., M. DelCogliano, A. Radde-Gallwitz, & L. Ayres, Trans.) (Vol. 43, p. 126). Yonkers, NY: St Vladimir's Seminary Press.

700 Athanasius of Alexandria. (1892). Four Discourses against the Arians. In P. Schaff & H. Wace (Eds.), J. H. Newman & A. T. Robertson (Trans.), *St. Athanasius: Select Works and Letters* (Vol. 4, p. 366). New York: Christian Literature Company.

701 Cyril of Alexandria. (2018). *Glaphyra on the Pentateuch, Volume 1 Genesis*. (N. P. Lunn, Trans.) (Vol. 137, p. 94). Washington, DC: The Catholic University of America Press.

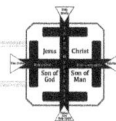

G. "When we consider the Father and the Son and the Holy Spirit, though we do truly assign them their own distinct subsistences, it is our habit to adorn them with a unity of nature. It is as though by means of this identity of essence we were raising up together[702] the length, the width, and the height by that one cubit, so completing the ark."[703]

H. "If the distinction between individuals makes no difference, let everything be mixed together with everything else. Let the traitor Judas be Peter or Paul, since he is consubstantial with Peter and Paul. . . . Being of the same substance will in no way remove the distinguishing characteristic of individuals who are in the same genus or species with each other."[704]

I. ". . . like Abel from Adam, who preserves the entire nature of his parent in himself and bears the complete principle of human nature."[705]

J. "He is both in the same person, combining in himself, so to speak, these natures which are so different."[706]

---

702   Var. "we were closely connecting."

703   Ibid. (p. 95)

704   Cyril of Alexandria. (2013–2015). *Commentary on John*. (J. C. Elowsky, T. C. Oden, & G. L. Bray, Eds., D. R. Maxwell, Trans.) (Vol. 1, p. 24). Downers Grove, IL: IVP Academic: An Imprint of InterVarsity Press.

705   Ibid. (p. 153)

706   Ibid. (Vol. 2, p. 67)

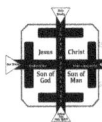

Definition of Attributes

I. "For you know yourselves, and no one can dispute it, that Like is not predicated of essence, but of habits, and qualities; for in the case of essences we speak, not of likeness, but of identity. Man, for instance, is said to be like man, not in essence, but according to habit and character; for in essence men are of one nature."[707]

II. "But a human differs from another human with respect to some knowledge, like grammar or something else like that. However, these differences do not touch the essence but clearly proceed from quite another cause. So a horse is faster than another horse or has a bigger or smaller body, but we will find that superiority or inferiority in these respects does not lie in the definition of essence . . . Therefore, natural properties exist in equal measure in every member of the same species. The qualities that inhere in them [the examples St Cyril just mentioned] are clearly different and are in them as external accidents... It is clear that the definition of every essence is not perfect in some but imperfect in others, but it is one and the same for all. We say, however, that accidents or qualities that are added in some way have different essences."[708]

---

707   Athanasius of Alexandria. (1892). Councils of Ariminum and Seleucia. In P. Schaff & H. Wace (Eds.), J. H. Newman & A. T. Robertson (Trans.), *St. Athanasius: Select Works and Letters* (Vol. 4, p. 478). New York: Christian Literature Company.

708   Cyril of Alexandria. (2013–2015). *Commentary on John*. (J. C. Elowsky, T. C. Oden, & G. L. Bray, Eds., D. R. Maxwell, Trans.) (Vol. 2, p. 205-206). Downers Grove, IL: IVP Academic: An Imprint of InterVarsity Press.

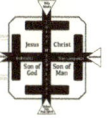

Specific Substantial Divine Attributes (possessed by all three Divine Hypostases)

I. Omnipotence (being all-powerful)

A. "The Father is Almighty; the Son is also Almighty."[709]

B. "He is almighty, and that while nothing has power over Him, He has power and rule over all."[710]

C. "It especially pertains to the most supreme Being of all to succeed in a matter without any effort at all."[711]

D. "God ever reigns, and is omnipotent."[712]

E. "The divine and omnipotent nature . . ."[713]

II. Omnipresence (being all-present)

A. "The Spirit fills all things and is present in the midst of all things through the Word."[714]

B. "But if the Son is everywhere because he is not in places assigned

709 Athanasius and Didymus. (2011). *Works on the Spirit: Athanasius's Letters to Serapion on the Holy Spirit, and, Didymus's on the Holy Spirit.* (J. Behr, Ed., M. DelCogliano, A. Radde-Gallwitz, & L. Ayres, Trans.) (Vol. 43, p. 108-109). Yonkers, NY: St Vladimir's Seminary Press.

710 Athanasius of Alexandria. (1892). <u>Against the Heathen</u>. In P. Schaff & H. Wace (Eds.), A. T. Robertson (Trans.), *St. Athanasius: Select Works and Letters* (Vol. 4, p. 19). New York: Christian Literature Company.

711 Cyril of Alexandria. (2018). *Glaphyra on the Pentateuch, Volume 1 Genesis.* (N. P. Lunn, Trans.) (Vol. 137, p. 207). Washington, DC: The Catholic University of America Press.

712 Cyril of Alexandria. (1859). *A Commentary upon the Gospel according to S. Luke.* (R. P. Smith, Trans.) (p. 333). Oxford: Oxford University Press.

713 Cyril of Alexandria. (2013–2015). *Commentary on John.* (J. C. Elowsky, T. C. Oden, & G. L. Bray, Eds., D. R. Maxwell, Trans.) (Vol. 2, p. 294). Downers Grove, IL: IVP Academic: An Imprint of InterVarsity Press.

714 Athanasius and Didymus. (2011). *Works on the Spirit: Athanasius's Letters to Serapion on the Holy Spirit, and, Didymus's on the Holy Spirit.* (J. Behr, Ed., M. DelCogliano, A. Radde-Gallwitz, & L. Ayres, Trans.) (Vol. 43, p. 94). Yonkers, NY: St Vladimir's Seminary Press.

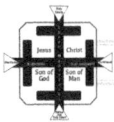

to him but in the Father, and if he is not a creature because he is outside of all things, then it cannot follow that the Spirit is a creature, because he is not in places assigned to him but fills all things and is outside of all things. For thus it is written: The Spirit of the Lord has filled the world [Wis 1.7]. And David sings in the psalm: Where can I go from your Spirit? [Ps 138.7]."[715]

C. "For this purpose, then, the incorporeal and incorruptible and immaterial Word of God comes to our realm, howbeit he was not far from us[716] before. For no part of Creation is left void of Him: He has filled all things everywhere, remaining present with His own Father."[717]

D. "Word as He was, so far from being contained by anything, He rather contained all things Himself; and just as while present in the whole of Creation, He is at once distinct in being from the universe, and present in all things by His own power. . . . For not even by being in the universe does He share in its nature."[718]

E. "He is in creation, and yet does not partake of its nature in the least degree."[719]

F. "And again men, being incapable of self-existence, are enclosed in place, and consist in the Word of God; but God is self-existent, enclosing all things, and enclosed by none; within all according to His own goodness and power, yet without all in His proper

715   Ibid. (p. 123-124)

716   Acts 17:27

717   Athanasius of Alexandria. (1892). <u>On the Incarnation of the Word</u>. In P. Schaff & H. Wace (Eds.), A. T. Robertson (Trans.), *St. Athanasius: Select Works and Letters* (Vol. 4, p. 40). New York: Christian Literature Company.

718   Ibid. (p. 45)

719   Ibid. (p. 60)

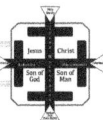

nature."[720, 721]

G. "For in place nothing is far from God,[722] but in nature only all things are far from Him."[723]

H. "No, it is impossible to be able to find heaven or earth ever void of the ineffable Godhead, for, as I said, the divine and consubstantial Trinity[724] fills all things."[725]

I. "And yet God fills everything, and in no way whatsoever is absent from anything that exists."[726]

J. "He fills all things with the unspeakable power of his divinity. He is present with the angels in heaven. He is with those on earth. And he does not even leave hell itself empty of his divinity. Since he dwells everywhere with everyone, he departs from no one."[727]

K. "Since I am true God, I am absent from no one, but I fill all things. And though I am with all things, I dwell especially in heaven,

---

720   Vid. also *Incarn.* § 17. This contrast is not commonly found in ecclesiastical writers, who are used to say that God is present everywhere, in substance as well as by energy or power. S. Clement, however, expresses himself still more strongly in the same way, 'In substance far off (for how can the originate come close to the Unoriginate?), but most close in power, in which the universe is embosomed.' *Strom. 2. circ. init.* but the parenthesis explains his meaning. Vid. Cyril. *Thesaur.* 6. p. 44. The common doctrine of the Fathers is, that God is present everywhere in *substance*. Vid. Petav. *de Deo,* iii. 8. and 9. It may be remarked, that S. Clement continues '*neither enclosing* nor enclosed.'

721   Athanasius of Alexandria. (1892). De Decretis or Defence of the Nicene Definition. In P. Schaff & H. Wace (Eds.), J. H. Newman & A. T. Robertson (Trans.), *St. Athanasius: Select Works and Letters* (Vol. 4, p. 157). New York: Christian Literature Company.

722   Vid. *de Decr.* 11, n. 5, which is explained by the present passage. When Ath. there says, 'without all in nature,' he must mean as here, 'far from all things in nature.' S. Clement *loc. cit.* gives the same explanation, as there noticed. It is observable that the *contr. Sab. Greg.* 10 (which the Benedictines consider not Athan.'s) speaks as *de Decr. supr.* Eusebius says the same thing, *de Incorpor.* i. init. *ap. Sirm. Op.* p. 68. vid. S. Ambros. Quomodo creatura in Deo esse potest, &c. *de Fid.* i. 106. and *supr.* § 1, n. 10.

723   Athanasius of Alexandria. (1892). Four Discourses against the Arians. In P. Schaff & H. Wace (Eds.), J. H. Newman & A. T. Robertson (Trans.), *St. Athanasius: Select Works and Letters* (Vol. 4, p. 406). New York: Christian Literature Company.

724   Θεία τε καὶ ὁμοούσιος Τριάς

725   Cyril of Alexandria. (1983). Answer to Tiberius: #2. L. Wickham (Trans.), *Cyril of Alexandria: Select letters* (p. 143). Oxford: Oxford University Press.

726   Cyril of Alexandria. (1859). *A Commentary upon the Gospel according to S. Luke.* (R. P. Smith, Trans.) (p. 624). Oxford: Oxford University Press.

727   Cyril of Alexandria. (2013–2015). *Commentary on John.* (J. C. Elowsky, T. C. Oden, & G. L. Bray, Eds., D. R. Maxwell, Trans.) (Vol. 1, p. 50). Downers Grove, IL: IVP Academic: An Imprint of InterVarsity Press.

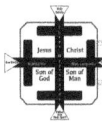

enjoying the company of the holy spirits."[728]

L. "He fills all things and is absent from nothing at all. He encompasses earth and heaven with his unspeakable power and does not leave the depth of the abyss. After all, where is God not present?"[729]

M. "Christ, who fills all things in his divine nature."[730]

N. The Divine Nature, Itself, is literally present *in* everything

1. "For pagan philosophers take a more religious view when they insist that the Godhead is incorporeal, without shape, quantity, parts or configuration, that it exists everywhere and is remote from nothing."[731]

2. "I am given to understand, then, that some are prompted by utter stupidity to take the line that the only- begotten Word of God on becoming man and having dealings in the flesh with men on earth, left heaven empty of his Godhead. This amounts to saying that he is quantitatively measurable, has a limited nature and occupies a position like bodies or the rest of created things. Perhaps they did not know that the Godhead is incorporeal, without configuration or parts, not quantitatively measurable, or limited by position but that it fills all and exists in all, being infinite by its very nature."[732]

3. "God who fills all things . . . attributes to Him the power to fill all things. . . . Yes, and the God of all himself shows us clearly that he does not have a nature circumscribed by place when he says this to the unholy Jews: '"Do I not fill heaven and earth?" says the Lord. What house will you build me? Or what is my resting

---

728   Ibid. (p. 329)

729   Ibid. (Vol. 2, p.197)

730   Cyril of Alexandria. (2008). *Commentary on the Twelve Prophets*. (T. P. Halton, Ed., R. C. Hill, Trans.) (Vol. 116, p. 184). Washington, DC: The Catholic University of America Press.

731   Cyril of Alexandria. (1983). Answer to Tiberius: #2. L. Wickham (Trans.), *Cyril of Alexandria: Select letters* (p. 141). Oxford: Oxford University Press.

732   Ibid. (Answer to Tiberius: #3, p. 147)

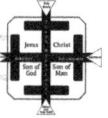

place? Heaven is my throne, and earth is my footstool.'"[733]

4. "No, as true God, he fills and cares for not only the heavens and the firmament beyond the heavens but also our world. And just as he was not absent from the heavens when he lived with human beings in this world in the flesh, so also we will hold, if we think rightly, that even though he has gone out of the world on account of his flesh, his divine and ineffable nature will be no less present to everyone in the world. And it rules over everything, being absent from nothing, neither leaving behind anything that exists, but present everywhere to everything. It fills the universe and whatever may be conceived of beyond the universe and is contained by itself alone."[734]

5. ". . . that Nature that is above all and through all and in all . . ."[735]

6. "The divine nature is not located in a place, and it is not absent from anything at all. It fills all things and goes through all things and is both outside and inside everything."[736]

O. God is not contained or limited by the things He is in

1. "Now, God would be sought by us, not in the sense of place—a fatuous notion, since the divinity is not localized."[737]

2. "The Divinity is not confined to a place, being neither bodily nor measurable."[738]

3. "Being incorporeal and infinite, and That Which fills all, but is

733 Cyril of Alexandria. (2013–2015). *Commentary on John*. (J. C. Elowsky, T. C. Oden, & G. L. Bray, Eds., D. R. Maxwell, Trans.) (Vol. 1, p. 325). Downers Grove, IL: IVP Academic: An Imprint of InterVarsity Press.

734 Ibid. (Vol. 2, p.30-31)

735 Ibid. (Vol. 2, p.154)

736 Ibid. (Vol. 2, p.290)

737 Cyril of Alexandria. (2007). *Commentary on the Twelve Prophets*. (T. P. Halton, Ed., R. C. Hill, Trans.) (Vol. 115, p. 204). Washington, DC: The Catholic University of America Press.

738 Cyril of Alexandria. (2008). *Commentary on the Twelve Prophets*. (T. P. Halton, Ed., R. C. Hill, Trans.) (Vol. 116, p. 368). Washington, DC: The Catholic University of America Press.

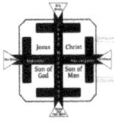

contained by none."[739]

4. "Now God exercises care for everything, and he must not be considered to be circumscribed by place; rather, as far as his own nature is concerned, he is completely uncontained by the things that exist."[740]

5. "God surpasses everything that comes into being, not by spatial exaltation (since it is silly and utterly senseless to conceive of something incorporeal in a place)."[741]

6. "Omnipresence is a God-befitting power and activity, ineffably filling heaven and earth, containing all things and being contained by none. God is not encompassed by a place or limited by distances or circumscribed within anything. The incorporeal nature that has no extent or quantity cannot experience such things."[742]

P. Saying God is far from, or not present in something can refer to:

1. The definition of His Nature being different from Creation

   a. "How then did He enter into the world? For He is separate from it, not so much in respect of place as of nature; for it is in nature that He differs from the inhabitants of the world."[743]

2. When He withholds His Grace (Divine Withdrawal)

   a. "While the divinity is completely uncircumscribed by place, he is said by some authors to be present when he confers

739   Cyril of Alexandria. (1859). *A Commentary upon the Gospel according to S. Luke.* (R. P. Smith, Trans.) (p. 285). Oxford: Oxford University Press.

740   Cyril of Alexandria. (2013–2015). *Commentary on John.* (J. C. Elowsky, T. C. Oden, & G. L. Bray, Eds., D. R. Maxwell, Trans.) (Vol. 1, p. 268). Downers Grove, IL: IVP Academic: An Imprint of InterVarsity Press.

741   Ibid. (p.331)

742   Ibid. (Vol. 2, p.287)

743   Cyril of Alexandria. (1859). *A Commentary upon the Gospel according to S. Luke.* (R. P. Smith, Trans.) (p. 9). Oxford: Oxford University Press.

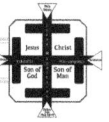

his benevolence, and likewise to be absent from sinners when he deprives them of it and cancels his clemency. You see, while words are used of God in human fashion, they should be understood in a way befitting him."[744, 745]

b. "God fills everything, and all things are full of his ineffable nature. Yet sometimes he is said to depart from sinners, though not separated from them by distance in a local sense, such a notion being extremely naïve; rather, it means by his no longer wishing to be well disposed or accord them pity and love. We refer to this as a display of wrath."[746]

III. Omniscience (being all-knowing)

A. "He who formed every breath knows all things."[747]

B. "And again, if all that is the Father's, is the Son's (and this He Himself has said),[748] and it is the Father"s attribute to know the day, it is plain that the Son too knows it, having this proper to Him from the Father."[749]

C. "For the divine Abraham was tested, though God was not ignorant of what would happen.[750] Indeed, nothing is beyond the notice

---

744   Anthropomorphic expressions in the biblical text require proper understanding, Cyril and other Fathers will insist.

745   Cyril of Alexandria. (2007). *Commentary on the Twelve Prophets*. (T. P. Halton, Ed., R. C. Hill, Trans.) (Vol. 115, p. 136). Washington, DC: The Catholic University of America Press.

746   Cyril of Alexandria. (2012). *Commentary on the Twelve Prophets*. (D. G. Hunter, Ed., R. C. Hill, Trans.) (Vol. 124, p. 166). Washington, DC: The Catholic University of America Press.

747   Prov 24:12 LXX

748   Jn 16:15

749   Athanasius of Alexandria. (1892). Four Discourses against the Arians. In P. Schaff & H. Wace (Eds.), J. H. Newman & A. T. Robertson (Trans.), *St. Athanasius: Select Works and Letters* (Vol. 4, p. 418). New York: Christian Literature Company.

750   Var. "of the mystery."

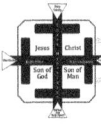

of the mind that knows everything . . . Consequently, it would be absolutely astounding and most improper if we should fail to understand the matter correctly by supposing that the God of all did not know what would happen, and that this was his reason for testing Abraham."[751]

D. "God knows everything."[752]

E. "He [God] knows all things before they happen."[753]

F. ". . . the omniscient God . . ."[754]

G. "Omniscience is an attribute of the true God."[755]

H. God's foreknowledge is not the same Thing as His Divine Will

   1. "The foreknowledge and telling of the future surely did not indicate the will and command of God."[756]

IV. Benevolence

A. "God is benevolent."[757]

V. Calmness

A. ". . . the calmness inherent in God . . ."[758, 759]

751   Cyril of Alexandria. (2018). *Glaphyra on the Pentateuch, Volume 1 Genesis*. (N. P. Lunn, Trans.) (Vol. 137, pp. 157-158). Washington, DC: The Catholic University of America Press.

752   Simonetti, M. (Ed.). (2002). *Matthew 14-28* (p. 85). Downers Grove, IL: InterVarsity Press.

753   Cyril of Alexandria. (1859). *A Commentary upon the Gospel according to S. Luke*. (R. P. Smith, Trans.) (p. 265). Oxford: Oxford University Press.

754   Ibid. (pp. 340–341)

755   Cyril of Alexandria. (2013–2015). *Commentary on John*. (J. C. Elowsky, T. C. Oden, & G. L. Bray, Eds., D. R. Maxwell, Trans.) (Vol. 2, p. 250). Downers Grove, IL: IVP Academic: An Imprint of InterVarsity Press.

756   Ibid. (p.289)

757   Cyril of Alexandria. (2008). *Commentary on the Twelve Prophets*. (T. P. Halton, Ed., R. C. Hill, Trans.) (Vol. 116, p. 163). Washington, DC: The Catholic University of America Press.

758   In place of "calmness" another manuscript speaks of God's "goodness."

759   Cyril of Alexandria. (2008). *Commentary on the Twelve Prophets*. (T. P. Halton, Ed., R. C. Hill, Trans.)

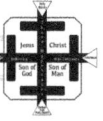

VI. Compassion

A. "Compassion . . . is an attribute of the divine nature."[760]

VII. Divinity[761]

A. ". . . the Divine Essence of the Word . . ."[762]

B. ". . . the Divine Essence . . ."[763]

C. "By his grace and through participation [with him], he will bring physical incorruptibility and the absolute security of divinity to the entire human race."[764]

D. ". . . the divine substance . . . "[765]

E. "... the substance that is divine..."[766]

VIII. Eternity

A. "To the King eternal, immortal, invisible, to God who alone is wise."[767]

B. "The Trinity is eternal, the Spirit is not a creature since he exists eternally with the Word and is in him."[768]

(Vol. 116, p. 59). Washington, DC: The Catholic University of America Press.

760   Cyril of Alexandria. (1859). *A Commentary upon the Gospel according to S. Luke*. (R. P. Smith, Trans.) (p. 108). Oxford: Oxford University Press.

761   Θεία

762   Athanasius of Alexandria. (1892). On Luke 10:22 (Mt 11:27). In P. Schaff & H. Wace (Eds.), A. T. Robertson (Trans.), *St. Athanasius: Select Works and Letters* (Vol. 4, p. 89). New York: Christian Literature Company.

763   Ibid. (Four Discourses against the Arians, p. 349)

764   Cyril of Alexandria. (2014). *Three Christological Treatises*. (D. Hunter, Ed., D. King, Trans.) (Vol. 129, p. 55). Washington, DC: The Catholic University of America Press.

765   Cyril of Alexandria. (2013–2015). *Commentary on John*. (J. C. Elowsky, T. C. Oden, & G. L. Bray, Eds., D. R. Maxwell, Trans.) (Vol. 1, p. 34). Downers Grove, IL: IVP Academic: An Imprint of InterVarsity Press.

766   Ibid. (p.349)

767   1 Tim 1:17

768   Athanasius and Didymus. (2011). *Works on the Spirit: Athanasius's Letters to Serapion on the Holy*

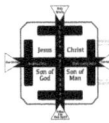

C. "Therefore, if the Father is eternal, the Son must also be eternal. For there can be no doubt that whatever we conceive as being in the Father is also in the Son, as the Lord himself said: All that the Father has is mine [Jn 16.15] and 'all that is mine is the Father's.' And so, the Father is eternal; the Son is also eternal."[769]

IX. Freedom

A. "For perfect freedom is the attribute of the divine and supreme substance only, and to be entirely separate from the yoke of servitude."[770]

X. Gentleness

A. ". . . the nature that is merciful and most gentle . . ."[771]

B. ". . . as would appease God. Who is gentle, and loveth mercy."[772]

XI. Goodness

A. "It is the property of the Father to be full of all good, and of such prerogatives as befit Deity: and this too belongs to the Son."[773]

1. "God, who is good by nature . . ."[774]

Spirit, and, Didymus's on the Holy Spirit. (J. Behr, Ed., M. DelCogliano, A. Radde-Gallwitz, & L. Ayres, Trans.) (Vol. 43, p. 126). Yonkers, NY: St Vladimir's Seminary Press.

769   Ibid. (p. 107)

770   Cyril of Alexandria. (1859). *A Commentary upon the Gospel according to S. Luke*. (R. P. Smith, Trans.) (p. 404). Oxford: Oxford University Press.

771   Cyril of Alexandria. (2013). *Festal Letters, 13–30*. (J. J. O'Keefe & D. G. Hunter, Eds., P. R. Amidon, Trans.) (Vol. 127, p. 95). Washington, DC: The Catholic University of America Press.

772   Cyril of Alexandria. (1859). *A Commentary upon the Gospel according to S. Luke*. (R. P. Smith, Trans.) (p. 501). Oxford: Oxford University Press.

773   Ibid. (p. 322)

774   Cyril of Alexandria. (2009). *Festal Letters, 1–12*. (J. J. O'Keefe, Ed., P. R. Amidon, Trans.) (Vol. 118, p. 132). Washington, DC: The Catholic University of America Press.

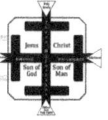

XII. Graciousness

A. "God is always gracious . . ."[775]

XIII. Holiness

A. "He who called you is holy . . ."[776]

B. "The Trinity must have one holiness, and it must have one eternity and immutable nature."[777]

C. "Furthermore, how will the divinity which is holy by nature give birth to an offspring from itself that is devoid of holiness and produce fruit that is its own but which is stripped of the properties that belong to it?"[778]

XIV. Honesty

A. "Being God, he is honest and incorruptible."[779]

XV. Immortality (Life)

A. "God is incorporeal and incorruptible, and immortal needing nothing for any purpose."[780]

---

775   Athanasius of Alexandria. (1892). Festal Letters. In P. Schaff & H. Wace (Eds.), H. Burgess & J. Smith Payne (Trans.), *St. Athanasius: Select Works and Letters* (Vol. 4, p. 540). New York: Christian Literature Company.

776   1 Pet 1:15

777   Athanasius and Didymus. (2011). *Works on the Spirit: Athanasius's Letters to Serapion on the Holy Spirit, and, Didymus's on the Holy Spirit*. (J. Behr, Ed., M. DelCogliano, A. Radde-Gallwitz, & L. Ayres, Trans.) (Vol. 43, p. 98-99). Yonkers, NY: St Vladimir's Seminary Press.

778   Cyril of Alexandria. (2013–2015). *Commentary on John*. (J. C. Elowsky, T. C. Oden, & G. L. Bray, Eds., D. R. Maxwell, Trans.) (Vol. 1, p. 79). Downers Grove, IL: IVP Academic: An Imprint of InterVarsity Press.

779   Cyril of Alexandria. (2012). *Commentary on the Twelve Prophets*. (D. G. Hunter, Ed., R. C. Hill, Trans.) (Vol. 124, p. 296). Washington, DC: The Catholic University of America Press.

780   Athanasius of Alexandria. (1892). Against the Heathen. In P. Schaff & H. Wace (Eds.), A. T. Robertson (Trans.), *St. Athanasius: Select Works and Letters* (Vol. 4, p. 16). New York: Christian Literature Company.

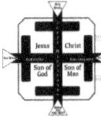

B. "Let us raise ourselves to the investigation of the Father's prerogatives and Attributes: those, namely, which specially belong to Him as God. God the Father is by nature Life, Light, and Wisdom. But the Son also is in like manner the same, as the divinely inspired Scripture everywhere testifies. For He is Light, and Wisdom, and Life. But if He be inferior to the Father, then of course He is indebted to Him for it, and that not in one particular only, but in every attribute that appertains to His substance."[781]

C. "Neither therefore the nature of angels, nor anything else whatsoever that was made, nor aught that from non-existence was brought into being, possesses life as the fruit of its own nature: but, on the contrary, life proceeds, as I said, from the Substance which transcends all: and to it only it belongs, and is possible that it can give life, because it is by nature life."[782]

D. "The ability to give life is a property of the divine nature which is in the Father and the Son alike."[783]

E. "Since the life-giving Word of God has taken up residence in the flesh, he has transformed it so that it has his own good attribute, that is, life."[784]

F. "After all, he will surely transform those who participate in the blessing so that they will have his own good attribute, that is, immortality."[785]

---

781 Cyril of Alexandria. (1859). *A Commentary upon the Gospel according to S. Luke*. (R. P. Smith, Trans.) (pp. 304–305). Oxford: Oxford University Press.

782 Ibid. (p. 666)

783 Cyril of Alexandria. (2013–2015). *Commentary on John*. (J. C. Elowsky, T. C. Oden, & G. L. Bray, Eds., D. R. Maxwell, Trans.) (Vol. 1, p. 148). Downers Grove, IL: IVP Academic: An Imprint of InterVarsity Press.

784 Ibid. (p. 232)

785 Ibid. (p. 237)

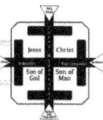

XVI. Immutability

A. "I am the Lord your God; I have not changed."[786]

B. "The Spirit is the same and unchangeable, and possesses the immutability of the Son."[787]

C. "The Son is immutable and unchangeable, just as the Father is."[788]

D. "It is impossible for that ineffable and supranatural substance[789] which is viewed as beyond all understanding and speech to be able to acquire any addition and especially not the addition of another nature from outside. It is utterly complete in its attributes and undergoes no diminution because it is ever unchangeable and unalterable, nor, as I said, does it need any addition."[790]

E. "The nature that is beyond all mind, and is the highest of all, knows no alteration."[791]

F. "The divine nature is truly stable in itself. It cannot experience a change into something else, but it is always the same, and it stands firm in its own superiority."[792]

XVII. Impartiality

A. "The impartiality and entire fairness of the unerring Nature . . ."[793]

---

786   Mal 3:6 LXX

787   Athanasius and Didymus. (2011). *Works on the Spirit: Athanasius's Letters to Serapion on the Holy Spirit, and, Didymus's on the Holy Spirit*. (J. Behr, Ed., M. DelCogliano, A. Radde-Gallwitz, & L. Ayres, Trans.) (Vol. 43, p. 94-95). Yonkers, NY: St Vladimir's Seminary Press.

788   Ibid. (p. 109)

789   οὐσίαν

790   Cyril of Alexandria. (1983). <u>Answer to Tiberius: #6</u>. L. Wickham (Trans.), *Cyril of Alexandria: Select letters* (p. 157). Oxford: Oxford University Press.

791   Cyril of Alexandria. (2013). *Festal Letters, 13–30*. (J. J. O'Keefe & D. G. Hunter, Eds., P. R. Amidon, Trans.) (Vol. 127, p. 27). Washington, DC: The Catholic University of America Press.

792   Cyril of Alexandria. (2013–2015). *Commentary on John*. (J. C. Elowsky, T. C. Oden, & G. L. Bray, Eds., D. R. Maxwell, Trans.) (Vol. 1, p. 64). Downers Grove, IL: IVP Academic: An Imprint of InterVarsity Press.

793   Cyril of Alexandria. (1859). *A Commentary upon the Gospel according to S. Luke*. (R. P. Smith, Trans.) (p. 557). Oxford: Oxford University Press.

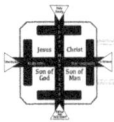

B. "God, who rules everything and who shows no partiality . . ."[794]

XVIII. Impassibility

A. "Nothing can grieve that nature which is incapable of passion, and of being affected by anything whatsoever of this kind."[795]

B. "The pure divine nature is above all suffering."[796]

C. "The divine nature is completely and entirely impassible."[797]

XIX. Incorporeality

A. "God is incorporeal and invisible and intangible by nature."[798]

B. "God is immaterial and incorporeal."[799]

C. "God, Who is an immaterial Being . . ."[800]

XX. Ineffability

A. ". . . the divine and ineffable nature . . ."[801]

B. "Although the divine nature comes down to our understanding

---

794   Cyril of Alexandria. (2013–2015). *Commentary on John*. (J. C. Elowsky, T. C. Oden, & G. L. Bray, Eds., D. R. Maxwell, Trans.) (Vol. 1, p. 136). Downers Grove, IL: IVP Academic: An Imprint of InterVarsity Press.

795   Cyril of Alexandria. (1859). *A Commentary upon the Gospel according to S. Luke*. (R. P. Smith, Trans.) (p. 427). Oxford: Oxford University Press.

796   Cyril of Alexandria. (2013–2015). *Commentary on John*. (J. C. Elowsky, T. C. Oden, & G. L. Bray, Eds., D. R. Maxwell, Trans.) (Vol. 1, p. 18). Downers Grove, IL: IVP Academic: An Imprint of InterVarsity Press.

797   Ibid. (Vol. 2, p.285)

798   Athanasius of Alexandria. (1892). <u>Against the Heathen</u>. In P. Schaff & H. Wace (Eds.), A. T. Robertson (Trans.), *St. Athanasius: Select Works and Letters* (Vol. 4, p. 19). New York: Christian Literature Company.

799   Ibid. (<u>De Decretis or Defence of the Nicene Definition</u>, p. 156)

800   Cyril of Alexandria. (1859). *A Commentary upon the Gospel according to S. Luke*. (R. P. Smith, Trans.) (p. 449). Oxford: Oxford University Press.

801   Athanasius of Alexandria. (1892). <u>On Luke 10:22 (Mt 11:27)</u>. In P. Schaff & H. Wace (Eds.), A. T. Robertson (Trans.), *St. Athanasius: Select Works and Letters* (Vol. 4, p. 90). New York: Christian Literature Company.

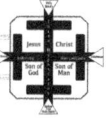

and makes itself intelligible to us, it still exists in both words and thoughts that are very far above us."[802]

XXI. Incorruptibility

A. "God is incorporeal and incorruptible, and immortal needing nothing for any purpose."[803]

B. "When humanity was made and brought into being by God, it did not have incorruptibility or indestructibility from its own nature. These belong essentially to God alone."[804]

XXII. Indivisibility

A. "Nor does He [God] have a nature that is divisible into parts."[805]

B. "It [the Holy Trinity] is self-consistent[806] and indivisible in nature."[807]

C. ". . . the Holy Trinity, Which is one indivisible Divinity . . ."[808]

D. "Their [Father and Son] nature also is one and indivisible."[809]

---

802   Cyril of Alexandria. (2013–2015). *Commentary on John*. (J. C. Elowsky, T. C. Oden, & G. L. Bray, Eds., D. R. Maxwell, Trans.) (Vol. 1, p. 170). Downers Grove, IL: IVP Academic: An Imprint of InterVarsity Press.

803   Athanasius of Alexandria. (1892). Against the Heathen. In P. Schaff & H. Wace (Eds.), A. T. Robertson (Trans.), *St. Athanasius: Select Works and Letters* (Vol. 4, p. 16). New York: Christian Literature Company.

804   Cyril of Alexandria. (2013–2015). *Commentary on John*. (J. C. Elowsky, T. C. Oden, & G. L. Bray, Eds., D. R. Maxwell, Trans.) (Vol. 1, p. 63). Downers Grove, IL: IVP Academic: An Imprint of InterVarsity Press.

805   Athanasius and Didymus. (2011). *Works on the Spirit: Athanasius's Letters to Serapion on the Holy Spirit, and, Didymus's on the Holy Spirit*. (J. Behr, Ed., M. DelCogliano, A. Radde-Gallwitz, & L. Ayres, Trans.) (Vol. 43, p. 78). Yonkers, NY: St Vladimir's Seminary Press.

806   Gk. ὁμοία ἑαυτῇ, lit. "like itself." See Serap. 1.17.1.

807   Athanasius and Didymus. (2011). *Works on the Spirit: Athanasius's Letters to Serapion on the Holy Spirit, and, Didymus's on the Holy Spirit*. (J. Behr, Ed., M. DelCogliano, A. Radde-Gallwitz, & L. Ayres, Trans.) (Vol. 43, p. 97). Yonkers, NY: St Vladimir's Seminary Press.

808   Ibid. (p. 104-105)

809   Athanasius of Alexandria. (1892). On Luke 10:22 (Mt 11:27). In P. Schaff & H. Wace (Eds.), A. T. Robertson (Trans.), *St. Athanasius: Select Works and Letters* (Vol. 4, p. 89). New York: Christian Literature Company.

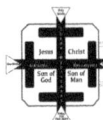

E. ". . . the impassible and impartitive nature of the Father"[810]

F. ". . . being the only Son proper and genuine from His Essence, and having with His Father the oneness of Godhead indivisible, as we said many times, being taught it by the Savior Himself."[811]

G. "The divine and indivisible nature . . ."[812]

H. Hence, because the Divine Essence is one undivided portion God is one

   1. ". . . but God is one . . ."[813]

   2. ". . . and there is one divinity, and one God 'who is over all and through all and in all.'"[814, 815]

   3. "In this way is the unity of the Holy Trinity preserved, and in this way is the one God preached in the Church."[816]

   4. "He [God] is one and not many."[817]

   5. ". . . the God of all, being one really and indeed and true."[818]

   6. ". . . thus there is one God and none other but He."[819]

   7. "There is one God and none other than He."[820]

---

810   Ibid. (De Decretis or Defence of the Nicene Definition, p. 157)

811   Ibid. (Four Discourses against the Arians, p. 370)

812   Cyril of Alexandria. (2013–2015). *Commentary on John*. (J. C. Elowsky, T. C. Oden, & G. L. Bray, Eds., D. R. Maxwell, Trans.) (Vol. 1, p. 227). Downers Grove, IL: IVP Academic: An Imprint of InterVarsity Press.

813   Gal 3:20

814   Eph 4:6

815   Athanasius and Didymus. (2011). *Works on the Spirit: Athanasius's Letters to Serapion on the Holy Spirit, and, Didymus's on the Holy Spirit*. (J. Behr, Ed., M. DelCogliano, A. Radde-Gallwitz, & L. Ayres, Trans.) (Vol. 43, p. 75). Yonkers, NY: St Vladimir's Seminary Press.

816   Ibid. (p. 97)

817   Athanasius of Alexandria. (1892). Against the Heathen. In P. Schaff & H. Wace (Eds.), A. T. Robertson (Trans.), *St. Athanasius: Select Works and Letters* (Vol. 4, p. 24). New York: Christian Literature Company.

818   Ibid. (Four Discourses against the Arians, p. 353)

819   Ibid. (Four Discourses against the Arians, p. 395)

820   Ibid. (Four Discourses against the Arians, p. 397)

8. "God is one."[821]

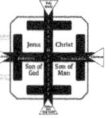

9. Yet, because of His Hypostases, God is a Trinity, or Triad

   a. "For the whole Trinity is one God."[822]

   b. "For thus we confess God to be one through the Triad, and we say that it is much more religious than the godhead of the heretics with its many kinds,[823] and many parts, to entertain a belief of the One Godhead in a Triad."[824]

   c. Consisting of the Father, Son and Holy Spirit

      1) ". . . the God and Father of our Lord Jesus Christ . . . our great God and Savior Jesus Christ . . . to lie to the Holy Spirit . . . you have not lied to men but to God."[825]

      2) "So, the Trinity is holy and perfect, confessed in Father and Son and Holy Spirit."[826]

      3) "For as the Trinity always was, so it is even now; and as it is now, so it always was: it is the Trinity, and in it are the Father and the Son and the Holy Spirit."[827]

      4) "There is a Trinity, Father, Son, and Holy Spirit."[828]

      5) "Let us acknowledge as consubstantial the Trinity of

821   Cyril of Alexandria. (1983). On the Creed. L. Wickham (Trans.), Cyril of Alexandria: Select letters (p. 103). Oxford: Oxford University Press.

822   Athanasius and Didymus. (2011). Works on the Spirit: Athanasius's Letters to Serapion on the Holy Spirit, and, Didymus's on the Holy Spirit. (J. Behr, Ed., M. DelCogliano, A. Radde-Gallwitz, & L. Ayres, Trans.) (Vol. 43, p. 79). Yonkers, NY: St Vladimir's Seminary Press.

823   [7] πολυειδοῦς.

824   Athanasius of Alexandria. (1892). Four Discourses against the Arians. In P. Schaff & H. Wace (Eds.), J. H. Newman & A. T. Robertson (Trans.), St. Athanasius: Select Works and Letters (Vol. 4, p. 402). New York: Christian Literature Company.

825   2 Cor 1:3, Titus 2:13, Act 5:3-4

826   Athanasius and Didymus. (2011). Works on the Spirit: Athanasius's Letters to Serapion on the Holy Spirit, and, Didymus's on the Holy Spirit. (J. Behr, Ed., M. DelCogliano, A. Radde-Gallwitz, & L. Ayres, Trans.) (Vol. 43, p. 97). Yonkers, NY: St Vladimir's Seminary Press.

827   Ibid. (p. 127)

828   Ibid. (p. 137)

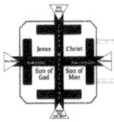

Father, Son, and Holy Spirit."[829]

I. Division would necessitate incompleteness

1. "What is divided, is not whole."[830]

XXIII. Invisibility

A. "He is by nature invisible and incomprehensible."[831]

B. "It is God's peculiar property at once to be invisible and yet to be known from His works."[832]

C. "The divine is intangible and invisible."[833]

D. "Now no one could gaze with physical eyes on that nature that is completely invisible to all creation."[834]

XXIV. Justice

A. "Tell me also, whether the God of the universe is not naturally God? Is he not naturally holy, just, good, life, light, wisdom, and power?"[835]

829 Cyril of Alexandria. (2013). *Festal Letters, 13–30*. (J. J. O'Keefe & D. G. Hunter, Eds., P. R. Amidon, Trans.) (Vol. 127, p. 113). Washington, DC: The Catholic University of America Press.

830 Athanasius of Alexandria. (1892). Four Discourses against the Arians. In P. Schaff & H. Wace (Eds.), J. H. Newman & A. T. Robertson (Trans.), *St. Athanasius: Select Works and Letters* (Vol. 4, p. 366). New York: Christian Literature Company.

831 Ibid. (Against the Heathen, p. 22)

832 Ibid. (On the Incarnation of the Word, p. 53)

833 Cyril of Alexandria. (2013). *Festal Letters, 13–30*. (J. J. O'Keefe & D. G. Hunter, Eds., P. R. Amidon, Trans.) (Vol. 127, p. 13). Washington, DC: The Catholic University of America Press.

834 Cyril of Alexandria. (2013–2015). *Commentary on John*. (J. C. Elowsky, T. C. Oden, & G. L. Bray, Eds., D. R. Maxwell, Trans.) (Vol. 2, p. 129). Downers Grove, IL: IVP Academic: An Imprint of InterVarsity Press.

835 Cyril of Alexandria. (2014). *Three Christological Treatises*. (D. Hunter, Ed., D. King, Trans.) (Vol. 129, p. 97). Washington, DC: The Catholic University of America Press.

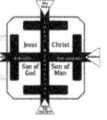

XXV. Light

A. "Proceed we then to consider the Attributes of the Father, and we shall come to know whether this Image is really His. The Father is eternal, immortal, powerful, light, King, Sovereign, God, Lord, Creator, and Maker. These Attributes must be in the Image, to make it true that he 'that hath seen' the Son 'hath seen the Father.'"[836, 837]

B. "The Father is almighty and the Son is also almighty. . . . The Father is Lord and the Son is also Lord. . . . The Father is light and the Son is also light. . . . The Father is life and the Son is also life."[838]

C. "If the Son alone is not 'true light,' but creation is too, this characteristic will clearly also be in us."[839]

D. "Illumination from above, when Christ imparts to the mind and heart a kind of bright ray, namely, grace from him."[840]

E. This is true illumination, knowledge, understanding or wisdom of God

1. "Now, to know Christ, who he is, how he became one of us, and what his manner of life was like subsequent to his Incarnation,[841] this, I say, is to receive into one's mind the light of the true divine vision."[842]

2. ". . . illumined by the divine light, in fact, and receiving into our

836   Jn 14:9

837   Athanasius of Alexandria. (1892). <u>Four Discourses against the Arians</u>. In P. Schaff & H. Wace (Eds.), J. H. Newman & A. T. Robertson (Trans.), *St. Athanasius: Select Works and Letters* (Vol. 4, p. 318). New York: Christian Literature Company.

838   Cyril of Alexandria. (2013–2015). *Commentary on John*. (J. C. Elowsky, T. C. Oden, & G. L. Bray, Eds., D. R. Maxwell, Trans.) (Vol. 1, p. 15). Downers Grove, IL: IVP Academic: An Imprint of InterVarsity Press.

839   Ibid. (p. 44)

840   Cyril of Alexandria. (2007). *Commentary on the Twelve Prophets*. (T. P. Halton, Ed., R. C. Hill, Trans.) (Vol. 115, p. 255). Washington, DC: The Catholic University of America Press.

841   Lit. "after the economy of flesh"

842   Cyril of Alexandria. (2018). *Glaphyra on the Pentateuch, Volume 1 Genesis*. (N. P. Lunn, Trans.) (Vol. 137, p. 265). Washington, DC: The Catholic University of America Press.

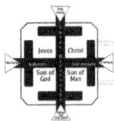

mind the beams of heavenly wisdom from on high."[843]

3. ". . . the light of the true knowledge of God . . ."[844]

4. ". . . enriched with the divine light in their mind, by means of which they attain unto the meaning of hidden truths."[845]

5. ". . . the light of the true knowledge of God . . ."[846]

6. "He gives light to the minds of all by filling them with divine knowledge."[847]

7. "God the Father imparts the inextinguishable light of the true knowledge of the true vision of God."[848]

8. "In this participation, he is wisdom and understanding (which is what light is called in rational creatures) so that things capable of reason may become rational and things capable of wisdom may have wisdom."[849]

9. ". . . the light from God, that is, illumination by the Spirit.'[850]

10. ". . . the spiritual ray, so to speak (I mean illumination by the Spirit)."[851]

F. Purity makes one ready to receive this Light

1. "To know God and to appropriate knowledge of him does not

---

843   Cyril of Alexandria. (2008). *Commentary on the Twelve Prophets*. (T. P. Halton, Ed., R. C. Hill, Trans.) (Vol. 116, p. 228). Washington, DC: The Catholic University of America Press.

844   Cyril of Alexandria. (1859). *A Commentary upon the Gospel according to S. Luke*. (R. P. Smith, Trans.) (p. 235). Oxford: Oxford University Press.

845   Ibid. P. 354)

846   Ibid. P. 373)

847   Ibid. (p. 377)

848   Ibid. (p. 613)

849   Cyril of Alexandria. (2013–2015). *Commentary on John*. (J. C. Elowsky, T. C. Oden, & G. L. Bray, Eds., D. R. Maxwell, Trans.) (Vol. 1, p. 39). Downers Grove, IL: IVP Academic: An Imprint of InterVarsity Press.

850   Ibid. (Vol. 2, p.21)

851   Ibid. (Vol. 2, p.42)

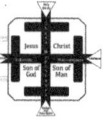

comes from the feeble effort of the frail, though he might see dimly as in a mirror. But it is achieved by the one who is brought to such a state of weakness, who reckons carnal and worldly things of no account, and who with a vigorous and active mind is able to strive for what is pleasing to God."[852]

2. "To the pure, the discourse on the vision of God will be clear. Christ shines in them (namely through his Spirit), guiding them with his light into everything they need, unveiling himself and making himself visible by a certain ineffable spiritual torchlight."[853]

3. "Those whose minds are bright with every virtue, however, and who are already able and fit to learn the divine and hidden mysteries, will receive the torch of the Spirit and behold with the eyes of their mind the Lord who has taken up residence in them."[854]

G. Any being that can think and reason can be filled with it

1. "Whatever is endowed with the power to reason and think is like a vessel most excellently fashioned by God, the master craftsman of all things, with the capacity to be filled with divine light."[855]

H. Is necessary to be able to have an unerring understanding

1. "The beloved light of the true vision of God, through which alone one may gain the correct and unobtainable knowledge of the sacred doctrines."[856]

---

852   Cyril of Alexandria. (2018). *Glaphyra on the Pentateuch, Volume 1 Genesis.* (N. P. Lunn, Trans.) (Vol. 137, p. 265). Washington, DC: The Catholic University of America Press.

853   Cyril of Alexandria. (2013–2015). *Commentary on John.* (J. C. Elowsky, T. C. Oden, & G. L. Bray, Eds., D. R. Maxwell, Trans.) (Vol. 2, p. 191). Downers Grove, IL: IVP Academic: An Imprint of InterVarsity Press.

854   Ibid. (p.193)

855   Ibid. (Vol. 1, p. 164)

856   Cyril of Alexandria. (2013). *Festal Letters, 13–30.* (J. J. O'Keefe & D. G. Hunter, Eds., P. R. Amidon,

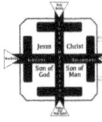

2. "whosoever would understand correctly and without error what He wishes to teach, are in need of divine light"[857]

3. "The divine light rises upon them, and they gain a correct and unerring knowledge of the sacred doctrines."[858]

4. "The Savior here calls the grace of the Holy Spirit 'water.' If anyone should become a participant of it, they will then have a supply of divine knowledge springing up in them so that they no longer need admonition from others. Instead, they will be sufficient and capable to exhort with ease those who thirst for the divine and heavenly word."[859]

5. "No one could progress toward the knowledge of the truth without the illumination of the Spirit, and no one could work out for themselves an accurate understanding of divine dogmas, at least with what is accessible to human beings."[860]

6. "As they were led easily by the light of the Spirit to perfect knowledge of the divinely inspired Scripture and the holy dogmas of the church."[861]

I. This can also be called God's glory

1. "He sent his own Son, not unclad and bodiless, nor dazzling in the fearsome, unapproachable light of his own divine glory"[862]

2. "The divine nature is completely invisible and unseen,

Trans.) (Vol. 127, p. 138). Washington, DC: The Catholic University of America Press.

857   Cyril of Alexandria. (1859). *A Commentary upon the Gospel according to S. Luke*. (R. P. Smith, Trans.) (p. 337). Oxford: Oxford University Press.

858   Ibid. (p. 640)

859   Cyril of Alexandria. (2013–2015). *Commentary on John*. (J. C. Elowsky, T. C. Oden, & G. L. Bray, Eds., D. R. Maxwell, Trans.) (Vol. 1, p. 121). Downers Grove, IL: IVP Academic: An Imprint of InterVarsity Press.

860   Ibid. (Vol. 2, p.295)

861   Ibid. (Vol. 2, p.296)

862   Cyril of Alexandria. (2013). *Festal Letters, 13–30*. (J. J. O'Keefe & D. G. Hunter, Eds., P. R. Amidon, Trans.) (Vol. 127, p. 94). Washington, DC: The Catholic University of America Press.

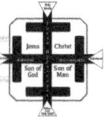

possessing a glory that is unapproachable (for 'he dwells in light inaccessible,' as Paul says).[863, 864]

3. "Therefore he brought the disciples to the mountain and showed them the glory with which he will shine on the universe in the future."[865]

4. "You may easily learn that our eyes could not have borne the glory of his holy body if Christ had chosen to reveal it, even before his ascension to the Father, if you consider the transfiguration that was displayed to the holy disciples on the mountain. The blessed Matthew the Evangelist writes that he once took 'Peter and James and John and went up to the mountain. And he was transfigured before them, and his face shone like lightning, and his clothes became white like snow.' But they could not bear the sight, and they fell to the ground. According to his wise plan, therefore, our Lord Jesus Christ did not yet transform his temple into the glory that was due and fitting for it but still appeared in his original form."[866]

XXVI. Limitlessness

A. "I am astonished at the ignorance and recklessness of people who think this and feel myself obliged to point out that they have made God's substance a quantity and are talking of it as confined, bounded and no longer unlimited and unconfined but as spatially finite and contained within dimensions . . . the Godhead is . . . infinite by its very nature."[867]

---

863   1 Tim 6:16

864   Cyril of Alexandria. (2013). *Festal Letters, 13–30.* (J. J. O'Keefe & D. G. Hunter, Eds., P. R. Amidon, Trans.) (Vol. 127, p. 152). Washington, DC: The Catholic University of America Press.

865   Simonetti, M. (Ed.). (2002). *Matthew 14-28* (pp. 62–63). Downers Grove, IL: InterVarsity Press.

866   Cyril of Alexandria. (2013–2015). *Commentary on John.* (J. C. Elowsky, T. C. Oden, & G. L. Bray, Eds., D. R. Maxwell, Trans.) (Vol. 2, p. 365). Downers Grove, IL: IVP Academic: An Imprint of InterVarsity Press.

867   Cyril of Alexandria. (1983). <u>Answer to Tiberius: #2</u>. L. Wickham (Trans.), *Cyril of Alexandria: Select letters* (p. 141). Oxford: Oxford University Press.

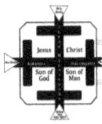

B. "The divinely inspired psalmist surely speaks the truth and declares hidden mysteries in the Spirit when he says that the Son is absent from no place at all, thereby attesting his incorporeal and unlimited nature and the fact that, as God, he is not confined to a place."[868]

XXVII. Lovingness

A. "The God of all ceases not to be kind: He is good and loving unto men."[869]

B. "God insists that kindness and incomparable love for humanity are his divine qualities."[870]

XXVIII. Mercy

A. "The inherent clemency and patience of the God of all."[871]

B. ". . . God's inherent clemency."[872]

C. ". . . God, who is naturally kind and merciful."[873]

---

868   Cyril of Alexandria. (2013–2015). *Commentary on John*. (J. C. Elowsky, T. C. Oden, & G. L. Bray, Eds., D. R. Maxwell, Trans.) (Vol. 2, p. 163). Downers Grove, IL: IVP Academic: An Imprint of InterVarsity Press.

869   Cyril of Alexandria. (1859). *A Commentary upon the Gospel according to S. Luke*. (R. P. Smith, Trans.) (p. 474). Oxford: Oxford University Press.

870   Cyril of Alexandria. (2013–2015). *Commentary on John*. (J. C. Elowsky, T. C. Oden, & G. L. Bray, Eds., D. R. Maxwell, Trans.) (Vol. 2, p. 23). Downers Grove, IL: IVP Academic: An Imprint of InterVarsity Press.

871   Cyril of Alexandria. (2008). *Commentary on the Twelve Prophets*. (T. P. Halton, Ed., R. C. Hill, Trans.) (Vol. 116, p. 27). Washington, DC: The Catholic University of America Press.

872   Ibid. (p. 152)

873   Cyril of Alexandria. (2012). *Commentary on the Twelve Prophets*. (D. G. Hunter, Ed., R. C. Hill, Trans.) (Vol. 124, p. 117). Washington, DC: The Catholic University of America Press.

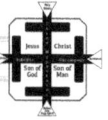

XXIX. Patience

A. "God is long-suffering."[874]

B. "The Lord of all is surely good and longsuffering by nature"[875]

XXX. Perfection

A. ". . . For God is not imperfect."[876, 877]

B. "God is deficient in nothing."[878]

C. "The Godhead exists in unchangeable perfection."[879]

D. ". . . the holy and consubstantial Trinity, the one Deity who possesses perfection, indeed total perfection in absolutely everything . . . the Deity, who though being single[880] is a perfection of perfections . . ."[881]

E. "He has reached the highest perfection in every good: for this is also an attribute of His by nature."[882]

F. "The substance of the Father is perfect in absolutely every

---

874   Cyril of Alexandria. (1859). *A Commentary upon the Gospel according to S. Luke*. (R. P. Smith, Trans.) (p. 496). Oxford: Oxford University Press.

875   Cyril of Alexandria. (2007). *Commentary on the Twelve Prophets*. (T. P. Halton, Ed., R. C. Hill, Trans.) (Vol. 115, p. 151). Washington, DC: The Catholic University of America Press.

876   See *Orat.* ii. § 24, 25, *De Decr.* § 8, and Harnack, *Dogmgesch.* (ed. 2) vol. 2. p. 208, note.

877   Athanasius of Alexandria. (1892). On Luke 10:22 (Mt 11:27). In P. Schaff & H. Wace (Eds.), A. T. Robertson (Trans.), *St. Athanasius: Select Works and Letters* (Vol. 4, p. 87). New York: Christian Literature Company.

878   Ibid. (Four Discourses against the Arians, p. 363)

879   Cyril of Alexandria. (2014). *Three Christological Treatises*. (D. Hunter, Ed., D. King, Trans.) (Vol. 129, p. 45). Washington, DC: The Catholic University of America Press.

880   Or "though existing in a monad [*monas*]."

881   Cyril of Alexandria. (2018). *Glaphyra on the Pentateuch, Volume 1 Genesis*. (N. P. Lunn, Trans.) (Vol. 137, p. 94). Washington, DC: The Catholic University of America Press.

882   Cyril of Alexandria. (1859). *A Commentary upon the Gospel according to S. Luke*. (R. P. Smith, Trans.) (p. 330). Oxford: Oxford University Press.

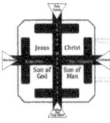

respect."[883]

XXXI. Self-existence

A. "God is incorporeal and incorruptible, and immortal, needing nothing for any purpose."[884]

B. "For if it is an admitted truth about God that He stands in need of nothing, but is self-sufficient and self-contained."[885]

C. ". . . the self-existent God . . ."[886]

D. "God does not need anything."[887]

E. ". . . the pure and self-subsistent divine nature . . ."[888]

F. "For the Deity has no need with respect to anything, but he has full perfection in himself. He does not receive power from anything outside of himself, nor does he get energy by means of physical food or drink. Rather, by his very nature he himself is power."[889]

XXXII. Simplicity (non-composite; not consisting of multiple parts)

A. "Being uncompounded in nature, He is Father of One Only Son."[890]

---

883   Cyril of Alexandria. (2013–2015). *Commentary on John*. (J. C. Elowsky, T. C. Oden, & G. L. Bray, Eds., D. R. Maxwell, Trans.) (Vol. 1, p. 17). Downers Grove, IL: IVP Academic: An Imprint of InterVarsity Press.

884   Athanasius of Alexandria. (1892). Against the Heathen. In P. Schaff & H. Wace (Eds.), A. T. Robertson (Trans.), *St. Athanasius: Select Works and Letters* (Vol. 4, p. 16). New York: Christian Literature Company.

885   Ibid. (p. 18)

886   Ibid. (To the Bishops of Egypt, p. 231)

887   Ibid. (Festal Letters, p. 545)

888   Cyril of Alexandria. (2014). *Three Christological Treatises*. (D. Hunter, Ed., D. King, Trans.) (Vol. 129, p. 134). Washington, DC: The Catholic University of America Press.

889   Cyril of Alexandria. (2018). *Glaphyra on the Pentateuch, Volume 1 Genesis*. (N. P. Lunn, Trans.) (Vol. 137, pp. 207-208). Washington, DC: The Catholic University of America Press.

890   Athanasius of Alexandria. (1892). De Decretis or Defence of the Nicene Definition. In P. Schaff & H. Wace (Eds.), J. H. Newman & A. T. Robertson (Trans.), *St. Athanasius: Select Works and Letters* (Vol. 4, p.

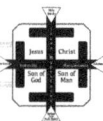

B. "Therefore the Lord himself ranked the Spirit together with the name of the Father in order to show that the Holy Trinity is not compounded of two different things, that is, Creator and creature, but that there is one divinity in the Trinity."[891]

C. ". . . if God be simple, as He is . . ."[892]

D. ". . . one is the Godhead"[893]

E. "The nature of the Godhead, which is simple and not composite, is never to be divided into two by the concepts of Father and Son."[894]

F. "The divine nature, perfectly simple and incomposite, has in itself the abundance of all perfection and is in need of nothing."[895]

G. "The Godhead is incorporeal, without configuration or parts, not quantitatively measurable, or limited by position but that it fills all and exists in all, being infinite by its very nature."[896]

H. "The Divine Nature is one."[897]

I. "The divine nature will not endure learning from anyone at all or endure being doubled by synthesis since simplicity is its own

157). New York: Christian Literature Company.

891 Athanasius and Didymus. (2011). *Works on the Spirit: Athanasius's Letters to Serapion on the Holy Spirit, and, Didymus's on the Holy Spirit*. (J. Behr, Ed., M. DelCogliano, A. Radde-Gallwitz, & L. Ayres, Trans.) (Vol. 43, p. 126). Yonkers, NY: St Vladimir's Seminary Press.

892 Athanasius of Alexandria. (1892). De Decretis or Defence of the Nicene Definition. In P. Schaff & H. Wace (Eds.), J. H. Newman & A. T. Robertson (Trans.), *St. Athanasius: Select Works and Letters* (Vol. 4, p. 165). New York: Christian Literature Company.

893 Athanasius of Alexandria. (1892). Four Discourses against the Arians. In P. Schaff & H. Wace (Eds.), J. H. Newman & A. T. Robertson (Trans.), *St. Athanasius: Select Works and Letters* (Vol. 4, p. 397). New York: Christian Literature Company.

894 Jurgens, W. A. (Trans.). (1970–1979). *The Faith of the Early Fathers* (Vol. 3, p. 210). Collegeville, MN: The Liturgical Press.

895 Ibid. (p. 214)

896 Cyril of Alexandria. (1983). Answer to Tiberius: #3. L. Wickham (Trans.), *Cyril of Alexandria: Select letters* (p. 147-149). Oxford: Oxford University Press.

897 Cyril of Alexandria. (2013–2015). *Commentary on John*. (J. C. Elowsky, T. C. Oden, & G. L. Bray, Eds., D. R. Maxwell, Trans.) (Vol. 1, p. 13). Downers Grove, IL: IVP Academic: An Imprint of InterVarsity Press.

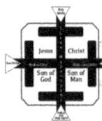

good and perfect property."[898]

J. "The divine nature is simple and free from all composition."[899]

XXXIII. Sovereignty

A. ". . . God, the King of all . . ."[900]

B. ". . . God, the universal King . . ."[901]

C. ". . . God, Who rules over all . . ."[902]

D. ". . . the Sovereign of the universe . . ."[903]

XXXIV. Supremacy

A. "Perceiving him to be God, to whom no name may properly apply . . ."[904]

B. ". . . the supreme Substance . . ."[905]

C. ". . . that nature Which transcends all, and is supreme . . ."[906]

D. ". . . solely to the supreme Substance . . ."[907]

---

898   Ibid. (p. 145)

899   Ibid. (p. 362)

900   Athanasius of Alexandria. (1892). <u>Festal Letters</u>. In P. Schaff & H. Wace (Eds.), H. Burgess & J. Smith Payne (Trans.), *St. Athanasius: Select Works and Letters* (Vol. 4, p. 531). New York: Christian Literature Company.

901   Cyril of Alexandria. (2009). <u>Festal Letters, 1–12</u>. (J. J. O'Keefe, Ed., P. R. Amidon, Trans.) (Vol. 118, p. 111). Washington, DC: The Catholic University of America Press.

902   Cyril of Alexandria. (1859). *A Commentary upon the Gospel according to S. Luke*. (R. P. Smith, Trans.) (p. 498). Oxford: Oxford University Press.

903   Ibid. (p. 536)

904   Cyril of Alexandria. (2018). *Glaphyra on the Pentateuch, Volume 1 Genesis*. (N. P. Lunn, Trans.) (Vol. 137, p. 266). Washington, DC: The Catholic University of America Press.

905   Cyril of Alexandria. (1859). *A Commentary upon the Gospel according to S. Luke*. (R. P. Smith, Trans.) (p. 16). Oxford: Oxford University Press.

906   Ibid. (p. 121)

907   Ibid. (p. 129)

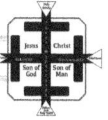

E. "... God alone, Who is supreme over all, and crowned with surpassing honors."[908]

F. "... the supreme and transcendent nature ..."[909]

G. "... for every created being is put under the feet of the divine and supreme nature, Which rules over all."[910]

H. "God transcends everything."[911]

XXXV. Truthfulness

A. "Constant truthfulness is characteristic of the divine nature."[912]

XXXVI. Uncreatedness

A. "He [God] is unmade."[913]

B. "But rather, as the Father's Attributes are Everlastingness, Immortality, Eternity, and the being no creature, it follows that thus also we must think of the Son."[914]

C. "God not only is not originated ..."[915]

D. "Now to the King eternal, immortal, invisible, to God who alone is wise, be honor and glory forever and ever. Amen."[916]

E. "Some, for instance, call what is, but is neither generated, nor has

---

908   Ibid. (p. 294)

909   Ibid. (p. 497)

910   Ibid. (p. 709)

911   Cyril of Alexandria. (2013–2015). *Commentary on John*. (J. C. Elowsky, T. C. Oden, & G. L. Bray, Eds., D. R. Maxwell, Trans.) (Vol. 2, p. 276). Downers Grove, IL: IVP Academic: An Imprint of InterVarsity Press.

912   Ibid. (Vol. 1, p. 110)

913   Athanasius of Alexandria. (1892). Against the Heathen. In P. Schaff & H. Wace (Eds.), A. T. Robertson (Trans.), *St. Athanasius: Select Works and Letters* (Vol. 4, p. 22). New York: Christian Literature Company.

914   Ibid. (On Luke 10:22 (Mt 11:27), p. 89)

915   Ibid. (De Decretis or Defence of the Nicene Definition, p. 171)

916   1 Tim 1:17

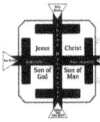

any personal cause at all, unoriginate; and others, the uncreate."[917]

F. "God is without beginning and unoriginate."[918]

G. ". . . the unoriginate and unmitigated Essence of God . . ."[919]

H. "Only the nature that is divine and above all things is suited to have no beginning or end."[920]

XXXVII. Unknowability in what the Divine Nature specifically is

A. "The nature of God is incomprehensible . . . human beings cannot understand God's nature."[921]

B. ". . . the incomprehensible nature [of God] . . ."[922]

C. "To comprehend what the essence of God is be impossible."[923]

D. ". . . the divine and inviolate nature, which is beyond all comprehension, and above reason and wonder."[924]

E. "No one will know what God is by nature."[925]

F. "No sober person would busy themselves trying to figure out what

---

917   Athanasius of Alexandria. (1892). Councils of Ariminum and Seleucia. In P. Schaff & H. Wace (Eds.), J. H. Newman & A. T. Robertson (Trans.), *St. Athanasius: Select Works and Letters* (Vol. 4, p. 475). New York: Christian Literature Company.

918   Ibid. (Four Discourses against the Arians, p. 343)

919   Ibid. (Four Discourses against the Arians, p. 362)

920   Cyril of Alexandria. (2013–2015). *Commentary on John*. (J. C. Elowsky, T. C. Oden, & G. L. Bray, Eds., D. R. Maxwell, Trans.) (Vol. 1, p. 33). Downers Grove, IL: IVP Academic: An Imprint of InterVarsity Press.

921   Athanasius of Alexandria. (1995) On Virginity. *Athanasius and Asceticism* (p. 309). Baltimore: The John Hopkins University Press.

922   Athanasius of Alexandria. (1892). On Luke 10:22 (Mt 11:27). In P. Schaff & H. Wace (Eds.), A. T. Robertson (Trans.), *St. Athanasius: Select Works and Letters* (Vol. 4, p. 89). New York: Christian Literature Company.

923   Ibid. (De Decretis or Defence of the Nicene Definition, p. 165)

924   Cyril of Alexandria. (2013). *Festal Letters, 13–30*. (J. J. O'Keefe & D. G. Hunter, Eds., P. R. Amidon, Trans.) (Vol. 127, p. 140). Washington, DC: The Catholic University of America Press.

925   Cyril of Alexandria. (2013–2015). *Commentary on John*. (J. C. Elowsky, T. C. Oden, & G. L. Bray, Eds., D. R. Maxwell, Trans.) (Vol. 1, p. 235). Downers Grove, IL: IVP Academic: An Imprint of InterVarsity Press.

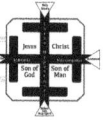

God really is by nature, since that is impossible to find out."[926]

G. "But in the case of God, it is not possible for us to grasp the logos or definition of his nature because we do not know what he is by nature."[927]

H. "But what the ineffable nature is in its essence is completely inaccessible to us and the other rational creatures."[928]

I. The complete truth of It is beyond our mind and reason

    1. "Our nature has no words or even ways of thinking that could accurately convey the mysteries that are above us or that could faultlessly explain matters that are fitting to God. So we will allow the divine nature superiority over our mind and our reason."[929]

    2. "We must concede supremacy to the divine and inexpressible nature over the power of language and the sharpness of every mind."[930]

    3. "The nature of originate beings approaches the sight of God to the point of conception alone, not surpassing the boundaries that are fitting for this nature, but it concedes to the divine nature, even unwillingly, that that nature is hidden in ineffable speech. But the Only Begotten, who arose from God the Father, sees his begetter completely in himself. And since he portrays the substance of his parent in his own nature, he knows him in a way that is impossible to say. For the things of God are unutterable."[931]

    4. Titles, or Attributes refer to His Essence but do not define It

        a. "Yet if we only understand that God is, and if Scripture

---

926   Ibid. (Vol. 2, p. 16)
927   Ibid. (Vol. 2, p. 18)
928   Ibid. (Vol. 2, p. 66)
929   Ibid. (p. 22)
930   Ibid. (p. 33)
931   Ibid. (p. 295)

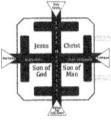

indicates Him by means of these titles, we, with the intention of indicating Him and none else, call Him God and Father and Lord. When then He says, 'I am that I am,' and 'I am the Lord God,' [932] or when Scripture says, 'God,' we understand nothing else by it but the intimation of His incomprehensible essence Itself, and that He Is, who is spoken of." [933, 934]

b. ". . . the very simple, and blessed, and incomprehensible essence itself of Him that is, (for though we be unable to master what He is, yet hearing 'Father,' and 'God,' and 'Almighty,' we understand nothing else to be meant than the very essence of Him that is)." [935, 936]

J. Only the Holy Trinity knows what the Divine Essence is

1. "For only the divine nature of the Trinity comprehends itself. Only the Father knows his own Son, the fruit of his own substance. Only the divine Son recognizes the One by whom he has been begotten. Only the Holy Spirit knows the deep things of God, the thought of the Father and the Son." [937]

2. "For the holy and consubstantial Trinity alone knows Itself, being far above all speech and understanding." [938]

---

932   Ex 3:14, 15

933   In like manner de Synod. § 34. Also Basil, 'The essence is not any one of things which do not attach, but is the very being of God.' contr. Eun. i. 10 fin. 'The nature of God is no other than Himself, for He is simple and uncompounded.' Cyril Thesaur. p. 59. 'When we say the power of the Father, we say nothing else than the essence of the Father.' August. de Trin. vii. 6. And so Numenius in Eusebius, 'Let no one deride, if I say that the name of the Immaterial is essence and being.' Præp. Evang. xi. 10.

934   Athanasius of Alexandria. (1892). De Decretis or Defence of the Nicene Definition. In P. Schaff & H. Wace (Eds.), J. H. Newman & A. T. Robertson (Trans.), St. Athanasius: Select Works and Letters (Vol. 4, p. 165). New York: Christian Literature Company.

935   De Decr. 29, note 7.

936   Athanasius of Alexandria. (1892). Councils of Ariminum and Seleucia. In P. Schaff & H. Wace (Eds.), J. H. Newman & A. T. Robertson (Trans.), St. Athanasius: Select Works and Letters (Vol. 4, p. 469). New York: Christian Literature Company.

937   Simonetti, M. (Ed.). (2001). Matthew 1–13 (pp. 231–232). Downers Grove, IL: InterVarsity Press.

938   Cyril of Alexandria. (1859). A Commentary upon the Gospel according to S. Luke. (R. P. Smith, Trans.)

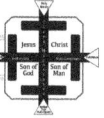

XXXVIII. Unquantifiability

A. "The divine nature is understood to be and is without size, without quantity and without body."[939]

B. "No one will suppose, even if they were a complete babbler, that the divine nature can be quantified or circumscribed by a shape or measured by an imprint or that the incorporeal can at all be subject to corporeal things."[940]

XXXIX. Will

A. The will can also be categorized as an attribute

1. "How could subjection itself be thought to subsist by itself without being in something else that exists? Ordinarily, such qualities are nothing but accidents of necessarily preexisting subjects in which they arise. They are seen to concern substances or are considered to be accidents in substances rather than subsisting by themselves . . . subjection to another's will, since it indicates a certain turning toward the necessity of being subject to others, will not be understood to exist in its own nature, but it will be (as a passion or will or desire, perhaps) in something that exists."[941]

B. The Will of the Trinity is:

1. One, through complete mutual agreement

    a. "The will and desire of Father and Son is one"[942]

(p. 304). Oxford: Oxford University Press.

939   Cyril of Alexandria. (2013–2015). *Commentary on John*. (J. C. Elowsky, T. C. Oden, & G. L. Bray, Eds., D. R. Maxwell, Trans.) (Vol. 1, p. 16). Downers Grove, IL: IVP Academic: An Imprint of InterVarsity Press.

940   Ibid. (p. 153)

941   Ibid. (p. 219)

942   Athanasius of Alexandria. (1892). On Luke 10:22 (Mt 11:27). In P. Schaff & H. Wace (Eds.), A. T. Robertson (Trans.), *St. Athanasius: Select Works and Letters* (Vol. 4, p. 89). New York: Christian Literature

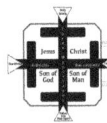

b. "Since he has one substance with the Father, he is called by certain physical laws, so to speak, to an identical will and power."[943]

c. "Since we understand the Father and the Son to have one divine nature, their will will certainly be the same also. Neither in the Father, nor in the Son nor in the Holy Spirit will the divine nature ever be understood to be at odds with itself; rather, whatever seems good to the Father, let's say, is the will of the entire divine nature."[944]

d. "We will refuse to think that the holy and consubstantial Trinity ever has a disagreement among himself, nor is he divided into different opinions, nor does he somehow parcel out what seems good to each, whether it be the Father, the Son or the Holy Spirit. They agree about everything because they are clearly from one divine nature. There is certainly always one and the same will in the entire holy Trinity."[945]

e. "Because there is one essence, there is indeed one will and one goal in every matter. There is no disagreement or division into different wills."[946]

2. Three, because each Divine Hypostasis has Its own Will

a. "The **wills** of the holy Trinity always coincide into one will and purpose."[947]

b. "If any should hold that the disciples are united in the same way the Father and the Son are one, not only in essence

---

Company.

943   Cyril of Alexandria. (2013–2015). *Commentary on John*. (J. C. Elowsky, T. C. Oden, & G. L. Bray, Eds., D. R. Maxwell, Trans.) (Vol. 1, p. 147). Downers Grove, IL: IVP Academic: An Imprint of InterVarsity Press.

944   Ibid. (p. 159)

945   Ibid. (p. 218)

946   Ibid. (Vol. 2, p. 191)

947   Ibid. (p. 218)

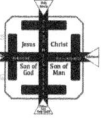

but also in will (since there is one will in the holy nature and one purpose in all matters), let them think this. They will not go astray from a fitting understanding, since anyone may see that there is an identity of will among those who are really Christians."[948]

3. Good and loving

    a. "The Father's will is good and loving."[949]

4. Never wrong

    a. ". . . the divine and faultless will . . ."[950]

C. God's will alone is sufficient to brings things into existence

1. "He willed only, and all things subsisted."[951]

2. "His mere will is sufficient for the framing of all things."[952]

3. ". . . God, who by his will and counsel crafted everything and set it in place."[953]

D. Nothing can resist God's absolute will

---

948   Ibid. (Vol. 2, p. 286)

949   Ibid. (p. 222)

950   Cyril of Alexandria. (1987). *Letters, 1–50*. (T. P. Halton, Ed., J. I. McEnerney, Trans.) (Vol. 76, p. 172). Washington, DC: The Catholic University of America Press.

951   Athanasius of Alexandria. (1892). Four Discourses against the Arians. In P. Schaff & H. Wace (Eds.), J. H. Newman & A. T. Robertson (Trans.), *St. Athanasius: Select Works and Letters* (Vol. 4, p. 361). New York: Christian Literature Company.

952   Ibid. (p. 364)

953   Cyril of Alexandria. (2013–2015). *Commentary on John*. (J. C. Elowsky, T. C. Oden, & G. L. Bray, Eds., D. R. Maxwell, Trans.) (Vol. 1, p. 141). Downers Grove, IL: IVP Academic: An Imprint of InterVarsity Press.

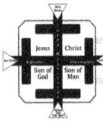

1. "The divinity is omnipotent, after all, and nothing will resist his will."[954]

2. "For He verily is the Lord of powers,[955] and nothing can offer resistance to His will."[956]

3. "There is nothing that can resist My will."[957]

E. Things that God allows to occur but are not His will occur by His permission

1. "What happens by God's permission is generally attributed to him, as with the statement, 'There is no evil in the city for which the Lord was not responsible'[958]—not that he causes evil, only allowing it to happen to cities' evildoers."[959]

---

954   Cyril of Alexandria. (2007). *Commentary on the Twelve Prophets*. (T. P. Halton, Ed., R. C. Hill, Trans.) (Vol. 115, p. 196). Washington, DC: The Catholic University of America Press.

955   This title of Deity, which is of very frequent occurrence in S. Cyril's works, is the Greek translation of "Jehovah Sabaoth," the Lord of Hosts, Ps 24:10; and this again the Latins render, "Dominus virtutum." By "powers" the Syrians understood an order of the angelic hierarchy, inferior only to the Cherubs and Seraphs. Among the MSS. obtained by the late Dr. Mill from the Syriac Christians of Malabar, I have found two lists of ecclesiastical and angelic dignities, in which they are ranked as follows: 1. Players on musical instruments. 2. Singers. 3. Doorkeepers. 4. Readers. 5. Subdeacons. 6. Deacons. 7. Priests. 8. Visitors. 9. Chorepiscopi. 10. Bishops. 11. Metropolitans. 12. Patriarchs. 13. Angels. 14. Archangels. 15. Principalities. 16. Dominions. 17. Thrones. 18. Lordships. 19. Powers. 20. Cherubs. 21. Seraphs. By visitors, though the title is taken from the Peschito version of 1 Pet 2:25, I imagine the περιοδευταὶ of the Greek Canons to be meant; and the Chorepiscopi, or Village-bishops, had no power to ordain any one above a subdeacon.

956   Cyril of Alexandria. (1859). *A Commentary upon the Gospel according to S. Luke*. (R. P. Smith, Trans.) (p. 232). Oxford: Oxford University Press.

957   Ibid. (p. 278)

958   Amos 3:6, the saying that Chrysostom also cites as a popularly misquoted text used to justify moral irresponsibility.

959   Cyril of Alexandria. (2008). *Commentary on the Twelve Prophets*. (T. P. Halton, Ed., R. C. Hill, Trans.) (Vol. 116, p. 392). Washington, DC: The Catholic University of America Press.

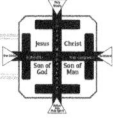

Hypostatic Attributes ("the Properties that strictly belong to each person")[960]

I. Fatherhood

A. "The argument of the just judge does not bring the father down to the place of sonship just because the father is of the same substance with the son, nor does it put the son in the position of fatherhood. It recognizes each one on his own. The father does not progress toward the son, and the son does not approach the father."[961]

B. "Even though the Son is the heir of all Attributes that are in the Father by nature, since he is from him by nature, even so he will never have the attribute of being Father. This is one thing that belongs to the Father alone. But the Son will remain without being deprived of anything in the Father even though he is not considered to be the Father. He has all the Attributes and special qualities of the Father's nature perfectly in himself."[962]

C. Generativeness

   1. "And as the Father is always good by nature, so He is always generative[963] by nature."[964]

II. Sonship

A. ". . . the divine and supra-mundane offspring, then, is identical in

---

960   Cyril of Alexandria. (2013–2015). *Commentary on John*. (J. C. Elowsky, T. C. Oden, & G. L. Bray, Eds., D. R. Maxwell, Trans.) (Vol. 1, p. 23). Downers Grove, IL: IVP Academic: An Imprint of InterVarsity Press.

961   Ibid.

962   Ibid. (p. 24)

963   *Or.* i. 14, n. 4; ii. 2, n. 3.

964   Athanasius of Alexandria. (1892). <u>Four Discourses against the Arians</u>. In P. Schaff & H. Wace (Eds.), J. H. Newman & A. T. Robertson (Trans.), *St. Athanasius: Select Works and Letters* (Vol. 4, p. 430). New York: Christian Literature Company.

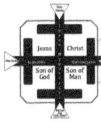

nature with the Father, differing from him only in his sonship."[965]

B. "He affirms that the Spirit is Lord: not as possessed of sonship; for He is the Spirit, and not the Son"[966]

C. "When we apply this same reasoning to the person of the Father, we say that he has all that belongs to the Son naturally, but he can never pass into sonship and be the Word."[967]

D. ". . . the Son possessing his own unique sonship and by the fact that he does not change into the Father, just as the Father does not change into the Son."[968]

III. Procession

A. "Each [Divine Hypostasis] having always His own peculiarity, plainly by reason of hypostatic considerations."[969]

B. The Holy Spirit being unique, or peculiar, in that It is the only Divine Hypostasis that proceeds.

IV. The hypostatic attributes are the only way to tell the Divine Hypostases apart

A. "The holy and consubstantial Trinity is distinguished by the differences in names and the qualities and attributes of the

965 Cyril of Alexandria. (1983). Answer to Tiberius: #3. L. Wickham (Trans.), *Cyril of Alexandria: Select letters* (p. 147). Oxford: Oxford University Press.

966 Cyril of Alexandria. (1859). *A Commentary upon the Gospel according to S. Luke*. (R. P. Smith, Trans.) (p. 405). Oxford: Oxford University Press.

967 Cyril of Alexandria. (2013–2015). *Commentary on John*. (J. C. Elowsky, T. C. Oden, & G. L. Bray, Eds., D. R. Maxwell, Trans.) (Vol. 1, p. 24). Downers Grove, IL: IVP Academic: An Imprint of InterVarsity Press.

968 Ibid. (p. 25)

969 Jurgens, W. A. (Trans.). (1970–1979). *The Faith of the Early Fathers* (Vol. 3, p. 215). Collegeville, MN: The Liturgical Press.

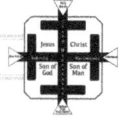

persons."[970]

Synonyms for the substantial Divine Attributes

I. Divine Activities

A. "To judge or to render judgment are activities or acts related to substances rather than truly substances themselves. When we give a judgment, we are acting; we are being what we are according to our own characteristics. . . . Just as God the Father has the ability to create and creates all things through the Son as through his own power and strength, so also he has the power to judge, and he will exercise that power through the Son as through his own righteousness."[971]

B. "No one would reasonably call heated iron fire, even though it contains the activity of fire from having been heated by the fire."[972]

C. ". . .let it have the unceasing activity of immortality."[973]

II. Divine Characteristics

A. "His substance cannot be created above all for this reason: it is capable of receiving the distinguishing marks[974] of God. Now his distinguishing marks are the characteristics by which God is

970 Cyril of Alexandria. (2013–2015). *Commentary on John*. (J. C. Elowsky, T. C. Oden, & G. L. Bray, Eds., D. R. Maxwell, Trans.) (Vol. 2, p. 146). Downers Grove, IL: IVP Academic: An Imprint of InterVarsity Press.

971 Ibid. (Vol. 1, p. 149-150)

972 Ibid. (Vol. 1, p. 242)

973 Ibid. (Vol. 1, p. 243)

974 Gk. τὰ ἴδια.

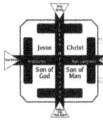

recognized. For example, that he is almighty, that he is, that he is immutable, and the other things mentioned earlier."[975]

III. Divine Energies

A. "It fully bore the attribute of him who dwelled in it and who was ineffably united to it, that is, life-giving energy."[976]

IV. Divine Fruit

A. "The Attributes that spring from the divine nature are the fruit of the highest essence."[977]

V. Divine Grace

A. ". . . heirs together of the grace of life . . ."[978]

B. ". . . that we, as built upon Him, might partake, as well-compacted stones, the life and grace which is from Him."[979]

C. "Giving life is characteristic of one who lives, and not of one who borrows that grace from another."[980]

D. "how could he give life as life since the divine nature has this as its own property and yields it to no one else?"[981]

---

975   Athanasius and Didymus. (2011). *Works on the Spirit: Athanasius's Letters to Serapion on the Holy Spirit, and, Didymus's on the Holy Spirit*. (J. Behr, Ed., M. DelCogliano, A. Radde-Gallwitz, & L. Ayres, Trans.) (Vol. 43, p. 111-112). Yonkers, NY: St Vladimir's Seminary Press.

976   Cyril of Alexandria. (2013–2015). *Commentary on John*. (J. C. Elowsky, T. C. Oden, & G. L. Bray, Eds., D. R. Maxwell, Trans.) (Vol. 2, p. 147). Downers Grove, IL: IVP Academic: An Imprint of InterVarsity Press.

977   Ibid. (p. 139)

978   1 Pet 3:7

979   Athanasius of Alexandria. (1892). Four Discourses against the Arians. In P. Schaff & H. Wace (Eds.), J. H. Newman & A. T. Robertson (Trans.), *St. Athanasius: Select Works and Letters* (Vol. 4, p. 389). New York: Christian Literature Company.

980   Cyril of Alexandria. (2013–2015). *Commentary on John*. (J. C. Elowsky, T. C. Oden, & G. L. Bray, Eds., D. R. Maxwell, Trans.) (Vol. 1, p. 226). Downers Grove, IL: IVP Academic: An Imprint of InterVarsity Press.

981   Ibid. (p. 34)

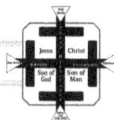

E. "Since the life-giving Word of God has taken up residence in the flesh, he has transformed it so that it has his own good attribute, that is, life."[982]

F. "Manifold indeed and beyond human conception are the instructions and gifts of grace which He has laid up in us; as the pattern of heavenly conversation, power against demons, the adoption of sons, and that exceeding great and singular grace, the knowledge of the Father and of the Word Himself, and the gift of the Holy Ghost."[983]

G. "Grace following from partaking of the Word."[984]

H. "Emmanuel wrought his grace in us, which is equivalent to a divine and spiritual fire, being like heat imparted through the Spirit."[985]

I. "... put on the heavenly grace from above, namely our incorruption."[986]

J. "Those who truly understand this are enriched through the precious divine grace, 'For as many as received him,' it says, 'he gave them the right to become children of God.'"[987]

K. ". . . those who drink the living water, that is, the grace poured out through the Holy Spirit, partake of Christ."[988]

L. "Creation borrows grace from him. . . . Why did he implant in

---

982   Ibid. (p. 232)

983   Athanasius of Alexandria. (1892). To the Bishops of Egypt. In P. Schaff & H. Wace (Eds.), M. Atkinson & A. T. Robertson (Trans.), *St. Athanasius: Select Works and Letters* (Vol. 4, p. 223). New York: Christian Literature Company.

984   Ibid. (On the Incarnation of the Word, p. 38)

985   Cyril of Alexandria. (2018). *Glaphyra on the Pentateuch, Volume 1 Genesis.* (N. P. Lunn, Trans.) (Vol. 137, p. 96). Washington, DC: The Catholic University of America Press.

986   Cyril of Alexandria. (2019). *Glaphyra on the Pentateuch, Volume 2 Genesis.* (N. P. Lunn, Trans.) (Vol. 138, p. 210). Washington, DC: The Catholic University of America Press.

987   Ibid. (p. 210)

988   Wilken, R. L., Christman, A. R., & Hollerich, M. J. (Eds.). (2007). *Isaiah: Interpreted by Early Christian and Medieval Commentators.* (R. L. Wilken, A. R. Christman, & M. J. Hollerich, Trans.) (p. 442). Grand Rapids, MI; Cambridge, UK: William B. Eerdmans Publishing Company.

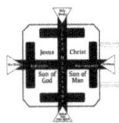

them his own good that belongs to him essentially?"[989]

M. ". . . transferring his grace to them . . ."[990]

N. "Will any sensible person claim that the Spirit-bearer is saying that the grace given to the Corinthians from above was given in the very substance of Christ?"[991]

O. The Divine Grace, possessed by the Holy Trinity, can be referred to as:

1. One (Single)

    a. "And the grace given is one, given from the Father in the Son, as Paul writes in every Epistle, 'Grace unto you, and peace from God our Father and the Lord Jesus Christ.'"[992,993]

    b. "There is one grace of the Trinity."[994]

    c. "There is one grace bestowed in the Trinity."[995]

    d. "We are all both partakers of the same one grace, and also have the same Lord of hosts as the Giver both of our existence and of our ability to do well."[996]

    e. "Now no one with any sense will think that the Father grants a certain amount of grace as his own, while the Son, in turn, grants his own partial grace, as it were. No, the grace

989   Cyril of Alexandria. (2013–2015). *Commentary on John*. (J. C. Elowsky, T. C. Oden, & G. L. Bray, Eds., D. R. Maxwell, Trans.) (Vol. 1, p. 47). Downers Grove, IL: IVP Academic: An Imprint of InterVarsity Press.

990   Ibid. (p. 189)

991   Ibid. (Vol. 2, p. 168)

992   Viz. Jn 14:23, and Jn 17:21; Rom 1:7

993   Athanasius of Alexandria. (1892). Four Discourses against the Arians. In P. Schaff & H. Wace (Eds.), J. H. Newman & A. T. Robertson (Trans.), *St. Athanasius: Select Works and Letters* (Vol. 4, p. 371). New York: Christian Literature Company.

994   Athanasius and Didymus. (2011). *Works on the Spirit: Athanasius's Letters to Serapion on the Holy Spirit, and, Didymus's on the Holy Spirit*. (J. Behr, Ed., M. DelCogliano, A. Radde-Gallwitz, & L. Ayres, Trans.) (Vol. 43, p. 125). Yonkers, NY: St Vladimir's Seminary Press.

995   Ibid. (p. 126)

996   Cyril of Alexandria. (1859). *A Commentary upon the Gospel according to S. Luke*. (R. P. Smith, Trans.) (p. 675). Oxford: Oxford University Press.

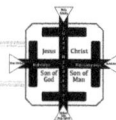

is one and the same, even though it is said to come through both of them. All blessings are given and the distribution of divine gifts is made by the Father through the Son to the worthy. The Son is not thought of in the category of a servant, as we have said, but he is considered and truly is a cogiver and cosupplier."[997]

2. Multiple

   a. "as good stewards of the manifold grace of God."[998]

   b. "the clothing of the divine graces"[999]

   c. "the abundant supply of graces bestowed by Christ upon the poor in spirit."[1000]

   d. "Him Who distributes these divine graces."[1001]

   e. "spiritual graces which are God's gift.[1002]"[1003]

   f. "he has placed faith also in the catalogue of spiritual graces."[1004]

   g. "From 'the fullness' of the Son, as from an ever-flowing spring, the gift of divine graces gushes forth to each soul that is shown worthy to receive it."[1005]

997   Cyril of Alexandria. (2013–2015). *Commentary on John*. (J. C. Elowsky, T. C. Oden, & G. L. Bray, Eds., D. R. Maxwell, Trans.) (Vol. 2, p. 175-176). Downers Grove, IL: IVP Academic: An Imprint of InterVarsity Press.

998   1 Pet 4:10

999   Cyril of Alexandria. (2008). *Commentary on the Twelve Prophets*. (T. P. Halton, Ed., R. C. Hill, Trans.) (Vol. 116, p. 319). Washington, DC: The Catholic University of America Press.

1000   Cyril of Alexandria. (1859). *A Commentary upon the Gospel according to S. Luke*. (R. P. Smith, Trans.) (p. 61). Oxford: Oxford University Press.

1001   Ibid. (p. 80)

1002   Heb 11:6

1003   Cyril of Alexandria. (1859). *A Commentary upon the Gospel according to S. Luke*. (R. P. Smith, Trans.) (p. 535). Oxford: Oxford University Press.

1004   Ibid. (p. 535)

1005   Cyril of Alexandria. (2013–2015). *Commentary on John*. (J. C. Elowsky, T. C. Oden, & G. L. Bray, Eds., D. R. Maxwell, Trans.) (Vol. 1, p. 67). Downers Grove, IL: IVP Academic: An Imprint of InterVarsity Press.

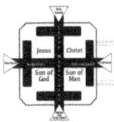

h.   "He will bestow the manifold grace of the Spirit."[1006]

i.   "He has promised to fill them with spiritual graces."[1007]

P.   Excommunication is losing a share in Grace

1.   ". . . having no share of grace, that is, excommunicated . . ."[1008]

VI. Divine Prerogatives

A.   "And if all that are called sons and gods, whether in earth or in heaven, were adopted and deified through the Word, and the Son Himself is the Word, it is plain that through Him are they all, and He Himself before all, or rather He Himself only is very Son, and He alone is very God from the very God, not receiving these prerogatives as a reward for His virtue, nor being another beside them, but being all these by nature and according to essence."[1009]

B.   "Now, He [the Son] has the prerogative of creating and making, of Eternity, of omnipotence, of immutability."[1010]

VII. Divine Properties

A.   "For it is God's peculiar property at once to be invisible and yet to

---

1006   Ibid. (p. 181)

1007   Ibid. (Vol. 2, p. 312)

1008   Cyril of Alexandria. (1987). *Letters, 51–110*. (T. P. Halton, Ed., J. I. McEnerney, Trans.) (Vol. 77, p. 98). Washington, DC: The Catholic University of America Press.

1009   Athanasius of Alexandria. (1892). <u>Four Discourses against the Arians</u>. In P. Schaff & H. Wace (Eds.), J. H. Newman & A. T. Robertson (Trans.), *St. Athanasius: Select Works and Letters* (Vol. 4, p. 329). New York: Christian Literature Company.

1010   Ibid. (<u>To the Bishops of Africa</u>, p. 492)

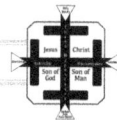

be known from His works . . ."[1011]

B. "Since he became like us (that is, a human being) in order that we might become like him (I mean gods and sons), he receives our properties into himself and he gives us his own in return."[1012]

C. "But God is incorruptible and eternal by nature. He does not obtain this by the will of someone else, like creation does; rather, he always exists in his own good properties, and this property is one of them."[1013]

VIII. Divine Titles

A. "This is why He has equality with the Father by titles expressive of unity, and what is said of the Father, is said in Scripture of the Son also, all but His being called Father.[1014] For the Son Himself said, 'All things that the Father hath are Mine' (John 16:15); and He says to the Father, 'All Mine are Thine, and Thine are Mine' (John 17:10),—as for instance,[1015] the name <u>God</u>; for 'the Word was God;'—<u>Almighty</u>, 'Thus says He that is, and that was, and that is to come, the Almighty' (John 1:1; Apoc. 1:8):—the being <u>Light</u>, 'I am,' He says, 'the Light' (John 8:12):—the <u>Operative Cause</u>, 'All things were made by Him,' and, 'whatsoever I see the Father do, I do also' (John 1:3; 5:19):—the being <u>Everlasting</u>, 'His eternal power and godhead,' and, 'In the beginning was the Word,' and, 'He was the true Light, which lighteth every man that cometh into

---

1011   Ibid. (<u>On the Incarnation of the Word</u>, p. 53)

1012   Cyril of Alexandria. (2013–2015). *Commentary on John*. (J. C. Elowsky, T. C. Oden, & G. L. Bray, Eds., D. R. Maxwell, Trans.) (Vol. 2, p. 363). Downers Grove, IL: IVP Academic: An Imprint of InterVarsity Press.

1013   Ibid. (p. 86)

1014   By 'the Son being *equal* to the Father,' is but meant that He is His 'exact image;' it does not imply any distinction of essence. Cf. Hil. *de Syn.* 73. But this implies some exception, for else He would not be like or equal, but the same. *ibid.* 72. Hence He is the Father's image in all things except in being the Father, πλὴν τῆς ἀγεννησίας καὶ τῆς πατρότητος. Damasc. *de Imag.* iii. 18. p. 354. vid. also Basil. *contr. Eun.* ii. 28; Theod. *Inconfus.* p. 91; Basil. *Ep.* 38. 7 fin. [Through missing this point the] Arians asked why the Son was not the beginning of a θεογονία. Supr. p. 319 a, note 1. vid. *infr.* note 8.

1015   Vid. *Orat.* iii. § 4.

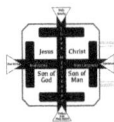

the world;'—the being <u>Lord</u>."[1016]

B. "We see many names predicated of God, but none of them seems to indicate what God is according to essence. Rather, they either show what He is not, or they indicate some condition distinct from another. For example, *incorruptible* and *immortal* indicate what He is not; but *Father* or *unbegotten*, that He is the begetter, which distinguishes Him from the Son, and that He is not produced; but neither of these is indicative of essence, as I said before, but indicates something of what surrounds the essence."[1017]

The Divine Attributes are:

I. Able to be learned from Holy Scripture

A. "One could easily find out what his Attributes are and are not by attending to the Holy Scriptures."[1018]

II. From God as Their Source

A. "For God is good, or rather is essentially the source of goodness."[1019]

B. "For Godhead is holy and is source, principle and origin of all

1016   Athanasius of Alexandria. (1892). <u>Councils of Ariminum and Seleucia</u>. In P. Schaff & H. Wace (Eds.), J. H. Newman & A. T. Robertson (Trans.), *St. Athanasius: Select Works and Letters* (Vol. 4, p. 476). New York: Christian Literature Company.

1017   Jurgens, W. A. (Trans.). (1970–1979). *The Faith of the Early Fathers* (Vol. 3, pp. 211–212). Collegeville, MN: The Liturgical Press.

1018   Cyril of Alexandria. (2013–2015). *Commentary on John*. (J. C. Elowsky, T. C. Oden, & G. L. Bray, Eds., D. R. Maxwell, Trans.) (Vol. 2, p. 16). Downers Grove, IL: IVP Academic: An Imprint of InterVarsity Press.

1019   Athanasius of Alexandria. (1892). <u>On the Incarnation of the Word</u>. In P. Schaff & H. Wace (Eds.), A. T. Robertson (Trans.), *St. Athanasius: Select Works and Letters* (Vol. 4, p. 37). New York: Christian Literature Company.

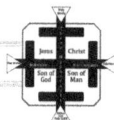

virtue."[1020]

C. "Deity is, indeed, in all that is fine and is the absolute source, root and origin of all virtue and from it comes to us what is good."[1021]

D. "The divine and ineffable nature is the source and origin of complete gentleness, and is goodness itself."[1022]

E. "Every good quality that we have is given, but that is not so with God. He is in himself the source of his own excellent Attributes, both glory and power, which belong to him alone."[1023]

III. Infinite and immeasurable

A. "The Father's goodness is inconceivable and immeasurable and far surpasses the limit of our understanding."[1024]

B. "His grace has no measure, as if someone else gave it to him, but it is true and perfect in the perfect one, that is, not imported or brought in from the outside as an addition, but it is in him essentially. It is the fruit of the Father's natural quality, which passes over to the Son who is from him."[1025]

IV. Eternal, having always existed in, or been possessed by, God; hence They are uncreated

A. "For just as He exists before creation, so before creation also He has what He has. . . . It is necessary, then, that we should perceive that in the Father reside Everlastingness, Eternity, Immortality.

1020   Cyril of Alexandria. (1983). Answer to Tiberius: #10. L. Wickham (Trans.), *Cyril of Alexandria: Select letters* (p. 165). Oxford: Oxford University Press.

1021   Ibid. (Answer to Tiberius: #14, p. 175)

1022   Cyril of Alexandria. (2007). *Commentary on the Twelve Prophets*. (T. P. Halton, Ed., R. C. Hill, Trans.) (Vol. 115, p. 109). Washington, DC: The Catholic University of America Press.

1023   Cyril of Alexandria. (2013–2015). *Commentary on John*. (J. C. Elowsky, T. C. Oden, & G. L. Bray, Eds., D. R. Maxwell, Trans.) (Vol. 2, p. 213). Downers Grove, IL: IVP Academic: An Imprint of InterVarsity Press.

1024   Ibid. (Vol. 1, p. 17)

1025   Ibid. (Vol. 1, p. 64)

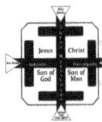

Now these reside in Him not as adventitious Attributes, but, as it were, in a well-spring they reside in Him, and in the Son."[1026]

B. "For though the grace which came to us from the Savior appeared, as the Apostle says, just now, and has come when He sojourned among us; yet this grace had been prepared even before we came into being, nay, before the foundation of the world."[1027]

C. "For God is good; and being good always"[1028]

D. "The like passages do not shew that the Son once had not these prerogatives—(for had not He eternally what the Father has, who is the Only Word and Wisdom of the Father in essence, who also says, 'All that the Father hath are Mine,'[1029] and what are Mine, are the Father's? for if the things of the Father are the Son's and the Father hath them ever, it is plain that what the Son hath, being the Father's, were ever in the Son),—not then because once He had them not, did He say this, but because, whereas the Son hath eternally what He hath, yet He hath them from the Father... He is not the Father, but the Father's Word, and the Eternal Son, who because of His likeness to the Father, has eternally what He has from Him, and because He is the Son, has from the Father what He has eternally... For if all things are delivered unto Him, first, He is other than that all which He has received; next, being Heir of all things, He alone is the Son and proper according to the Essence of the Father... as receiving all things, He is other than them all, and alone proper to the Father. Moreover that 'Was given' and 'Were delivered' do not shew that once He had them not."[1030]

1026   Athanasius of Alexandria. (1892). On Luke 10:22 (Mt 11:27). In P. Schaff & H. Wace (Eds.), A. T. Robertson (Trans.), *St. Athanasius: Select Works and Letters* (Vol. 4, p. 88-89). New York: Christian Literature Company.

1027   Ibid. (Four Discourses against the Arians, p. 389)

1028   Ibid. (Four Discourses against the Arians, p. 390)

1029   Jn 16:15; 17:10

1030   Athanasius of Alexandria. (1892). Four Discourses against the Arians. In P. Schaff & H. Wace (Eds.), J. H. Newman & A. T. Robertson (Trans.), *St. Athanasius: Select Works and Letters* (Vol. 4, p. 413). New York: Christian Literature Company.

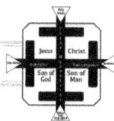

E. "Rather then is the Word faithful, and all things which He says that He has received, He has always, yet has from the Father; and the Father indeed not from any, but the Son from the Father. . . . For the Father, having given all things to the Son, in the Son still[1031] hath all things; and the Son having, still the Father hath them; for the Son's Godhead is the Father's Godhead, and thus the Father in the Son exercises His Providence over all things."[1032]

F. "For He was and is God Good by Nature and Compassionate and Merciful always, and hath not become this in time but was so manifested to us."[1033]

G. "Father's eternal foreknowledge."[1034]

H. "He must be omnipotent, and that this glorious attribute is, so to speak, His without a beginning, and without end."[1035]

1031 πάλιν. vid. *Or.* i. 15, n. 6. Thus iteration is not duplication in respect to God; though *how* this is, is the inscrutable Mystery of the Trinity in Unity. Nothing can be named which the Son is in Himself, as distinct from the Father; we are but told His *relation* towards the Father, and thus the sole meaning we are able to attach to Person is a relation of the Son towards the Father; and distinct from and beyond that relation, He is but the One God, who is also the Father. This sacred subject has been touched upon *supr. Or.* iii. 9, n. 8. In other words, there is an indestructible essential relation existing in the One Indivisible infinitely simple God, such as to constitute Him, viewed on each side of that relation (what in human language we call) Two (and in like manner Three), yet without the notion of number really coming in. When we speak of 'Person,' we mean nothing more than the One God in substance, viewed relatively to Him the One God, as viewed in that Correlative which we therefore call another Person. These various statements are not here intended to explain, but to bring home to the mind *what* it is which faith receives. We say 'Father, Son, and Spirit,' but when we would abstract a general idea of Them in order to number Them, our abstraction really does hardly more than carry us back to the One Substance. Such seems the meaning of such passages as Basil. *Ep.* 8, 2; *de Sp. S.* c. 18; Chrysost. *in Joan. Hom.* ii. 3 fin. 'In respect of the Adorable and most Royal Trinity, 'first' and 'second' have no place; for the Godhead is higher than number and times.' Isid. *Pel. Ep.* 3, 18. Eulog. *ap.* Phot. 230. p. 864. August. *in Joan.* 39, 3 and 4; *de Trin.* v. 10. 'Unity is not number, but is itself the principle of all things.' Ambros. *de Fid.* i. n. 19. 'A trine numeration then does not make number, which they rather run into, who make some difference between the Three.' Boeth. *Trin. unus Deus,* p. 959. The last remark is found in Naz. *Orat.* 31, 18. Many of these references are taken from Thomassin *de Trin.* 17.

1032 Athanasius of Alexandria. (1892). <u>Four Discourses against the Arians</u>. In P. Schaff & H. Wace (Eds.), J. H. Newman & A. T. Robertson (Trans.), *St. Athanasius: Select Works and Letters* (Vol. 4, p. 414). New York: Christian Literature Company.

1033 Cyril of Alexandria. (1881). *Five Tomes against Nestorius; Scholia on the Incarnation; Christ Is One; Fragments against Diodore of Tarsus, Theodore of Mopsuestia, the Synousiasts* (p. 97). London; Oxford; Cambridge: James Parker and Co.; Rivingtons.

1034 Cyril of Alexandria. (2009). *Festal Letters, 1–12.* (J. J. O'Keefe, Ed., P. R. Amidon, Trans.) (Vol. 118, p. 97). Washington, DC: The Catholic University of America Press.

1035 Cyril of Alexandria. (1859). *A Commentary upon the Gospel according to S. Luke.* (R. P. Smith, Trans.) (p. 333). Oxford: Oxford University Press.

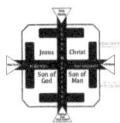

I.   "He was always holy by nature as God."[1036]

J.   "The divine admits no turning at all or change to anything unrighteous, but it always shines forth in its eternal Attributes."[1037]

K.   The Divine Attributes always exist regardless of whether They are being actualized

  1.   "Qualities that inhere in natures or happen to be possessed by them are most clearly manifested when they are brought to actuality. Fire, for example, possesses its heat by nature, but when it acts on wood, that is when we see what kind of power it has and how great that power is. Likewise someone who has obtained knowledge of grammar, let's say, or some other such discipline, would not be admired when silent, I think, but rather when they display the excellence of their learning for others to see. So it is with the divine and ineffable nature. When it actualizes any of its qualities or natural properties, that is when it shows itself more clearly for what it is and is thereby perceived by us as well."[1038]

V.   The only way created beings can know God

A.   "His substance cannot be created above all for this reason: it is capable of receiving the distinguishing marks[1039] of God. Now his distinguishing marks are the characteristics by which God is recognized. For example, that he is almighty, that he is, that he is immutable, and the other things mentioned earlier."[1040]

1036   Cyril of Alexandria. (2013–2015). *Commentary on John*. (J. C. Elowsky, T. C. Oden, & G. L. Bray, Eds., D. R. Maxwell, Trans.) (Vol. 1, p. 83). Downers Grove, IL: IVP Academic: An Imprint of InterVarsity Press.

1037   Ibid. (Vol. 2, p. 290)

1038   Ibid. (Vol. 2, p. 70)

1039   Gk. τὰ ἴδια.

1040   Athanasius and Didymus. (2011). *Works on the Spirit: Athanasius's Letters to Serapion on the Holy Spirit, and, Didymus's on the Holy Spirit*. (J. Behr, Ed., M. DelCogliano, A. Radde-Gallwitz, & L. Ayres, Trans.) (Vol. 43, p. 111-112). Yonkers, NY: St Vladimir's Seminary Press.

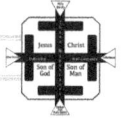

B. "For the divine is by nature invisible. For it is written, 'No one has ever seen God.'"[1041] But he is known by us, as far at least as that is attainable, from his mighty works, his unspeakable power, and his supreme pre-eminence. . . . From his mighty, godlike power, therefore, which transcends all discourse, it is possible in a way to receive knowledge concerning his ineffable divinity."[1042]

C. "The divine and ineffable nature is grasped by us (as far as possible) in no other way than through what it accomplishes and works."[1043]

VI. Able to be manifested:

A. Towards someone

1. Ex: God shows authority over someone by limiting their actions

2. "The rulers are constrained by divine activity that puts a bridle on their unholy deeds and allows their plans to advance only to the point of attempting them."[1044]

B. Through someone

1. Example: someone manifests goodness, that was received through partaking, towards another person

2. "So He indeed is good, or the good absolutely, but angels and men are good, only by being made, as I said, partakers of the good God. Let therefore the being good be set apart as the special property of God over all alone, essentially attached to His nature, and His peculiar attribute... to be a mere man, one

---

1041   Jn 1:18

1042   Cyril of Alexandria. (2013). *Festal Letters, 13–30.* (J. J. O'Keefe & D. G. Hunter, Eds., P. R. Amidon, Trans.) (Vol. 127, p. 183). Washington, DC: The Catholic University of America Press.

1043   Cyril of Alexandria. (2013–2015). *Commentary on John.* (J. C. Elowsky, T. C. Oden, & G. L. Bray, Eds., D. R. Maxwell, Trans.) (Vol. 1, p. 171). Downers Grove, IL: IVP Academic: An Imprint of InterVarsity Press.

1044   Ibid. (p. 296)

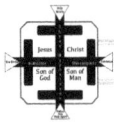

that is who never is invested with goodness, the property of the unchangeable nature, but only gains it by the assent of the divine will."[1045]

3. "Now, this would be appropriate in God's case, and specifically and characteristically his alone; even if there are many holy people and rational powers, including people on earth, they are nevertheless styled holy on the basis of participation in the one who is holy by nature, and who alone is truly so. Just as it is he who is true light, remember, but gave the privilege also to others, saying, 'You are the light of the world,' so too the one who alone is holy together with the God and Father and the Holy Spirit gives it, as from his fullness, to those sharing holiness with him."[1046]

VII. Able to be shared with created beings through a process called partaking[1047]

A. Partaking is when a substance receives an attribute from another substance

1. "Being the good Offspring of Him that is good, and true Son, He is the Father's Power and Wisdom and Word, not being so by participation,[1048] nor as if these qualities were imparted to Him from without, as they are to those who partake of Him and are made wise by Him, and receive power and reason in Him."[1049]

1045   Cyril of Alexandria. (1859). *A Commentary upon the Gospel according to S. Luke*. (R. P. Smith, Trans.) (pp. 566–567). Oxford: Oxford University Press.

1046   Cyril of Alexandria. (2008). *Commentary on Isaiah*. (R. Hill, Trans.) (Vol. 3, p. 201-202). Brookline: Holy Cross Orthodox Press.

1047   μετοχή, μέθεξιν or κοινωνός; 'participation' can also be used as a synonym for partaking

1048   μετοχή, cf. *de Syn.* 48, 51, 53. This was held by Arians, but in common with Paul Samos, and many of the Monarchian heretics. The same principle in Orig. on Ps. 135 (Lomm. xiii. 134) οὐ κατὰ μετουσίαν ἀλλὰ κατ' οὐσίαν θεός.

1049   Athanasius of Alexandria. (1892). <u>Against the Heathen</u>. In P. Schaff & H. Wace (Eds.), A. T. Robertson (Trans.), *St. Athanasius: Select Works and Letters* (Vol. 4, p. 29). New York: Christian Literature Company.

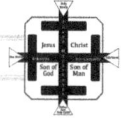

2. "Emmanuel wrought his grace in us, which is equivalent to a divine and spiritual fire, being like heat imparted through the Spirit."[1050]

3. "Fire is hot by nature, and other things are hot by participating in its activity, like iron or wood."[1051]

4. "In its Greek form, 'participation' (methexis, metousia, or metoche) is a philosophical term with both a weak and a strong sense. In the weak sense it means 'sharing in the attributes of another.' In the strong sense it is used to account for whatever has no being in its own right, whatever is not self-caused: things exist 'by participation' when they depend on something else. . . . In our examination of 2 Pet 1:4 ('partakers of the divine nature') we saw how the sense of 'partakers' (in this instance koinonoi) moved from the weak form in the New Testament author (sharing in the divine attributes of glory, goodness and incorruption) to the strong form in Cyril of Alexandria (human nature transformed in Christ)."[1052]

B. This process must be initiated by God alone, it cannot be initiated by creatures

1. "For it is the sole and peculiar property of the Substance That transcends all, to be able to bestow on men the indwelling of the Holy Ghost, and make those that draw near unto It partakers of the divine nature."[1053]

2. "If, however, you understand 'knowledge' to mean relationship

---

1050   Cyril of Alexandria. (2018). *Glaphyra on the Pentateuch, Volume 1 Genesis*. (N. P. Lunn, Trans.) (Vol. 137, p. 96). Washington, DC: The Catholic University of America Press.

1051   Cyril of Alexandria. (2013–2015). *Commentary on John*. (J. C. Elowsky, T. C. Oden, & G. L. Bray, Eds., D. R. Maxwell, Trans.) (Vol. 1, p. 241). Downers Grove, IL: IVP Academic: An Imprint of InterVarsity Press.

1052   Russell, Norman. (2009). Chapter Six: Participation in the Divine Life. *Fellow Workers with God: Orthodox Thinking on Theosis*. (p. 127). Crestwood: SVS Press

1053   Cyril of Alexandria. (1859). *A Commentary upon the Gospel according to S. Luke*. (R. P. Smith, Trans.) (p. 39). Oxford: Oxford University Press.

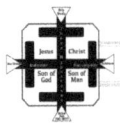

or kinship, then we say this: It was not we who initiated this knowledge but the only begotten God, who is from God. After all, we did not pursue the divinity above our nature, but he who is by nature God laid hold of the seed of Abraham, as Paul says, and became a human being in order to become like his brothers in all things except sin and to bring into relationship those who did not have it of themselves, that is, humanity."[1054]

VIII. Not the same Thing as the Divine:

A. Essence

1. "If that which pertains to God alone is inevitably also His essence, He will be composed of many essences. For there are many things that pertain by nature to God alone and to no other being. Indeed, the divine Scriptures call Him King, Lord, incorruptible, invisible, and say many thousands of other things about Him. If, then, each of His Attributes is ranked with essence, how can the simple God not be composite? But this is a most absurd view to hold."[1055, 1056]

2. ". . . that substance and glory which are beyond everything."[1057]

3. ". . . every attribute that appertained to the divine substance. . . . those who are of the same nature and substance are, of course, equal to one another in all those qualities which belong to them as pertaining to their substance"[1058]

4. "The properties of the divine nature are difficult to utter and

1054 Cyril of Alexandria. (2013–2015). *Commentary on John*. (J. C. Elowsky, T. C. Oden, & G. L. Bray, Eds., D. R. Maxwell, Trans.) (Vol. 2, p. 68). Downers Grove, IL: IVP Academic: An Imprint of InterVarsity Press.

1055 *Treasuries* 31 (P.G. LXXV, 444BC)

1056 Gregory Palamas. (1995). *Philokalia*. (G.E.H. Palmer, P. Sherrard & K. Ware, Trans.) (Vol. 4, p. 402). United States: Faber & Faber.

1057 Cyril of Alexandria. (2013). *Festal Letters, 13–30*. (J. J. O'Keefe & D. G. Hunter, Eds., P. R. Amidon, Trans.) (Vol. 127, p. 202). Washington, DC: The Catholic University of America Press.

1058 Cyril of Alexandria. (1859). *A Commentary upon the Gospel according to S. Luke*. (R. P. Smith, Trans.) (p. 304). Oxford: Oxford University Press.

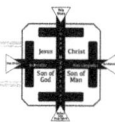

even more difficult to explain clearly."[1059]

5. "For example, the sun in the sky is bright, and silver from the earth is likewise bright, but the nature of the things mentioned is different."[1060]

B. Hypostases

1. "There are not some things in the Father and other things in the Son, but that which is in the Father is in the Son. And what you see in the Son is what you see in the Father."[1061]

2. "For if all things are delivered unto Him, first, He is other than that all which He has received."[1062]

3. "It is impossible to be able to find heaven or earth ever void of the ineffable Godhead, for, as I said, the divine and consubstantial Trinity[1063] fills all things."[1064]

1059   Cyril of Alexandria. (2013–2015). *Commentary on John.* (J. C. Elowsky, T. C. Oden, & G. L. Bray, Eds., D. R. Maxwell, Trans.) (Vol. 1, p. 5). Downers Grove, IL: IVP Academic: An Imprint of InterVarsity Press.

1060   Ibid. (p. 151)

1061   Athanasius and Didymus. (2011). *Works on the Spirit: Athanasius's Letters to Serapion on the Holy Spirit, and, Didymus's on the Holy Spirit.* (J. Behr, Ed., M. DelCogliano, A. Radde-Gallwitz, & L. Ayres, Trans.) (Vol. 43, p. 108-109). Yonkers, NY: St Vladimir's Seminary Press.

1062   Athanasius of Alexandria. (1892). Four Discourses against the Arians. In P. Schaff & H. Wace (Eds.), J. H. Newman & A. T. Robertson (Trans.), *St. Athanasius: Select Works and Letters* (Vol. 4, p. 413). New York: Christian Literature Company.

1063   Θεία τε καὶ ὁμοούσιος Τριάς

1064   Cyril of Alexandria. (1983). Answer to Tiberius: #2. L. Wickham (Trans.), *Cyril of Alexandria: Select letters* (p. 143). Oxford: Oxford University Press.

Glory be to the Incomprehensible Holy Trinity: The Father, Son and Holy Spirit. One Triune God, indivisible and uncompounded in His Essence, diverse in His Attributes. Amen.

Please pray for my weak self

References

Athanasius and Didymus. (2011). *Works on the Spirit: Athanasius's Letters to Serapion on the Holy Spirit, and, Didymus's on the Holy Spirit.* (J. Behr, Ed., M. DelCogliano, A. Radde-Gallwitz, & L. Ayres, Trans.), Vol. 43. Yonkers, NY: St Vladimir's Seminary Press.

Athanasius of Alexandria. (1892). *St. Athanasius: Select Works and Letters.* P. Schaff & H. Wace (Eds.), A. T. Robertson (Trans.), Vol. 4. New York: Christian Literature Company.

Athanasius of Alexandria. (1995). *Athanasius and Asceticism.* Baltimore: The John Hopkins University Press.

Burns, J. P., Jr., Newman, C., & Wilken, R. L. (Eds.). (2012). *Romans: Interpreted by Early Christian Commentators.* (J. P. Burns Jr. & C. Newman, Trans.). Grand Rapids, MI; Cambridge, UK: William B. Eerdmans Publishing Company.

Cyril of Alexandria. (1859). *A Commentary upon the Gospel according to S. Luke.* (R. P. Smith, Trans.). Oxford: Oxford University Press.

Cyril of Alexandria. (1872). *The Three Epistles of S. Cyril, Archbishop of Alexandria: English Text.* (P. E. Pusey, Ed.). Oxford; London: James Parker and Co.

Cyril of Alexandria. (1881). *Five Tomes against Nestorius; Scholia on the* Incarnation; Christ Is One; Fragments against Diodore of Tarsus, Theodore *of Mopsuestia, the Synousiasts.* London; Oxford; Cambridge: James Parker and Co.; Rivingtons.

Cyril of Alexandria. (1970–1979). *The Faith of the Early Fathers.* Jurgens, W. A. (Trans.), Vol. 3. Collegeville, MN: The Liturgical Press.

Cyril of Alexandria. (1983). *Cyril of Alexandria: Select letters.* L. Wickham (Trans.). Oxford: Oxford University Press.

Cyril of Alexandria. (1987). *Letters, 1–50.* (T. P. Halton, Ed., J. I. McEnerney, Trans.), Vol. 76. Washington, DC: The Catholic University of America Press.

Cyril of Alexandria. (1987). *Letters, 51–110.* (T. P. Halton, Ed., J. I. McEnerney, Trans.), Vol. 77. Washington, DC: The Catholic University of America Press.

Cyril of Alexandria. (1995). *On the Unity of Christ.* (J. Behr, Ed., J. A. McGuckin,

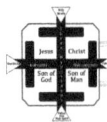

Trans.), Vol. 13. Crestwood, NY: St Vladimir's Seminary Press.

Cyril of Alexandria. (2004). *Against Those Who Are Unwilling to Confess that the Holy Virgin Is Theotokos*. Protopresbyter G. Dragas (Ed. & Trans.), Rollinsford: Orthodox Research Institute.

Cyril of Alexandria. (2007). *Commentary on the Twelve Prophets*. (T. P. Halton, Ed., R. C. Hill, Trans.), Vol. 115. Washington, DC: The Catholic University of America Press.

Cyril of Alexandria. (2008). *Commentary on Isaiah*. (R. Hill, Trans.), Vol. 3. Brookline: Holy Cross Orthodox Press.

Cyril of Alexandria. (2008). *Commentary on the Twelve Prophets*. (T. P. Halton, Ed., R. C. Hill, Trans.), Vol. 116. Washington, DC: The Catholic University of America Press.

Cyril of Alexandria. (2009). *Festal Letters, 1–12*. (J. J. O'Keefe, Ed., P. R. Amidon, Trans.), Vol. 118. Washington, DC: The Catholic University of America Press.

Cyril of Alexandria. (2012). *Commentary on the Twelve Prophets*. (D. G. Hunter, Ed., R. C. Hill, Trans.), Vol. 124. Washington, DC: The Catholic University of America Press.

Cyril of Alexandria. (2013). *Commentary on John*. (J. C. Elowsky, T. C. Oden, & G. L. Bray, Eds., D. R. Maxwell, Trans.), Vol. 1. Downers Grove, IL: IVP Academic: An Imprint of InterVarsity Press.

Cyril of Alexandria. (2013). *Festal Letters, 13–30*. (J. J. O'Keefe & D. G. Hunter, Eds., P. R. Amidon, Trans.), Vol. 127. Washington, DC: The Catholic University of America Press.

Cyril of Alexandria. (2014). *Three Christological Treatises*. (D. Hunter, Ed., D. King, Trans.), Vol. 129. Washington, DC: The Catholic University of America Press.

Cyril of Alexandria. (2015). *Commentary on John*. (J. C. Elowsky, T. C. Oden, & G. L. Bray, Eds., D. R. Maxwell, Trans.), Vol. 2. Downers Grove, IL: IVP Academic: An Imprint of InterVarsity Press.

Cyril of Alexandria. (2018). *Glaphyra on the Pentateuch, Volume 1 Genesis*. (N. P. Lunn, Trans.), Vol. 137. Washington, DC: The Catholic University of America Press.

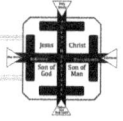

Cyril of Alexandria. (2019). *Glaphyra on the Pentateuch, Volume 2 Genesis.* (N. P. Lunn, Trans.), Vol. 138. Washington, DC: The Catholic University of America Press

Gregory Palamas. (1995). *Philokalia.* (G.E.H. Palmer, P. Sherrard & K. Ware, Trans.), Vol. 4. United States: Faber & Faber.

Heen, E. M., & Krey, P. D. W. (Eds.). (2005). *Ancient Christian Commentary on Scripture: Hebrews.* Downers Grove, IL: InterVarsity Press.

Liddell, H. G. (1996). *A lexicon: Abridged from Liddell and Scott's Greek-English lexicon.* Oak Harbor, WA: Logos Research Systems, Inc.

Patriarch Callistus and Ignatius of Xanthopoulos. (1992). *Writings from the Philokalia on Prayer of the Heart.* (Kadloubovsky E., G.E.H. Palmer, Trans.). New York: Faber and Faber, Inc.

Russell, Norman. (2009). *Fellow Workers with God: Orthodox Thinking on Theosis.* Crestwood: SVS Press.

Simonetti, M. (Ed.). (2001). *Ancient Christian Commentary on Scripture: Matthew 1–13.* Downers Grove, IL: InterVarsity Press.

Wilken, R. L., Christman, A. R., & Hollerich, M. J. (Eds.). (2007). *Isaiah: Interpreted by Early Christian and Medieval Commentators.* (R. L. Wilken, A. R. Christman, & M. J. Hollerich, Trans.). Grand Rapids, MI; Cambridge, UK: William B. Eerdmans Publishing Company.

www.ingramcontent.com/pod-product-compliance
Lightning Source LLC
Chambersburg PA
CBHW030932090426
42737CB00007B/399